PSI SUCCESSFUL BUSINESS LIBRARY

The BUYER'S GUIDE To BUSINESS INSURANCE

DON BURY
LARRY HEISCHMAN

Edited by
Camille Akin

OASIS PRESS

The Oasis Press® / PSI Research
Grants Pass, Oregon

Published by The Oasis Press

Editor: Camille Akin

Assistant Editors: Linda Pinkham and Vickie Reierson

Editorial Assistance: Rosanno Alejandro

Book Design: Constance Dickinson and Jan Olsson

Page Formatting: Darrin Clay

Cover Design: Ark Stein

Please direct any comments, questions, or suggestions regarding this book to The Oasis Press®/PSI Research:

Editorial Department
300 North Valley Drive
Grants Pass, OR 97526
(503) 479-9464
(800) 228-2275

The Oasis Press® is a Registered Trademark of Publishing Services, Inc., an Oregon corporation doing business as PSI Research.

Library of Congress Cataloging-in-Publication Data
Bury, Don, 1955–
The buyer's guide to business insurance / Don Bury, Larry Heischman ; edited by Camille Akin.
p. cm.
Includes index.
ISBN 1-55571-310-6 : $39.95 (binder). -- ISBN 1-55571-162-6 : $19.95 (trade paper)
1. Insurance, Business--United States--Handbooks, manuals, etc.
2. Small business--United States--Handbooks, manuals, etc.
I. Heischman, Larry, 1947– . II. Akin, Camille. III. Title.
HG8059.B86 1994
368.8'1'00973--dc20 94-17498
CIP

Printed in the United States of America
First edition 10 9 8 7 6 5 4 3 2 1 0 Revision Code: 94AA

Printed on recycled paper when available.

This book is dedicated to all buyers of business insurance, to our loving wives Linda Heischman and Sharon Bury, and to Conrad E. Imhaus who persuaded buyers to prove our methods work.

—*Larry Heischman and Don Bury*

About the Authors

Don Bury operates a business consulting practice called Imhaus & Bury–Insurance Optimizers in San Rafael, California. He is an insurance broker-agent, with more than 20 years experience serving the insurance-buying public. His years of interviewing insurance buyers and negotiating with insurance companies contribute to the strategies presented in this book. He has carefully observed a wide variety of trial and error methods applied by many clients and companies. He has worked both as an exclusive agent — representing only one insurance company — and as an independent insurance broker, giving him unusual insight into the opportunities available in the insurance marketplace. He holds a bachelors degree in business and finance from San Francisco State University.

Larry Heischman has 18 years experience in insurance agency operations and in the technical aspects of insurance. He has worked in the marketing department of three property and casualty insurance companies. He has visited and observed hundreds of independent insurance agencies of all sizes, in many states. He has worked in several different insurance agencies, and is currently licensed as an insurance broker for property and casualty insurance, and as an agent for life and health insurance. Larry teaches insurance courses for one of the nation's largest nonprofit insurance education organizations and holds the designation of Chartered Property Casualty Underwriter (CPCU) from the American Institute of Property and Liability Underwriters. In addition, he holds the Associates in Risk Management (ARM) from the Insurance Institute of America. Together with his wife, Linda, they own and operate LinLar Services developing and presenting educational seminars and insurance consulting.

Preface

Buying business insurance is just one of the many responsibilities faced by business owners and managers in today's complex business environment. Typically, the issue of buying business insurance gets a priority somewhere below taxes, but slightly above supply ordering. Whether you are a one-person operation, an owner-operator of a small family business, or responsible for buying insurance for several large corporations, your business insurance is a crucial element of your business' security and survival. As the business insurance buyer, your decisions can make the difference in your business' continued survival.

This book was written to help insurance buyers get better results from their insurance purchasing efforts. We have observed a wide variety of purchasing strategies from the perspectives of insurance companies and brokerages. Many of the buying strategies tried by business owners failed to produce the desired results, while some surprised us with their effectiveness. We carefully examined the most effective strategies, and from these, have derived what has proven to be a very effective purchasing system.

This book was written to help insurance buyers get better results from their insurance purchasing efforts.

During our years of working in the insurance business, we both developed a desire to teach the buying public how to get better results in dealing with the insurance industry. We wanted to share so much with every buyer with whom we spoke — about what they should do and when they should do it. Economies of time and money prevented us from sharing our insights on a one-to-one basis. Clearly, a book was needed to serve as a guide and reference for the buyers we could not personally advise during their many critical decision points in dealing with the insurance industry.

Our major goal in presenting this book is to help buyers save time, money, and effort. The purchasing strategies included in this book will help buy-

We have watched buyers save thousands of dollars, add needed coverages, and command the full attention of their brokers by using the techniques found in this guide.

ers receive quality coverage and superior service at the lowest prices. As consultants, we have tested the methods from the buyer's side, and have been delighted with the overall effectiveness of these methods. We have watched buyers save thousands of dollars, add needed coverages, and command the full attention of their brokers by using the techniques found in this guide.

The guide was written to help business insurance consumers deal with the following coverages:

- Commercial general liability
- Commercial property
- Commercial automobile
- Workers' compensation
- Inland marine
- Umbrella liability
- Boiler and machinery

More specifically, this guide helps you:

- Save time and money by using simple, yet powerful buying procedures, designed for hurried businesspeople.
- See beyond what any one agent or broker can represent because no commission considerations influence what is disclosed; industry truths are candidly presented.
- Benefit from the lessons and insights gained from years of experience in the specialized field of business insurance.
- Direct insurance people to work for you by using prepared letters and forms. You control the buying process and your policy service by being fully informed with the industry's inside information.
- Avoid expensive mistakes commonly made by even the most skillful buyers of business insurance.

We welcome your comments and suggestions based on your experiences after using the techniques in this book. Any comments are invaluable to our continuing efforts to improve business insurance purchasing strategies and the results achieved by implementing the strategies. We are committed to helping people save money and effort, increase their chances of being properly insured when a loss occurs, and increase the quality of current and future services.

Don Bury
Larry Heischman
July 1994

Table of Contents

Section III — After the Purchase

Section IV — Helpful Resources

Worksheets and Forms

How to Use this Book

How this Book Is Organized

Whether you are a start-up business looking for a first-time policy or an existing business looking for better rates, every insurance buyer should be prepared to approach the insurance marketplace so he or she can get the best possible coverage and service for a reasonable amount of money. Because all this information and process can be overwhelming to most, *The Buyer's Guide to Business Insurance* has been written and organized to explain key issues and procedures in a reader-friendly format.

Taking you from the initial insurance basics you will need to know before making your insurance purchase to the post-purchase tips on how to maintain service and quality from your particular agent and insurance company, this guide is comprehensive in content and easy to follow. The book's first three sections respectively cover the beginning, middle, and ending of the insurance buying process. Each section features practical, yet valuable tips on how to make the best buying decision for your particular business, but you won't get lost in industry jargon because the definitions are contained within the chapters' text, as well as the book's Glossary, which is located in Section IV. Section IV also contains the Appendix of Sample Letters. These samples are designed to further assist you in your quest for quality in your insurance coverage and procedure.

Take the time to read how each section specifically will contribute to making you a more informed insurance buyer. Don't be overwhelmed with the topic and task ahead, take each section at a time and carefully glean the information and advice to your advantage.

Section I – Before the Purchase

Section I has six chapters that show you the key players and parts of the insurance industry. This section is designed to introduce you to some insurance basics, such as why and how you should reevaluate your insurance coverage; how to go about researching the insurance marketplace; and what aspects of your business you need to consider covering in your policy. In addition, you will learn how to:

- Present your business in the best possible light to the insurance industry;
- Prepare the necessary data to make the shopping process relatively painless and effective;
- Manage your potential for losses through effective risk management;
- Compare the credentials of those who want to insure your business;
- Control all the various property, liability, automobile, and workers' compensation coverages needed for your business;
- Prepare for the insurance industry's cycles and how you can manage a fluctuation in insurance costs; and
- Discover common misconceptions of what the policies do and don't cover.

In addition, several worksheets and forms are built into each chapter of this section. These worksheets assist you in making the right insurance purchase for your business. This section give you a head start on protecting your business from future danger and puts you in control — not your agent or broker — of your insurance purchase.

Section II – The Purchase

Section II helps you make the right decision to get the needed coverage at the best possible price. Specifically, this section shows you how to:

- Deal effectively with insurance people to get the service for which you are paying;
- Make sound buying decisions by quickly identifying differences in coverages and locating only the important issues in your quotes; and
- Negotiate and set up a strategy for pricing and installment terms.

Section III – After the Purchase

Section III give you ideas on how you can manage your insurance policies after your purchase. Often, business insurance buyers will pay an exorbitant amount of money for a policy and once the deal is done, never communicate with their agents or brokers again until renewal time. This section tells you how you can take a proactive approach to handling your insurance policy year-round. This section will give you tips on how to:

- Avoid expensive mistakes commonly make by even the most experienced buyers and their agents and brokers;

- Implement a scheduled service plan for your agent or broker to eliminate surprises; and
- Handle any claims that may arise if your business suffers a loss.

Section IV – Helpful Resources

Section IV provides you with a wealth of resources you can use in your search for the right coverage at the right price. In this section you will find:

- An appendix of sample letters that can be used to expedite your purchase.
- A comprehensive glossary for a quick reference to complex insurance terms; and
- A complete index of major insurance topics covered in each chapter.

Other Helpful Aspects of this Book

Because an insurance purchase can seem like an overwhelming task, this book was created to simplify the purchasing process for you. As a result, you will find several other helpful resources to guide you through the various steps.

Worksheets and Forms

By using the worksheets and forms in this book, you can make agents work more to your benefit. Often, business insurance buyers are inundated with varying quotes in different types of formats. Also, when you leave the insurance selection process in the hands of an agent or broker, you may inadvertently transfer control of your purchase to someone who may not share in providing the best interests of your business.

If you use the simple, user-friendly forms in this book, you will remain the one in control of your purchase. You will communicate to agents, brokers, and underwriters that you are a serious and informed buyer. Also, the worksheets give you a standardized format for reviewing bids from different agencies and brokerages.

To assist you, each worksheet is located on a right-hand page, with a corresponding left-hand instructions page. This format allows you easy reference to understanding all the necessary aspects of your insurance purchase. The forms in this book are your only copies, so you are reminded to reproduce as many copies as you need and reserve the forms in this book as your master copies.

Side Quotes – Highlighted Expert Advice

You will easily locate tips from the authors that give you the cutting edge in dealing with insurance people. This advice is sprinkled throughout the book in side columns within each chapter. Look for these quotes for guidance, because this information is key to protecting your business from harm.

Look for these quotes for guidance, because this information is key to protecting your business from harm.

Sample Letters

Communication is essential to effectively manage your insurance program. To expedite much of this communication, 24 sample letters are ready for your use. The letters provide you with critical communication tools for each aspect of your insurance purchase and are fully referenced in their respective chapters. You are encouraged to use these letters for a variety of insurance needs throughout your policy year.

In addition, the sample letters can be installed on your computer by using this book's companion software, *The Insurance Assistant.*

Italicized Terms

Throughout each chapter, you will find that many insurance terms are called to your attention by *italicized text treatment.* By knowing some of the insurance jargon, you will communicate that you are an informed buyer to quoting agents and brokers. When you see the italicized insurance terms, keep them in mind when analyzing your insurance needs and talking "insurance" with the insurance industry's people. Complex insurance terms are defined for you in the text following an italicized word. Otherwise, you can refer to the glossary for help.

Companion Software

If you are like many insurance buyers, you have streamlined much of your operations by using a computer system. To follow suit with the automated needs of today's business owners, this book's companion software – *The Insurance Assistant* – is available through special order. To learn more about *The Insurance Assistant,* contact:

The Oasis Press
(800) 228-2275

Acknowledgments

We would like to acknowledge the following people for their persistent encouragement and support to complete this project:

Thomas Jordan
Ted Potter
Gary and Nuala Ruddell
Fred and Eileen Bury
Erica Young
Jeff and Dawn Stone
Michael Imberman-Stern
Rod and Janice Roche
Michael Anderson
Dan and Barbara Paicopolis
Stacey N. Conlin
Ron and Risa Hearn
George and Eunice Jones
Bob and Brenda Jones
Morton and Ann Feld
Mark and Carol Rogers
Dennis and Jeannie Jensen
Bob and Barbara Powell
Sandy Masters
Carol and Ralph Greco
Cindy Davidson
Jan King
Mike and Susan Green

Before the Purchase

Section I

Chapter 1
Why Reevaluate Your Insurance?

Chapter 2
The Issue of Risk Management

Chapter 3
Know the Marketplace

Chapter 4
Prepare Your Business for Action

Chapter 5
Know Your Business Insurance Coverage Options

Chapter 6
Know Your Workers' Compensation Issues

Chapter 1

Why Reevaluate Your Insurance?

An Ideal Marketplace Versus Today's Realities

In an ideal insurance marketplace, you could submit your insurance requirements to a central service, and within 24 hours have quotes from every insurance company willing to write your type of business. Ideally, the quotes would:

- Be standardized in a simple format, making them easy to compare so your optimal choices would be obvious;
- Eliminate confusion for you when purchasing business insurance; and
- Enable you to quickly make better choices in spending your premium dollars.

To get a partial example of an ideal marketplace — a marketplace of all the insurance companies willing and able to write your insurance — visit an insurance brokerage equipped with an automated, comparative auto insurance rating system. A data input person will enter your driver and vehicle information once, and in about a minute, you will get 20 auto insurance quotes, ranked in order of cost. In addition, you will get pricing detail, so you can select your company, limits, and deductibles from the many variations quoted. For example, if you are curious about the insurance costs of buying a different car, it takes only seconds to requote to see exactly how that vehicle will affect your rates. If the insurance industry would apply auto insurance's powerful, standardized approach to business insurance, pricing would intensify price competition, and the task of purchasing business insurance would be much simpler.

Of course, the real world is not set up for such rampant competition for your business. For agents, brokers, and insurance companies, price shopping generally is considered an ugly practice in the business insurance community, and is discouraged and frowned upon.

Price shopping forces agents and brokers to work to retain their business and this costs them time and money. They want you to value their professional services of identifying needs and selecting coverages, and trust them to keep your pricing competitive. If the agents and brokers don't retain their accounts, they must seek out and sell new ones, which is much harder than simply renewing existing business. Apples for apples comparisons are rare, because insurance companies have been busily producing:

- Unique, customized policies with coverage variations and unique labels to literally separate them from the competition; and
- Unique forms and questionnaires on which your circumstances must be described, causing extra work that discourages agents from price shopping.

These subtle differences and variations slow the quoting process and muddle price comparisons. These complications cloud the vital issue — what is the least amount of money you will have to spend to adequately insure your business?

Today's insurance marketplace epitomizes the concept of "Let the buyer beware."

The confusion causes you to depend on insurance agents who are paid commissions, for what you hope is wise advice and proper coverage. Today's insurance marketplace epitomizes the concept of "Let the buyer beware," because the confusion prevents you from obtaining rock bottom prices.

Obtain Regular and Competitive Quotes

Insurance costs on your profit and loss (P&L) statement can be significant and surprisingly volatile. Shop regularly to defend yourself against paying too much, and against shocking price hikes. Of course, shopping may result in reducing your insurance costs, which directly improves your bottom line profits. But you may not recognize your vulnerability to an insurance marketplace that can change quickly, resulting in painful premium increases or lack of coverage availability. Defensively, handle your insurance to guard yourself against the decisions and actions of companies and agencies. Remember, these firms focus on maximizing their profit, not yours.

The key to defensively handling your insurance is to develop concrete alternatives before a crisis arises.

The key to defensively handling your insurance is to develop concrete alternatives before a crisis arises — which would demand a sudden change in your existing program. Because there is a wide range in pricing for commercial insurance coverage, it is possible to pay double or triple the lowest available price for your commercial insurance program. Further, a set of quote specifications taken to the insurance marketplace will frequently result in widely varying price quotes. Often, it is hard to believe that the quoting insurance companies are all looking at the same account. This broad variation in pricing is seldom seen in any industry other than commercial insurance.

Pricing is influenced by the information your agent presents to describe your business operations, which can vary depending on each individual agent's understanding of your situation. Underwriters — employees of insurance companies who determine whether to quote your insurance and at what price — elect to apply credits or surcharges to the pricing. Underwriters depend on very subjective reasoning, which may have little to do with the merits of your particular risk. Also, prices can be responsive to the relationship between the agent and the underwriter. If the underwriter enjoys a profitable relationship with the agent, your price may be more competitive. In addition, no set pattern exists for individual underwriters within a company when judging accounts. For example, if the underwriter is in a bad mood the morning your submission arrives, you may get a less competitive quote. To help influence pricing in your favor, present your business as completely and favorably as possible. To achieve this goal, Chapter 4 shows you how to complete the Underwriting Information Questionnaire, to fully inform quoting agents and companies about your business' operations.

To help influence pricing in your favor, present your business as completely and favorably as possible.

The quality and quantity of service widely varies among agencies and customers. You may not realize you are getting bad service until you experience terrific service. On occasion, you may encounter outstanding service, brightly contrasting the norm. Service varies across a broad spectrum, including:

- The intensity of effort applied to getting prices down and getting claims paid;
- The level of communication and followup;
- The speed and skill with which problems are solved; and
- The range of issues handled skillfully.

The level of service you receive varies upon the background and attitude of the individuals handling your account. The information in this book will help you select the right agency and increase your knowledge, so you can receive the best from insurance service people.

Get the best from insurance service people by learning how to select the right agency and to increase your business insurance knowledge.

Winning Requires Knowledge and Skill

With the broad range of pricing and services available in the marketplace, only a few buyers have the skills to consistently win low prices and high levels of service. Time and again statistics show:

- Only a small percentage of buyers enjoy the best pricing and service;
- Most buyers endure average pricing and service; and
- Few buyers suffer excessively in the purchasing of their coverages.

Of the very few buyers enjoying the best pricing and services, some arrived there by accident, and in time, they will end up with average service. An informed few arrived there by design, because they knew what they were doing and why they were doing it. The informed few will consistently tend to win the best values and optimum service, because they practice many of the actions suggested throughout this book.

Be an Informed Buyer

Ignorance about what the competition offers can be very expensive.

If you are complacent, you simply may be uninformed. Ignorance about what the competition offers can be very expensive. Hundreds of people might say they are perfectly satisfied with their insurance programs, only to find their programs are riddled with shortcomings. When alternative opportunities become apparent, they find greater satisfaction than they or their agent had imagined possible. When handling insurance, you can pay a high price for being misinformed or underinsured.

Most businesses do an inadequate job shopping their insurance accounts. A large number of small business owners hope their agents have their best interests at heart. Other businesses try to be thorough, and occasionally may shop several places. They find the whole process frustrating and time consuming, and decide to move on to more productive efforts.

Most businesses have invented their own purchasing methods, based on limited trial and error efforts. Many of the methods do not adequately address the problems. You need to know how to effectively shop the marketplace and systematically manage business insurance.

Naturally, the profit-making providers of insurance services have not taught people how to get a less expensive deal elsewhere. In practice, agents and brokers do not work for you, or for an insurance company — they work for themselves. While the agents know they must have your price low enough to win and keep your business, further reductions in price directly reduce their commission paychecks. How many agents are willing to put in extra time and effort only to reduce the size of their own paychecks?

If you are prepared with concrete alternatives, then you can help convince underwriters to apply maximum discounts.

When writing your account, insurance company underwriters want the premium you pay to be as high as the market permits. Most underwriters do not volunteer their best available bargains; however, for those agents who know how to ask the right questions, an underwriter may reluctantly grant any available bargain. Most underwriters are not fond of a soft market, in which the prices spiral downward. To keep writing business in the soft market conditions, the underwriters slightly undercut their competition — just enough to reach their stated corporate objectives of increased written premiums. For instance, when faced with losing an account, they are sometimes willing to make concessions in your favor — which can be very meaningful to you — while serving their own interests. If you are prepared with concrete alternatives, you can help convince underwriters to apply maximum discounts.

The insurance marketplace is simply too large for any one person to be aware of all the possible solutions for every situation. Further, the gargantuan size of the marketplace dictates that no single agent can know all there is about where to find the best possible deal for your account. With hundreds of insurance companies, and the corresponding number of individual retailers, it is unlikely you will stumble into the best bargain on your first insurance purchase. Many people are required to sift through the industry and extract the best possible values.

It is unlikely you will stumble into the best bargain on your first insurance purchase.

An Ever-Changing Industry

The insurance industry is in a constant state of change. The only way to be sure past realities — such as coverage options and pricing — are valid now is to investigate the insurance marketplace again. Keep in mind depending on only one agent to keep up with this continually changing marketplace can be expensive. Because of the all the constant changes in the industry, know the following:

The only way to be sure last year's realities are valid this year is to investigate the alternatives again.

- You may not have the same agent year after year because of employee turnover.
- Your agent may be slacking when working on your account this year, even though the agent worked hard for you last year.
- Your agent may have found a more lucrative specialized area and is now paying less attention to your type of account.
- You might not know if the agency has improved or fallen apart.

Remember, you may never be told what changes are really taking place, so regularly cross check the marketplace by getting other opinions.

Not all agents or brokers have the same access to all the market opportunities. Brokers are not able to shop the entire market because industry practices forbid this type of shopping. For example, the many *exclusive companies* — insurance companies with their own exclusive agents — can be accessed only through their appointed agents. Brokers cannot connect you with these markets, unless they go through one of the insurance company's exclusive agents. Because of these obstacles, brokers find it difficult to be informed about the strengths and weaknesses of exclusive companies.

In today's insurance marketplace, brokers are placing more of their business with fewer insurance companies due to financial pressures in the industry. Insurance companies insist on growth in premium volume from their agents and brokers because the insurance companies find it more profitable to do business with fewer, larger volume agencies. If the volume requirements are not met, the agent-broker relationships are terminated by the insurance companies. In their efforts to meet the rising volume requirements, brokers have consolidated their clients' premium dollars into fewer companies. Agents hope to be rewarded for their volume with greater commissions, and special concessions in placing business with less formality and paperwork. Agencies also find that consolidating their business with fewer insurance companies simplifies daily business routines and reduces operating costs. This consolidation satisfies the companies and keeps brokers in business, but it denies your account access to the larger marketplace.

If you do not shop the market yourself, the job may not get done.

Brokers may know valuable opportunities from which you could profit, but for one reason or another, and for their own undisclosed reasons, they may not offer them to you. It is imperative you methodically and efficiently check the marketplace yourself, beyond your broker's capacities, to find the pleasant surprises hidden along the way. This means getting more than one quote from more than one agent. If you do not shop the market yourself, the job may not get done.

Inside Industry Information Is Poorly Communicated

Agents do not know everything their own insurance companies will and will not do for their clients.

The way information is disseminated in the insurance industry can cost you money. Competitive information tends to be poorly communicated to agents, so agents are often uninformed about the possibilities available to you. Information flows inconsistently from insurance companies and is often delayed and incomplete in getting to agents. Suppose a great bargain is now available from ABC Insurance Company, which its underwriters learned about at a meeting weeks ago. The underwriter mentions the great bargain when talking to agent Y, who seizes the opportunity for a client — who happens to be your biggest competitor. Unfortunately, you are with loyal agent X, who places your policy with a different company at a higher price, completely unaware of the opportunity to save you money. The way information is disseminated throughout the industry leaves agents with incomplete information. They do not know everything their own insurance companies will and will not do for their clients.

Know What Your Agent Does for You

All agents' knowledge are limited to their own individual experience. The agents' knowledge is directly related to their time in the business, their interest in serving their clients, and the effort they put into staying informed about what their companies offer. They may know very little about the marketplace beyond their immediate reach. They will tell you they are giving you the best deal. At best, this is true only to the extent of their knowledge and experience, and the support they get from their agency staff.

Your challenge is to overcome human inertia, awaken people, and get them to work for you.

The work you need insurance people to put in to reduce your price is tedious, time consuming, and stressful. The work will get done only if you make sure it gets done. Your challenge is to overcome human inertia, awaken people, and get them to work for you. Consider the effort it takes to quote your account.

- Your current detailed information must be collected, evaluated, and set up on current applications.
- The applications are sent to various selected insurance companies with cover memos.
- Each company's underwriter usually wants to discuss some aspect of your account, which usually involves a rally of phone tag with your agent.
- You will often have to be reached for some additional detail.
- The quotes have to be assessed and evaluated, then decisions must be made about what to tell you.
- A proposal must be prepared.
- Finally, you are called for an interview to explain and sell the recommendations.

Compare this with how much easier it is to simply send a memo to the current company to "Renew as is!"

The truth is, you will be lucky to get most agents to thoroughly quote three companies. They must be motivated to call underwriters, request special credits, and quote variations in coverage that may work to your advantage. To get the most for your money, follow these guidelines.

- Manage insurance people just like employees.
- Set clear instructions and performance standards.
- Measure the results to make sure you are getting what you want.

The Insurance Assistant, this book's companion software makes the quoting process much faster and easier. The software is designed to save you time and effort when submitting your business' information to quoting agencies. This eliminates needless phone tag rallies and cuts interview time in half. For more information, contact:

The Oasis Press
(800) 228-2275

Stay in Contact with Your Agent

You need to apply corrective measures when your agent's performance falls short of the possibilities. Of course, be considerate of his or her needs.

To protect your business' assets, take control of your insurance, and have your agency's work regularly checked by their competitors.

If you encounter negligence or lethargy from insurance people, you and your business may be affected significantly. Their actions or inactions can be a financial detriment. For instance, maybe you could have saved a few hundred dollars, but you didn't have the opportunity because your agent didn't act on the savings. Perhaps a few thousand dollars slipped away because he or she was not paying attention. Ultimately, your business could be ruined by an uninsured loss. To protect your business' assets, take control of your insurance, and have your agency's work regularly checked by their competitors.

You are vulnerable to disservice when only one agent is quoting your account.

Incompetence can obstruct your path to your best values. Agents may be unqualified to handle your account, but will not risk commission income by telling you their weakness. The industry has its share of misguided and misinformed workers who may be new in the business or deeply entrenched in old ways. Also, the information your agent presents about you could have come from someone who did not know or care about your situation. For example, one weary underwriter may not give you a desired premium. Meanwhile, at the next desk, a more alert and informed underwriter grants the identical premium to one of your biggest competitors. Keep in mind you are vulnerable to disservice when only one agent is quoting your account.

Your account may be considered unprofitable by your agency, and, as a result, receive second class treatment. If this is the case, you are usually the last one to find out. The business that pays smaller premiums and generates lower commissions may find the following especially true:

- Your agency may feel it cannot afford to put the time into researching the marketplace on your account, when that time can be better spent on larger accounts.
- The smaller your account is, the more susceptible you are to disservice.
- Accounts paying below $25,000 per year are increasingly susceptible to neglect, in both cost conservation and professional attention, especially on renewals. Stronger agents tend to gravitate to the larger accounts.

Shop Your Account

Shopping your account helps you increase the odds of being insured if a loss occurs. Just like getting a second opinion from a doctor, having several competent agents look over your exposures and recommend coverages can prove worthwhile. Most coverage packages can be improved, and a second agent hoping to win your account may be more alert and innovative with coverage suggestions. For instance, you may find your premium dollar can be better applied to meet your objectives through some coverage changes. Many businesses are purchasing coverages for exposures they could easily handle without insurance, while being exposed to hazards that could ruin them.

As you accumulate alternative quotes, you gain valuable negotiating power. With multiple quotes in hand, you have the power to change agents, and select the agency you want to handle your account. If you are renewing your policy, you can tell your current agent you have a more competitive quote. Watch as the agency scrambles to find new ways to lower its current quote and offer you new and improved services. If the agency does not try to get you a lower quote or better service, maybe it is time you change agencies anyway. Since you have the necessary alternate quotes, you can do so quickly and conveniently. Having concrete alternatives puts you in the driver's seat when the time comes to negotiate your renewal.

Most businesses should regularly shop their insurance for many valuable reasons. Even when you are getting excellent service, it pays to have your agency's work regularly inspected by other agencies. You can remain satisfied with your favorite agent, while you maintain a focus on your competitive position. For instance, you may make a tough decision to save money by purchasing your insurance this year from your agent's competitor. At least when the time arrives, your former agent may be motivated to do everything possible to win you back. While all businesses should regularly obtain competitive quotes, the situations discussed below demand immediate attention.

Shopping your account helps you increase the odds of being insured should a loss occur.

Twelve Danger Signs that Alert You to Act Now!

You can be alerted to problems relating to your account, if you know what to look for. If any of the following conditions apply to you, take heed. These conditions warn you that you need to prepare to find an alternative agent, company, and quote.

Having concrete alternatives puts you in the driver's seat when the time comes to negotiate your renewal.

Sign 1 – Insurance Companies Aren't Interested in You

If you are canceled or nonrenewed by your current carrier, the remaining players could try to extract unreasonably high premiums from you. You could find yourself without coverage, and effectively out of business until the situation is remedied. Take every possible step to develop contingency plans, including finding the right people in the insurance industry who can help with your situation. One of these agents could end up rescuing you just in time, should you end up in distress.

If you are canceled or nonrenewed by your current carrier, the remaining players could try to extract unreasonably high premiums from you.

Sign 2 – Your Agency Is Probing for Price Sensitivity Near Expiration

When your friendly agency asks whether you are aware of any lower-price alternatives, consider the questioning a bad sign. This may indicate a lack of confidence in the competitiveness of their price. Perhaps no effort has been expended towards reducing your price, and the agency wonders whether to work on your account. When this happens, get quotes for your renewal from at least one other agency.

Sign 3 – You Have Not Shopped for Several Years

Staying with the same company year after year suggests the renew-as-is syndrome, wherein you could be missing some dramatic price savings or increased coverages. Make shopping your account a priority this year.

Sign 4 – Rising Insurance Prices or Companies Withdrawing from the Field

When trade publications report a rise in insurance prices or insurance companies withdrawing from the field, these industry reports suggest a hardening insurance market — where it becomes vital for you to aggressively handle your insurance to maintain status quo. Since you could be heading for a significant increase in renewal premiums or problems with coverage availability, develop as many alternatives as possible before expiration.

Sign 5 – A Significant Claim or Series of Smaller Losses

If you have had a significant claim or series of smaller losses within this past year, prepare to fortify yourself against an unhappy surprise. The company may not renew your policy or want a significant premium increase. You will be pleased you developed alternatives ahead of time, should these events transpire.

Sign 6 – Your Premium Has Risen over Previous Years

Premium increases may suggest your insurance company is disenchanted with your business. Perhaps the company believes your type of business is causing a loss in profits, or that you were undercharged in the past. Whatever the case, collect other quotes, as other carriers may not have reached the same conclusion

Sign 7 – Significant Changes in Your Operation

If your operation has changed significantly since the company last checked your status, be ready for surprises at renewal time when the agency becomes aware of your new or reduced exposures. Perhaps you added a location, or expanded operations to include an additional product or service. Your insurance company may decide to cancel you or increase your rates. Your best bet is to develop alternative plans prior to the renewal date.

Sign 8 – Your Agent Pays Less Attention to You Now than before

If you fear the agency is taking you for granted, your suspicions may be correct. Perhaps you never communicate with the agency, and the only regular contact you get is an invoice. If the agents were working hard for you, they would call you and tell you about it. Assume your file has been put away; if you want any progress, you will have to initiate the progress.

Sign 9 – Your Agency Says "It Cannot Be Done"

Your agent may be correct, but it is wise to get opinions from other qualified people. Your agency may not be able to deliver what you want, though it is readily available through other channels. Perhaps the individual with whom you are dealing is simply uninformed.

Sign 10 – Your Agency Is Slow to Respond to Your Requests

Apparently, other matters are more important than responding to your inquiries. For whatever reason, you have moved down on the list of priority customers. Slow response time suggests your account is being neglected.

When an agent is slow to respond to your requests, be assured you are not getting special attention.

Sign 11 – Your Renewal Quote Arrives Late or after the Expiration Date

This is a potentially costly situation. Your agent could arrive on your doorstep with an outrageous renewal quote. Should you try to cancel a month later to go to a lower-priced competitor, you could be responsible for a *short-rate cancellation charge*. By developing competitive quotes well ahead of renewal, you avoid being trapped by your agency.

Sign 12 – Your Total Premium Outlay Is Under $25,000

Often, these small size accounts increasingly are neglected as they are passed around from one agency to another through acquisitions and mergers. Agencies have trouble making a profit on these lower-priced accounts. If you are in this premium range, regularly check your alternatives to make sure you are not neglected, or do not overpay.

If you have never seriously tested the marketplace, immediately do so. Follow the suggestions in this book and you will find out how your present program can be improved. You will be glad you did!

Beware of Reliance on One Agency

If you think only one agency should handle your account for several years, you may have made some dangerous assumptions. Perhaps you have been with your current agency for many years, and have developed a sense of trust in the agency, and feel you have established a valuable relationship. You are confident the agency is watching out for your needs, and is annually shopping your insurance among the available companies. Recognize that you are assuming:

- Your agency has access to the best available companies to quote your coverages.
- Your agency is actively pursuing the best rates for your business.
- Your agency has done a good risk management analysis of the needs of your business.

Obviously, you would like those assumptions to be valid, but this may not be the case. To illustrate the dangers of relying on the *one-agency concept* — renewing with the same people year after year — study the following two examples.

Genesis Corporation, a manufacturer of widgets, was prospering and flourishing. However, the business was exposed to potential liability problems — because these widgets could remove fingers under the wrong conditions. They took their insurance problem to a wise insurance broker who had set up an attractive program with a preferred insurance company. The total premium they paid for the program was $149,000.

The following year, an aggressive and resourceful insurance broker persuaded them to shop their account. The broker found an exceptional program that was substantially less than the incumbent company's program. The aggressive new broker found some important gaps in Genesis' coverage that was not included in their existing program. Although they missed these important coverages, the owners of Genesis were quite fond of their old broker. To be fair, Genesis' owners showed the new proposal to their existing broker, who showed it to the incumbent company. The incumbent company found a way to match the new quote by reducing their premium by forty percent!

In another example, Joe, the owner of a retail operation with approximately twelve business locations, kept his insurance business with the same agent for many years. Each year, Joe was assured the agent:

- Had shopped the insurance marketplace thoroughly;
- Was confident the bids were as low as the insured could find anywhere; and
- Placed the coverage with the best company possible.

The agent depended on the fact the insurance company was one of the industry's best. After all, the insurance company had Best's top rating. See Chapter 3 for an explanation of what a Best rating is and how it applies to insurance companies.

Eventually, Joe gave another agent a chance to quote the business, and saved thirty percent of the premium. The replacement company also enjoyed the same high financial rating, and significantly improved Joe's coverages.

In addition, small businesses can achieve surprising cost reductions. Consider the examples below of smaller, widely varied operations and you will see why almost any business should apply the strategic purchasing methods presented in this book.

- A baker's premium was reduced by fifty percent by allowing a new agent to quote the renewal — because the new agent used an aggressive insurance company that competed for bakeries.
- A beautician saved thirty percent after finding an insurance company that specialized in writing beauticians.
- A landscaper found welcome relief in the landscape gardener's association program.
- An owner of a start-up business discovered not all companies declined to quote, or surcharge insurance rates because of lack of business experience.

- A printer saved $1,600 by splitting the coverages between two different insurance companies.
- A pharmacist discovered special professional liability coverage could be obtained by switching to another carrier at no extra cost.
- An apartment owner saved twenty percent after discovering the buildings were overinsured for the past five years.
- A restaurant owner discovered the square footage of the facility was miscalculated and received a welcome savings.

Beyond premium savings, many business owners have learned their current policy coverages could be greatly improved, as evidenced by the following:

Agents commonly quote one price, and then find they can reduce it by applying some additional effort.

- A glass shop owner learned a new and improved program contained much broader property insurance coverage.
- A mechanic discovered coverage for damage to customers' cars was sorely lacking.
- A trucker learned one of his vehicles was uninsured because it was not on the schedule included in the insurance policy.
- A manufacturer found her existing coverage would not pay for a loss of income resulting from a fire. This would have likely meant bankruptcy had the coverage not been changed and her business suffered a fire.

Like the wise insurance buyers previously discussed, you can receive significant savings on your insurance if you realistically approach the marketplace.

A Realistic Approach

A creative and ambitious agent may find a way to reclassify a risk or has a unique connection in the marketplace.

Experienced agents realize that the marketplace is bigger than they are. Because there are so many opportunities to find bargains, and because the entire marketplace is in a constant state of change, no single individual can have all the answers. In many cases, businesses will get very similar quotes, and then stumble across a quote that is half the price of others — because a creative and ambitious agent found a way to reclassify the risk or had a unique connection in the marketplace. It is not uncommon for agents to quote one price, and then find they can reduce it by applying some additional effort.

You may be wondering if your time and effort in shopping your insurance will guarantee an immediate and dramatic savings. Although you may not see an immediate savings, if you consistently employ the practices presented in this book, you put the odds in your favor. In the long term, you may win a dramatic price reduction, avoid a rate increase, or have a loss fully covered, which otherwise might have been underinsured. While it is difficult to say exactly when your profits will arrive, no one will disagree that insurance purchasing is a burdensome business expense that can be significantly reduced with the proper knowledge and skill.

Notes

Chapter 2

The Issue of Risk Management

Defining Risk Management

Have you ever wondered what the term, "risk management," means to you and your business? If asked, can you define the various risk management techniques? If not, you are not alone. Currently, risk management is an insurance industry buzz word. One of the problems with a buzz word is its meaning often becomes confused, as people attempt involvement in or connection with the new concept attached to the buzz word.

Risk management is no exception. The term is used as a general description of a variety of differing services performed on behalf of those insured — people like you, the insurance buyers. Although this book is not a study of risk management, you will learn various risk management techniques throughout the following chapters. To make the risk management discussions easily identifiable, briefly review the following risk management issues.

Understanding the Risk Management Process

Risk management is a process of determining the acceptable level of loss your business is willing to tolerate in all the various aspects of its existence. To do this, you must first identify potential loss exposures of your business and set the acceptable level of loss for each aspect of the business' operations. Your next step is to develop various alternatives to prevent or minimize your losses. Once you develop a list of alternatives, you:

Identify potential loss exposures of your business and set the acceptable level of loss for each aspect of the business' operations.

- Select the best alternative;
- Implement the alternative selected; and
- Monitor the outcome.

If you don't achieve your desired outcome, repeat the process until the you achieve your predetermined acceptable level of loss.

Risk management covers every conceivable possibility of loss.

You may notice the definition is not limited to the loss of tangible property. In its pure form, risk management covers every conceivable possibility of loss. For example, it is equally useful to deal with the problems of a phonograph manufacturer in preparing for the obsolescence of its products, as it is handling the possibility of minor theft from a local convenience store. To effectively prepare for loss, you can use several different methods. One such method involves four steps. Your identification of the acceptable level of loss your business is willing to tolerate in all the various aspects of its existence is a major project. Frequently, just determining the areas of potential loss is the most difficult task, and it is accomplished after reviewing every part of your business' operations. This review should include everything from the possible loss of your building due to fire, to the possible loss of your investor's capital that allows expansion of your business.

Step 1 – Identify Potential Losses

Your first step in finding loss exposures is to review your business' day-to-day operations by examining every step involved. To help, you can construct flow charts that show the flow of your operation; this often proves to be a revealing process. The charts should include:

- The names of any key people involved in the operation;
- All the specific items needed to accomplish a task; and
- Other necessary elements for task completion, such as electrical power needed to operate machinery.

You should scrutinize every aspect of your business for the possibility of loss.

The completed charts should point out areas where your losses can occur, and help you identify the potential magnitude of the losses. If yours is an elaborate or large operation, you may need a simplified block diagram, where each department of your business completes a flow chart of its specific operation. Once all the departmental charts are assembled, you can thoroughly study your business' overall operations. An investigation beyond the physical necessities into the financial, human resources, marketing, and sales operation of your business is more difficult. But ideally, you should scrutinize every aspect of your business for the possibility of loss.

Step 2 – Determine the Acceptable Level of Risk

Once you have determined the areas of potential loss, decide the acceptable level of loss you are willing to assume. Normally, this level is determined in dollars, although it can be expressed in other terms — such as sick days or hours of down time. To determine the appropriate level of loss, you may need to review your business goals and current financial conditions. Goals can relate to everything from your monetary earnings and growth, to your commitments to good citizenship in your community. When deciphering your current financial condition, you may consider your current cash flow, borrowing power, stock price, bond interest rate, and other financial variables. Frequently, these decisions are made by the owners or top management. Once you make your decisions, you don't have to convey the information to the public or the other employees of your business, except on a need-to-know basis.

You may consider your current cash flow, borrowing power, stock price, bond interest rate, and other financial variables.

Step 3 – Identify Alternatives by Prioritizing and Categorizing Risks

When you begin developing various alternatives to prevent or minimize losses, project the frequency and severity of losses occurring under the present set of circumstances. At this point, your task is to identify alternatives to minimize the frequency and severity of losses and to bring the potential impact of overall losses in line with your acceptable business goals. You can use a model that categorizes and prioritizes all aspects of your business. This prioritizing method gives ways to handle a risk of loss, depending on the frequency with which it occurs and the severity of the loss when it does occur. The two main variables are frequency and severity.

Take a careful look at the following risk categorization model. You can effectively identify your insurance alternatives by prioritizing and categorizing your risks. You will notice that as the severity and frequency of a loss increases, the need to avoid or transfer the risk becomes greater. In like manner, as the severity, or impact, and the frequency decreases, you can utilize other methods, such as reducing or retaining the risk.

As previously discussed, you will want to scrutinize each aspect of your business and its potential for loss. This model gives you a starting point to deal with your potential losses and provides a standardized method to help you choose the appropriate insurance for your business.

Model to Prioritize and Categorize Your Risks

Severity of Loss	Not Frequent	Very Frequent
Very Severe	**Not Frequent/Severe** **Action: Transfer the risk**	**Frequent/Severe** **Action: Avoid the risk**
Not Severe	**Not Frequent/Not Severe** **Action: Retain the risk**	**Frequent/Not Severe** **Action: Reduce the risk**

Frequency of Occurrence

Evaluate the following four alternatives for dealing with your risks.

- Avoid the Risk Labeled Frequent/Severe — The risks of loss that are categorized as frequent/severe usually happen with such frequency and are so severe, they cannot be tolerated by your business. You must make arrangements to completely avoid these types of losses. For instance, if one of your operations causes frequent and severe fires, then your only alternative is to avoid that particular part of the operation. Perhaps the fire-causing portion of your operation can be subcontracted to a company that is better qualified to handle the operation or is better prepared to meet the losses.

Loss prevention measures strive to stop losses from occurring, thus reducing frequency.

- Reduce the Risk Labeled Frequent/Not Severe — The risks of loss that are categorized as frequent/not severe occur with great frequency, but fortunately are not severe — such as minor thefts at a retail store. If this applies to your type of business, to bring this type of loss into the acceptable level, you can take steps to reduce the number of these losses. For example, you can install mirrors, closed circuit television monitors, or schedule more people on each work shift. In the insurance industry, these actions are called loss prevention measures. *Loss prevention measures* strive to stop losses from occurring, thus reducing frequency. The same measures used for loss prevention can be referred to as loss control measures as well. Loss controls are used to reduce the severity of a loss when it does occur.
- Retain the Risks Labeled Not Frequent/Not Severe — The risks of loss that are categorized as not frequent/not severe happen infrequently and are minor, so you can treat the losses as nuisances and normal costs of doing business. For example, you may experience the inconvenience of a phone system, copier, or computer breakdown. Normally, an equipment breakdown is an infrequent occurrence and is handled by paying for the repair out of the normal cash flow of your business. But if an item continues to break with more frequency, you probably want to label it as frequent/not severe or frequent/severe — depending on how your day-to-day operations are affected. In a greater priority category, you can take more appropriate actions to handle the risk. Perhaps the failing equipment needs replacement or its task subcontracted to another business.

What may appear to be avoidance of the issue is actually effective risk management.

- Transfer the Risks Labeled Not Frequent/Severe — The risks of loss that are categorized as not frequent/severe happen infrequently. But, because the risks are so severe, they should be transferred to someone else. What may appear to be avoidance of the issue is actually effective risk management. For instance, suppose you own a building and lease space to other tenants. If a visitor slips and falls while on your premises, the potential for lawsuit is great. As the owner of the building, you can transfer the risk to the lessee through a skillfully written hold harmless agreement — where the owner transfers the risk of loss to the lessee as part of the lease. If the risk from owning a building is the chance it may suffer a fire loss, then you can easily transfer that risk to your insurance company. By purchasing a fire insurance policy, with enough coverage to replace the building in the event of a fire loss, you will have minimal personal monetary risk of loss.

Step 4 – Implement and Monitor the Appropriate Solutions

Once you have categorized your risks and their corresponding solutions, implement and monitor the appropriate alternatives. Using the model on page 17, you will either transfer, retain, avoid, or reduce the risk. Usually, you can track the losses and compare the dollars of loss from year to year. Obviously, differing periods of time can be used depending on your type of business. If your desired level of loss is not achieved, then the quadrant prioritizing process must be repeated from the point of determining alternatives through monitoring the risks again.

Ultimately, all forms of risk are managed using one of the four actions or a combination of these tactics. Sometimes, your actions will be thoughtfully selected, while other times, your course of action is by default from lack of attention to your risks of losses. For instance, suppose you neglect to insure a valuable part of your business. At this point, you have two options. You can learn to operate without the important part of the business, or you can replace the loss from your business' current cash flows, borrowing power, or sales of assets. Your decision will rest on the importance of the lost part to your overall business success.

Your Best Choice — Transference

Insurance is normally the most cost-effective and convenient method of transference of potential loss available to your business. As a business owner, you may have insurance options available and wonder how much risk of loss you should transfer to your insurance company and how much you should retain yourself. Retaining risk can be somewhat unpredictable, since the causes of loss are usually accidental in nature.

Fortunately, insurance packages usually cover accidental losses, so insuring is normally an available option if you can afford and locate the right coverage. When confronted with the question of how much risk to transfer — or how much insurance coverage to buy, and how much risk to retain — your decision will hinge on the cost of the insurance and the amount of available money you have to spend on insurance. To help you make an appropriate choice, you will want to know what coverages are necessary for your business.

Insuring is normally an available option if you can afford and locate the right coverage.

Know What Coverages Are Necessary

If you have not selected several insurance professionals to assist you, refer to Chapter 3. Once selected, insurance professionals should assist in identifying the types of insurance coverages available and the costs of each. To choose the most important coverages, understand the significance of each item subject to risk of loss as either:

- Critical — Our business cannot continue without this and we cannot afford to replace it.

- Important — Our business cannot continue without this item and we will have to borrow or sell assets to replace it.
- Optional — Our business can continue without this item, or can be replaced with current cash flows.

The following worksheet will help you list the items that are necessary to your business' operation and that would need repair or replacement if lost or damaged. You will want to identify your items as critical, important, and optional insurance risks based on their necessity to continue operations. For example, suppose your business consists of one building and its contents — or business personal property — and one trucking vehicle. You only have enough money to insure some of these items and still continue to operate within your budgeted amount for insurance. You will need to decide which, if any, of these items you can repair or replace without the help of insurance in the event of a loss.

For instance, if your business requires the actual building to continue operating, or requires insurance as a condition of the lease, then it must be insured. The building should be labeled as critical. If the truck is not deemed critical to the continuance of your business, categorize it as optional — meaning the truck will be repaired or replaced as cash flow permits. After some additional thought, you may label the business personal property as important. Further, you can decide which of the business personal property items are critical, important, or optional. You can assess each item in this same manner and assign each item one of the priority categories for the purpose of determining the need to insure.

Throughout the remaining chapters, many insurance-risk management techniques are discussed without specifically referring to them as such. Keep in mind the techniques' usefulness is not diminished by the lack of distinguishing them as risk management concepts. As you learn the importance of reevaluating your insurance program on a regular basis, you can begin to apply key strategies presented in this book. You will surely reap the benefits of lower premiums and eliminate the risk of uninsured losses and poor service.

On the following pages, you will find the Risk Categorization Worksheet. Carefully read the instruction sheets on the corresponding pages. Make enough photocopies for your business' purpose.

Risk Categorization Worksheet

Worksheet Instructions

Worksheet

Risk Categorization Worksheet Instructions

Before you attempt to use this worksheet, read Chapter 2. The worksheet is a reproducible copy. Make enough photocopies for your business' purposes.

1. Enter the item that you must consider risk of loss. Describe the item accurately. For example, if the item is a building or personal property, say, "A building with masonry walls, wood roof with hot mop tar and gravel, a concrete slab floor. The ground floor is used as our store and the second floor is used as two apartments that are rented to long-term tenants. Built in 1944; 2,400 square feet."
2. In consideration of the worst case scenario, be honest, yet somewhat conservative. Consider the possible problems your community would face at the same time you experience the problems. For example, an earthquake, tornado, or hurricane could devastate the entire area. After a major disaster, virtually everyone looks for financing, low interest loans, and available building space. Remember, all prices rise immediately after a major natural disaster.
3. Consider your geographic location. Is your property near an earthquake faultline or in a coastal region prone to hurricanes?
4. After your thoughtful analysis of questions one through three, you can categorize your risky loss as critical, important, or optional. Refer to Chapter 2 for further help, if you are still undecided.
5. At this point, you are probably ready for a cost-benefit analysis. This is the final decision point for you to decide how you will handle your risk. If the risk is critical to insure but insurance is not available to you because you can't afford it, then the risk becomes either one you must avoid or transfer by another manner. See the discussion on avoidance, transference, reduction, and retention in Chapter 2.
6. Will you take a loan, sell assets, use current cash flow, or divert funds from other areas, such as expansion plans? You must take a proactive approach to your ability to finance before loss occurs.
7. Explain how you will take action as a result of a loss. If you do, can you finance it out of cash flow? If not, how will you proceed? If this risk of loss truly is optional, you may decide no action is necessary.

Risk Categorization Worksheet

1. **The item at risk of loss:**

____

____

____

____

2. **The worst case scenario, if the item is not insured and a loss occurs:**

____

____

____

____

3. **The probability of such a loss occurring: (check one)**

☐ High probability ☐ Moderate ☐ Low ☐ Will not happen

4. **The risk is:**

☐ Mandatory ☐ Important ☐ Optional

5. **Insurance available for the mandatory risk:**

☐ Yes ☐ No

The price is:

☐ Affordable ☐ Unaffordable

6. **How will we finance the loss of an important item?**

____

____

____

____

7. **How will we finance the loss of an optional item?**

____

____

____

____

Notes

Chapter 3

Know the Marketplace

Introduction to the Marketplace

As an informed business insurance buyer, you need a thorough knowledge of the marketplace, including:

- The different types of insurance sellers;
- The correct ways to find a good insurance company; and
- The types of service and coverage to look for.

This chapter provides you with a good basis for knowing the insurance industry's key players, so you can confidently approach the insurance marketplace. A useful and practical evaluation and comparison form — Insurance Agency Profile — is located at the end of this chapter for your use.

Find Superior Agents and Brokers

Hundreds of different property and casualty insurance companies do commercial insurance business in the United States. The insurance companies sell insurance in a variety of ways; however, the majority use agents and brokers to market to the general public. Accordingly, each state has thousands of agents and brokers, representing hundreds of commercial insurance companies. Before starting your search for the right company and agency, be familiar with the different kinds of companies and agencies.

Being informed about different types of agencies will alert you to the agents' or brokers' positions and will help you effectively deal with them. Also, being informed will help you when selecting agencies to quote your account. Many agencies want you to think they have the policy and price

Many agencies quote your account, and recommend you purchase their insurance program; but until you shop the marketplace, you don't know where your best buy is hiding.

you need. They may quote your account, and recommend you purchase their insurance program; but until you shop the marketplace, you don't know where your best buy is hiding.

Types of Insurance Agents and Agencies

Insurance is marketed in basically three ways, two of which involve agents and brokers. The terms agents and brokers, although technically different, are synonymous and interchangeable in the insurance marketplace. First, there are *exclusive agents* who represent one company or group of companies. These are frequently referred to as *captive agents* or *direct writers*. Next, there are agencies called *independent agencies* who represent more than one company and usually represent more than five insurance companies. Finally, some insurance companies use no agents at all, but sell directly through the mail or through association programs offered by telemarketing contact. These are true *direct writers*.

The two most common types of agents are the exclusive agents and the independent agents. Continuing competition between these two types of distribution systems is prevalent as each claims to be superior to the other. The exclusive agents generally offer only the products and coverages their one company offers. In contrast, the independent agents can shop the various companies they represent to get you a greater variety of quotes. The exclusive agent system is thought to be a less expensive method of distribution, and the savings can be passed along to you. These two distribution systems are constantly in a price war. If you can get one exclusive agency and one independent agency quoting against one another, you can make this work to your advantage to get the lowest possible premium.

Ask for a list of the insurance companies your agents contacted to quote your account, and the results to help you identify companies that want your business.

When choosing between the two types of agents, one consideration involves claim disputes. The theory is independent agents may be able to fight on your behalf to resolve a disputed claim, because they have other insurance companies in which to place your business. The insurance company disputing the claim does not want to risk losing not only your business, but all of the business the agency has with the company. This threat of business movement can be a powerful motivator to help the independent agent get the claim settled.

In contrast, exclusive agents have no flexibility to move to another company, and may even be employees of the company they represent, with little or no power to bargain on your behalf. Exclusive agents may have developed a relationship through years of association with the company, and the insurance company may pay the claim on the merits of this relationship. In reality, most large claims that are disputed go to arbitration or litigation, and the agent is not a significant factor in its resolution. Truthfully, an agent's power is usually only a factor in small claims handling.

The smaller and less complex your business, the greater the likelihood it can be insured competitively in an exclusive agency company, and done correctly. The exclusive agency companies generally have not ventured into the larger and more complex product lines of the commercial business insurance yet. The exclusive agents historically have been the personal product lines — homeowners and personal use auto — insurance writers. In the past 15 years, the exclusive agents and companies have made very strong gains in the commercial insurance marketplace, and their importance varies by state and region of the country. In *Best Review's* October 1991 study, insurance companies marketing commercial insurance through independent agencies account for approximately eighty percent of the total marketplace in a common commercial policy called the Commercial Multi-peril Line by premium volume. (*Best Review* p. 36)

Know Your Insurance Company's Rating

Informed buyers want to be certain they are insured by a financially sound and well-managed insurance company. To determine this on your own seems an impossible task unless you enjoy perusing financial statements. Fortunately, there is another, more simple way to gain information on the quality of an insurance company.

A company called A.M. Best publishes the *Best's Key Rating Guide-Property and Casualty Insurance.* Best assigns insurance companies a letter grade similar to the types used in today's educational system. The letter grade (A++, A+, A, A-, B++, and so on, down to D, E, and F) is an indication of a company's financial performance, its overall management, and the quality of business it writes. For example, A++ is the highest rating any company can receive. From there, the rating can fall to an F rating. The size of a company is shown by roman numeral — I (one) is the lowest rating, and XV (fifteen) is the highest — to give an indication of its policyholder surplus or assets. Thus, the top rating available is an A++XV. This shows a company of superior quality and the largest size, per Best's rating. Keep in mind Best rates companies based largely on the data that companies submit to the state insurance departments. This means Best's does not audit or guarantee the accuracy of the information. Further, you should easily find a company with a high rating, since over 1,300 companies are rated A- or higher.

In addition, the two leading investment services — Moody's Investor Service and Standard & Poor's Corporation — also rate insurance companies. Typically, they rate only companies whose stock trades in the public sector, or who use bonds as a means of accumulating capital. Your public library will have at least one of these sources available, as should many insurance agencies.

Many insurance organizations are interested in writing all or part of your commercial insurance program. With the large number of companies in the marketplace, it is unlikely you will discover the best possible price and coverage combination by obtaining only one or two quotes. Approach

It is unlikely you will discover the best possible price and coverage combination by obtaining only one or two quotes.

several companies with your specific situation so they can inform you of their ability to serve your needs.

Admitted Versus Nonadmitted Insurance Companies

All insurance companies are formed as either domestic, foreign, or alien companies depending on where they are formed or organized.

- Domestic company — A company that is formed or organized under the laws of your state.
- Foreign company — A company that is formed under laws of a state other than your state.
- Alien company — A company that is formed or organized under laws of another country.

Many states are encouraging their citizens to only purchase insurance from admitted companies.

Many states are making it more difficult for nonadmitted companies to do business in their state and are encouraging their citizens to only purchase insurance from admitted companies.

By knowing the various types of business formation, you will be alerted to the importance of dealing with domestic or foreign insurance companies whenever possible. Insurance companies that have formed or organized in one of the states of the United States allow that state's insurance department to exercise jurisdiction over the insurance company and to monitor its financial condition. A state insurance department's jurisdiction doesn't guarantee that a company won't go bankrupt or that it will pay your claim quickly. However, you are assured state government control over an insurance company.

In contrast, an alien company can be formed and located on a remote island or country. Such alien companies may be operated by a part-time employee who receives mail from a postal box. In recent history, some poorly financed alien companies have gone bankrupt, leaving many insured people with unpaid claims; however, not all alien companies are financially impaired. Many alien companies are in outstanding financial condition, and are among the world's largest insurance companies.

No matter where an insurance company is formed, an insurance company must decide if it wants to become an admitted company in your state. *Admitted* means the insurance company will apply to your state to become licensed to do business in your state. The licensing process subjects a company to financial scrutiny and requires that annual financial reports be filed with the state every year. To be an admitted insurance carrier, the company must:

- Allow the insurance department of its residing state to examine its books;
- Comply with state laws; and
- Participate in the state's guarantee funds for insurance company insolvency.

If an admitted insurance company goes bankrupt, those people it insures will have some amount of their claims paid by the state guarantee funds — a practice only done for admitted insurance companies.

In the United States, no state or federal laws exist that say insurance companies must become admitted carriers. An insurance company can opt to be *nonadmitted* — meaning the company is not licensed by the state to transact insurance through agents or brokers. Nonadmitted companies normally can only do business through surplus line brokers — those who specialize in certain areas. Historically, nonadmitted companies have been willing to insure more hazardous types of risks and often served as a market for the least desirable types of insurance risks, such as vacant buildings and hazardous operations like building demolition. Many states are making it more difficult for nonadmitted companies to do business in their state and are encouraging their citizens to only purchase insurance from admitted companies.

You can distinguish the good alien companies from the bad ones by contacting your state insurance department. Look in your local phone book under state offices or call general information for your area. Once you have located the department and appropriate person with whom to talk, ask if the insurance company you are interested in is on an approved list, or if the company has any complaints. In addition, the National Association of Insurance Commissioners created a list of alien companies they feel are qualified to meet your needs. See if your state has this list or its own list. Another way you can check out a company's status is to look in the *Best's Key Rating Guide*, which features a section that shows the states in which companies are licensed and the state of their domicile. If you are really curious, call the insurance company's marketing department and ask if the company is an admitted insurance carrier in your state. An insurance company marketing representative should be able to answer this question. Finally, discuss the insurance company with quoting agents or brokers with whom you are working, to see if they have any factual information on the company.

Ideally, insure with admitted companies — whether domestic, foreign, or alien. Remember, if you are insured with an admitted company, you will have some hope of getting claims paid by your state's guarantee fund in the event the company should go bankrupt. However, the guarantee funds of most states do not return the premiums you have paid in advance. So if your old insurance company goes bankrupt, you will lose that money and begin paying all over again with your new company.

Ideally, insure with admitted companies — whether domestic, foreign, or alien.

How Insurance Cycles Affect You

As an informed business insurance buyer, you need to know how insurance cycles affect you. With a better understanding of these cycles, you will be better prepared to approach the marketplace and make your buying decision.

A soft insurance market is when the insurance industry has surplus investment capital and insurance is plentiful, with heavy competition among insurance companies.

Insurance cycles are caused by two major factors — profit and investment capital. As soon as insurance companies generate a healthy income, they cut their pricing to attract more buyers. Unfortunately, claims continue to be a direct percentage of the number of written policies. Soon the losses from claims increases far greater than the premium income. As this happens, companies begin to lose profits and eventually may lose money. To remain in competition with the lower rates, other companies will also cut their pricing to retain their clients and attract new ones. So the whole industry starts to spiral downward in a pricing war and downward in profitability. Like a domino effect, insurance industry investors will note the lack of profitability and move their money to other investment industries. As a result, the insurance industry will lack necessary capital to allow it to write an increasing amount of insurance. The result is reduced availability of insurance and profitability.

A hard market is when a lack of investment capital makes insurance scarce and prices increase.

An insurance downward trend can be remedied in two steps. In step one, the companies examine the policies they write and cancel any they fear may produce losses. Those that looked attractive enough to write in the soft market — when the insurance industry has surplus investment capital and insurance is plentiful, with heavy competition among insurance companies — may now look like bad gambles. If you are viewed in this negative light, expect a notice of cancellation or nonrenewal. The cancellation can result from no fault of your own, but rather an insurance company's management decision that your type of business needs to be removed to avoid losses. Step two involves accounts that survive this scrutiny. They are offered renewals with significant price hikes. When these circumstances occur, you know you are dealing with the classic hard market — when a lack of investment capital makes insurance scarce and prices increase.

After prices have been high for some time, and insurance companies have properly priced and placed the difficult-to-insure risks, they will return to profitability. Investors will return to the high profit industry and once again, a large supply of money will be available for the companies to write all the insurance they desire. Then a company will decide the only way to make more money is to attract more insurance clients, and the prices will fall again. Keep in mind your ideal purchase is in a soft market — where the prices fall and insurance is readily available.

Market cycles affect you because your premiums and the availability of insurance coverages will fluctuate in direct correlation to the insurance marketplace. You can capitalize on this by shopping your insurance during a soft market, so you can get the best coverage available for the lowest possible price. Further, during a soft market you can prepare for the hard market — much higher prices later — by accumulating your savings from the relatively lower prices. You can take advantage of the lower premiums by carefully spending money on the precautions that sensible loss control and risk management call for, to make your business more attractive to insurance companies.

Bear in mind, as you implement sensible loss prevention measures, you will find insurance companies more willing to insure you regardless of the market conditions.

Four Ways to Find the Right Insurance Organization

Considering the large number of companies and agents available, how can you find the right agent, broker, or company to handle your business? The most common ways to find prospects from which you can make a final selection of agencies to quote your insurance are by networking, affiliation with an association, direct mail or phone solicitation, and by simply consulting the Yellow Pages.

Networking

Networking with businesses similar to yours enables you to compare notes with your peers. Networking can become a valuable source of information for the best service and pricing for your type of business. Ask your business acquaintances who they use for their business insurance, and compare results with them. If your business acquaintances also read this book, you and your associates can collect completed Insurance Agency Profiles provided at the end of this chapter, and identify the agencies in your area which may better serve your needs. Remember to network with businesses similar to yours, which are the same size or slightly larger than your own.

Associations and Organizations

You probably belong to various associations or organizations that have endorsed certain insurance companies and their specific programs. These programs may be available to you through local agents or directly from the companies. The association may have literature or brochures available, giving you the name and phone number to call.

Phone or Mail Solicitation

For insurance companies and agencies, direct mail advertising and telemarketing are efficient methods of contacting a target class of business. When you receive an attractive mail advertisement from an agency or company, file it for later reference. Similarly, ask telemarketers to send information on their agency; you may use it in the future.

Yellow Pages

By looking in the Yellow Pages under "Insurance," you will find many listings and advertisements of both agencies and insurance companies. You may recognize insurance company logos, which distinguish them from the agencies. Under these insurance logo listings, the company will frequently list the various agencies representing them in your local community. You can also call the insurance company directly and ask them for names of the agencies in your area with whom they do business.

Advertisements do little to reveal how empowered any particular firm is to help you.

When browsing through the Yellow Pages, keep in mind that advertisements do little to reveal how empowered any particular firm is to help you. The strength of the agency and the competence of its staff are functions of the insurance companies it represents. Some excellent agencies display modest-sized advertisements that may seem disproportionate for the agencys' size. These agencies don't need to spend large amounts of money on this type of advertising, because their major source of new business is client referrals.

Be "Size-Wise" When Selecting Agencies

When selecting your insurance agency, there are some fundamental factors you need to keep in mind. Once of these factors is the size of your business. You don't want to waste your time dealing with an insurance company that caters more to large corporations when you operate a small business. Some "size-wise" tips for when you are getting to know your marketplace are discussed below.

Exclusive Agents

Exclusive agents tend to operate out of small offices with one or two licensed agents and support staff. Usually, the total number of employees in the office is one to eight people. This means you have one insurance company and only a handful of people to serve you. If your business and your service demand is small, an exclusive agent may suit your needs. In this case, you probably will deal with the principals more frequently, and probably will receive attentive, personal service.

Small Independent Agencies

The smaller your business, the more likely you are to receive superior service from a smaller insurance agency.

Small independent agencies are firms with a limited number of insurance company appointments and are frequently no larger than the exclusive agency. During the last 15 years, many of these smaller agencies have been purchased and merged into larger firms, to gain competitive advantages. The strengths of the small independents will be relatively the same as the exclusive agency, except they will have more companies to quote your insurance.

Whether you choose an exclusive agent or a small independent agent, be aware of their limited capacity to serve you as your business grows. Their limited access to insurance companies can keep you from saving significant dollars with programs they cannot offer you. Their limited financial resources keep them from aggressive innovation and progressive steps that help serve you. For example, they may not purchase available computerized information services that may help you. Often, personalized attention hypnotizes buyers into accepting their agency's programs and recommendations without shopping the rest of the marketplace.

If you are currently buying your business insurance through one of these smaller agencies, obtain quotes from some larger independent insurance agencies. This will give you the price comparison you are seeking. The real question is your size. If you are a small business, you will normally receive better service from the smaller insurance agencies.

If you are currently buying your business insurance through a smaller agency, obtain quotes from some larger independent insurance agencies, for price comparisons.

Medium- to Large-Size Independent Agencies

Medium- to large-size independent agencies are writing significant amounts of commercial business these days. The large-size agencies:

- Place business with fifty or more insurance companies and are fully automated;
- Plan special arrangements with insurance companies that can benefit you, such as increased binding authorities, or the ability to commit the insurance company to insure a risk, and special rating programs;
- Use computerized rating systems to shop the markets more efficiently;
- Hire highly skilled staff; and
- Utilize personnel development systems.

Know who the larger agencies are in your area, and put them to work for you, if that is being size-wise in your situation.

National Insurance Brokerages

National insurance brokerages are the largest of the independent agencies. These firms have multiple offices and are located in many, if not all of the states. They have the ability to provide the service you need and deserve as your business grows. In fact, the largest of these firms now have offices or affiliations overseas to help their large multinational clients. Look for the national firms to be subtly listed in the Yellow Pages under "Insurance."

Have at least three agencies, and optimally five agencies quote your insurance. Include both independent agencies and exclusive agencies.

How Educated Is Your Agent?

The insurance industry has tried to encourage its members to involve themselves in continuing education programs to show a commitment to the industry and to professionalism. Insurance agents take courses to increase their knowledge, just like other professionals. When insurance professionals successfully complete a prescribed program of courses, they earn special designations, which are usually abbreviated after their names. Courses vary in length and difficulty by a wide margin. Examine the following list of some of the most common acronyms. The list is presented with no comment on their quality except for the number of course parts needed to achieve each title. Obviously, more course parts entail

Agents holding designations may deliver more complete and accurate coverage recommendations than those who never took the time to take the courses.

more effort. Usually, the presence of credentials adds credibility to the agent's commitment to the business and coverage recommendations.

- Chartered Property and Casualty Underwriter (CPCU) — Ten parts
- Associates in Risk Management (ARM) — Three parts
- Accredited Advisor in Insurance (AAI) — Three parts
- Certified Insurance Counselor (CIC) — Five parts
- Chartered Life Underwriter (CLU) — Ten parts
- Chartered Financial Planner (CFP) — Six parts

All courses require that the student successfully complete examinations. Many now encourage or require continuing education activity to retain the designation.

How Financially Stable Is the Agency?

Financially weak agencies usually cause trouble for their clients and for their insurance companies. Normally, the exclusive writers have little or no trouble with this situation because they directly control their agencies and many of their activities. The independent agency system has an occasional problem with the continued financial soundness of some of its agencies. If you are observant, you usually can spot warning signs. Below you will find a list of signals that may indicate an agency is experiencing financial difficulties.

- Personnel reductions and layoffs;
- Frequent personnel turnover;
- Relocation to smaller quarters;
- Loss of company appointments — you get notices of nonrenewal indicating the agency is "no longer appointed" by a specific company;
- Slow refund of premiums due from the agency, not the company;
- Lack of *errors and omissions* coverage — an agent's liability coverage for negligence in rendering service;
- Phone service interrupted or phone numbers changed; and
- No return of phone call messages.

Naturally, any or all of these conditions can occur while an insurance agency is perfectly healthy. Be candid with your agent, or check with others who do business with the agency, to identify their financial status. If you suspect your agency is about to collapse, immediately take steps to establish a relationship with a competing agency. Contact your insurance company directly and ask which agencies in your area represent them. If you decide to leave your agency, you can easily assign another as your agent.

How to Decide which Agency to Quote Your Insurance

The Insurance Agency Profile — located at the end of this chapter — helps you evaluate and compare the agencies you interview. Simply complete one profile for each agency you interview. By completing a form on each agency, you will develop a feel for your local insurance community. You may find friends and associates willing to trade profile information with you, thus multiplying your observation power.

Filling out an Insurance Agency Profile on the first meeting with an agent may seem reasonable to the agent, or it may seriously chill the relationship. You must decide how to handle the interview based on your own personal style. The questions asked on the profile are very pertinent and reveal much about an agency. Try to learn all you can about the agency. You may choose to wait until the agent leaves to make your notes on the profile, based on what you have learned in the interview. You can always call agents with specific questions; they may appreciate your interest. You eliminate those agents who are less qualified to serve you by asking intelligent, penetrating questions of new agents. Those who seem qualified should be encouraged to put their full efforts into winning your business.

By asking intelligent, penetrating questions of new agents, you eliminate those agents who are less qualified to serve you.

Shopping your insurance every year is not essential. By getting several opinions about your coverage selections, you do a thorough job and succeed in obtaining a competitive price this year. It may make sense to simply renew the following year — provided the market prices hold steady. Be certain, however, to carefully review your coverages every year, so your policy keeps pace with your changing business. At the very least, conduct a complete market survey every three years.

In your attempts to thoroughly shop the insurance marketplace, ask quoting agents to inform you of each insurance company intend to approach for your quote. This avoids the mistake of allowing more than one agent to approach the same company. Take note, when underwriters see the same account coming from several agents, they infer the account is being shopped all over the marketplace. This discourages underwriters, who may decide not to quote, or quickly prepare a high quote. These underwriters feel time spent quoting your account will probably result in a "no sale" anyway. Be aware of which insurance companies are looking at your account, so you can present your business in the best possible light to the underwriters.

Thoroughly shop your insurance, and select your optimal coverage combination at a low price. Your next renewal may require only updating coverage limits, unless the rates go up. Shop thoroughly at least every three years.

Notes

Insurance Agency Profile

Profile Instructions

Profile

Insurance Agency Profile Instructions

Use Sample Letter H in the Appendix for asking agents to provide information by mail.

1. Attaching their business card can save a little effort writing down the basic information.
2. Obtain both the street location and mailing address.
3. Write down their toll-free 800 number if they have one.
4. Self-explanatory.
5. This is the person you will work with, so you must be comfortable with that thought. Would you hire this person as an employee?
6. Information here should also include what year the agent first became licensed to transact insurance and how long the agent has been in the insurance business.
7. You should know how long the agency has been in business.
8. Check the designations held. If other than suggested below, ask for clarification. Refer to the discussion on how educated is your agent in Chapter 3, for definitions.
9. Check one. See discussion on types of agencies in Chapter 3.
10. For the sake of argument, consider a small agency to be under $5 million written premium, medium $5 million to $25 million, or a large business in excess of $25 million.
11. Know who to contact if you need answers from top management.
12. Appointed means able to contact and write insurance on a direct basis, without the use of an intermediary such as an excess or surplus lines broker.

Insurance Agency Profile

1. **Name of agency:** ______________________________
2. **Addresses:** ______________________________
3. **Phone number:** ______________________________
4. **Fax number:** ______________________________
5. **Name of agent contact:** ______________________________
6. **Number of years licensed:** ______________________________
7. **Age of the firm:** ______________________________
8. **Credentials and designations of agent:**

   Check those applicable: ☐ CPCU ☐ ARM ☐ AAI ☐ CIC ☐ CLU ☐ CFP ☐ Other: __________

   ____
9. **Type of agency: (check one)**

   ☐ Independent agency

   ☐ Exclusive agency
10. **To get a sense of the size of the agency, indicate the number of:**

    _____ Producers (sales agents)

    _____ Customer service representatives

    _____ Claims personnel

    $__________ Gross premium written by the agency (in millions)
11. **Name of agency president, manager, or current owners:**

    ____
12. **Our agency is appointed with the following insurance companies:**

    ____

    ____

    ____

Insurance Agency Profile Instructions (continued)

13. This helps you understand who you are really doing business with. An agency may have access to many companies, but may try to put most of their volume with only a few.
14. This is professional liability coverage for insurance agents and brokers, to defend and indemnify for losses caused by agent's negligence in the rendering of services. Some agents have it, and some do not. Naturally, you are more secure with firms that carry this coverage. The more money you spend on insurance, the more reasonable it is to ask for specifics on errors and omissions coverage. In all cases, it is reasonable to ask the agent if coverage is provided. The coverage is so expensive, some agencies run without it, and others carry low limits.
15. It doesn't hurt to ask which insurance company provides the errors and omissions insurance. It makes sense for larger businesses to ask agencies to provide certificates of insurance from the errors and omissions insurance company. The insurance company can be looked up in Best's for financial soundness, as discussed in Chapter 3.
16. New systems seem to always have problems. A new system may mean slow or poor service until the problems are resolved.
17. Ask to see a sample billing statement. Check for clarity and ease of understanding the bills. Manual accounting systems can be cumbersome, and less responsive to your inquiries, such as requests for statements summarizing your account.
18. A system that has the client files on-line can result in fast, efficient service. This is particularly true when the computer system has been working over a year, so the difficulties that often arise from new computer systems have been resolved.
19. If the applications are on the system, this can be a plus, because the agency can efficiently shop your account, so it is more likely to do so. Applications on the computer system indicate a progressive business that can keep pace with the fast-changing world.
20. Get names and phone numbers of clients with similar needs to yours. If the firm is unable to produce referrals, consider this a serious concern. While you can't measure the character of agents by looking at them, you can place a quick call to the referrals to confirm they are authentic. The call should reveal any serious problems.

Insurance Agency Profile (continued)

13. Which three insurance companies are used most often for businesses like ours?

____

____

____

14. Limit of errors and omissions coverage: $____________________

15. Insurance company providing errors and omissions coverage:

____

16. Automated billing system: ☐ Yes ☐ No

Age of current automation system: _____ years

17. Accounting system automated: ☐ Yes ☐ No (Attach a sample of your billing statement.)

18. Are client files on the system: ☐ Yes ☐ No

19. Are applications stored on the system: ☐ Yes ☐ No

20. References of agency's customers with businesses similar to ours:

Business	Contact	Phone

Notes

Chapter 4

Prepare Your Business for Action

How You Can Prepare

With a basic knowledge of the marketplace and having reevaluated your current service, you are now ready to prepare your business for action and possibly slash prices. Truly, you can now take up your sword and armor to protect yourself against the many dangers found in the insurance industry. By completing the Underwriting Information Questionnaire at the end of this chapter, you will be safer from the dangers of high prices, weak coverage design, and inferior professional service.

A few hours is all it takes to assemble the pertinent information about your business. With the questionnaire thoroughly and accurately completed, you have increased power for minimizing your insurance expenses, while maximizing coverages. The completed questionnaire serves as your indispensable time-saving tool. It enables you to have even your new receptionist dispatch experienced agents to grind the insurance companies down for you. The agents will be fully equipped with the details they will need to negotiate your prices as much as possible.

The Underwriting Information Questionnaire was designed to save you time and money. The easy-to-complete questionnaire and corresponding, side-by-side instructions at the end of this chapter are easy to follow. In addition, the use of several sample letters, located in the Appendix, will expedite the process and get you on your way to better protection.

By completing the Underwriting Information Questionnaire at the end of this chapter, you will be safer from the dangers of high prices, weak coverage design, and inferior professional service.

Better yet, you can use *The Insurance Assistant*, this book's companion software. Simple to install and user-friendly, the software cuts your work time in half. The software allows you to plug in the data appropriate to your business. No photocopying or needless typing is involved — and, best yet, the information remains electronically stored. Whenever you make any changes to your operation or inventory, simply add the new information and update your Underwriting Information Questionnaire. For more information, contact:

The Oasis Press
(800) 228-2275

Nine Reasons to Complete the Questionnaire

At this point, you still might not be convinced of the necessity of completing a seven-part questionnaire. To give you a better idea of your buying position once you have completed the Underwriting Information Questionnaire, here are some of the main reasons to fill-in-the-blanks.

Avoid Lengthy Initial Interviews and Get a Faster Start

When an agent begins to quote your account, you skip the fifty questions on the agency's form — because your answers are ready. You eliminate wasted time hunting around for information the agency needs — because you have already prepared it. You eliminate call backs for information the agency forgot to ask — because your information is complete. You accomplish in 10 or 15 minutes what normally consumes over 90 minutes. And your efficiency enables you to engage as many agencies as necessary to fully sample the marketplace.

Control Your Insurance Purchase

Your preparation and organization tells the agency that you demand excellent service. Also, any additional interview time you elect to invest in can be directed toward determining the agency's qualifications to serve you. See the Insurance Agency Profile in Chapter 3. Further, it may be worthwhile to invest some time to establish rapport with the agencies to convince them to work extra hard on your account. Or you can discuss specific issues that need attention, and gather ideas and information. You also may use this opportunity to communicate with the agents regarding your service agenda, including:

- The date the quote is needed;
- The feedback you desire about which companies are interested in your account;
- The coverage variations for which you want prices; and
- The Coverage Checklist you want included with their quotes. (A full discussion on service scheduling is found in Chapter 10.)

Direct the time agents spend on your account away from gathering your basic information and toward obtaining competitive quotes.

You direct the time agents spend on your account away from gathering your basic information and toward obtaining competitive quotes. This effectively leverages your time, as well as the agents' time, to better serve your purposes. This leverage becomes possible when you have your completed Underwriting Information Questionnaire ready for action!

Improve the Quality of the Policy You Ultimately Purchase

Your policy will be designed by agents equipped with a complete understanding of your operation. Coverages you may now be missing will be identified by the better agents, so you can choose whether to purchase them. You minimize the chances of being needlessly exposed because of omitted information — a frequent occurrence for ill-prepared buyers. Your preparation protects you from forgetting to include all your business operations, equipment, property, vehicles, and employees. The questionnaire passes to agents some responsibility for your satisfaction and adequate protection because it documents what you have informed them about your business.

The questionnaire passes to agents some responsibility for your satisfaction and adequate protection because it documents what you have informed them about your business.

Reduce the Odds of Inadvertently Purchasing Unnecessary Coverages

Without your preparation, it is all too easy to overinsure a building, overstate inventory values, or include equipment you sold last year. You might purchase unnecessary coverage for physical damage on older vehicles. You might waste money on needless automobile medical payments coverage, while all those using the vehicles are insured by workers' compensation. An accurate presentation of the facts of your business helps avoid coverage excesses and redundancies.

Avoid Cancellations, Surprise Rate Increases and Audit Billings

By providing the complete information about your business at the initial interview, you avoid surprises. The insurance company and the agent enter the transaction fully informed, so there tends to be fewer disagreements during the policy year. Your filed copy of the questionnaire serves as powerful documentation about your representations. This protects you from claims that are later denied on the basis of "you never told us that."

Your filed copy of the questionnaire serves as powerful documentation about your representations — which protects you from claims that are later denied on the basis of "you never told us that."

Get Competitive Pricing from Quoting Companies

Your questionnaire provides the underwriters with the information they need to get you discounts. You earn all the premium credits you are due by volunteering every possible bit of favorable information about your business. You inform them in writing about such things as your sprinklers, fire extinguishers, loss-free history, burglar alarms, superior construction, safety meetings, financial strength, and experience in your line of work. Favorable details can reduce your rates — so make sure none are overlooked in your completed questionnaire.

Improve Your Chances for a Quote from Preferred Insurance Companies

In thinking through the answers, you learn the importance of incidental details. For instance, you can inadvertently give the wrong impression by

Inform agents and underwriters in writing about favorable details that can reduce your rates.

overemphasizing a negative aspect of your operation, while neglecting to emphasize all the positive aspects. Often, a company will decline to quote an account based on a poor presentation, yet change its position when additional positive information is obtained. With your completed questionnaire, a very selective company known for its terrific prices can be persuaded to quote your business' coverages. This could mean a dramatic improvement in your pricing.

Identify Operational Improvements that Can Help Your Insurance Pricing

For example, housekeeping and maintenance can go a long way toward attracting the better deals from insurance companies. In addition, some operations get more interest when equipped with certain alarm systems or other protection. By completing the Underwriting Information Questionnaire, you become more astute in establishing procedures that affect insurance pricing.

Receive a Superior Level of Responsiveness

Agents almost never meet clients as prepared as you will be, and they will tend to respond to your presentation with more competitive service than usual.

Agents almost never meet clients as prepared as you will be, and they will tend to respond to your presentation with more competitive service than usual. They will recognize that you are not looking for a baby sitter to help you get your facts together. Rather, you are looking for tangible results in price reductions, coverage improvements, and superior service. If the agents are ill-prepared to serve you, they may surrender to what they see as obvious exposure to competition and save time for both of you. Only the stronger agents will compete for your account, quietly knowing that the strength of their pricing and service will be tested on a level playing field by a worthy client.

You would waste your accountant's costly minutes by going to your tax preparation interview without all your vital income and expense information readily available. It is equally wasteful and expensive to interview insurance agents without being prepared. In shopping your account, you are going to get your business' information together one way or the other, completely or incompletely. The use of the suggested methods and forms in this book will prove to be the most productive and efficient way to enter the marketplace.

Red Flags to Underwriters

The existence of the red flag will either cause your business to be uninsurable or cause you to pay higher than normal premiums for coverage.

As an insurance buyer, it is important to see your business operations through the eyes of insurance company loss control inspectors and underwriters. Through identifying the red flags that cause concern, you can avoid future problems and appear less of a risk to insure. If you have taken proper corrective actions, then add proof of those actions to your permanent insurance shopping file, including photographs and copies of contracts for safety services.

What is a red flag? A red flag is a condition or operation listed on an underwriter's list of unacceptable characteristics of a risk submitted for insurance. The existence of the red flag will either cause your business to be uninsurable or cause you to pay higher than normal premiums for coverage. Some examples of red flags are presented on the following pages by the type of insurance coverage they affect.

Red Flags Relating to All Types of Coverage

When it comes to insurance, all businesses will need specific coverages based on their unique operations. As a business insurance buyer, you can be alerted to the red flags that relate to all types of coverage. By knowing what prospective underwriters look for, you can avoid a negative rating by insurance companies that might be interested in insuring your business. Try to avoid sending a red flag to a prospective insurer by carefully handling the following aspects of your business.

New Ventures

New ventures concern underwriters because they know the dangers awaiting inexperienced management. To alleviate underwriters' fears if you are insuring a new venture, sell them on your capabilities and experience with prior, similar operations. Emphasize your background experience — a good indicator of what has prepared you for your current venture. Remember, business management and people management skills are important, as are skills in managing money. Strong financial backing also encourages underwriters to forgive the concerns related to a new venture.

Moral Hazards

Insurance company underwriters avoid exposure to moral hazards. Moral hazards are those that may motivate an insured to cause a loss and collect the money from the insurance company. If any of the following examples apply to you, offset them with as much positive information as possible.

Frequent red flags for moral hazards include:

- Slow payment of premiums;
- A weak financial statement;
- Noncompliance with governing laws and regulations — such as being an unlicensed contractor;
- Poor maintenance of your property, including shoddy appearance, peeling paint, dry rot, pot holes, piles of debris, and trash;
- Poor credit, such as in Dun and Bradstreet reports; and

- High loss frequency and patterns of theft, fires, or any other claims that appear to be repetitious.

Morale Hazards

Another major concern for all insurance companies is the existence of morale hazards. Morale hazards are indicated by a poor general management attitude toward maintaining a safe and efficient working environment. Never immediately reject the recommendations of insurance company inspectors or auditors. Display a cooperative attitude toward any reasonable idea that may reduce your exposure to risks and subsequently reduce your premium.

Recent Claims

For any claims in the past three years, demonstrate the steps you have taken to prevent recurrence.

For any claims in the past three years, demonstrate steps you have taken to prevent recurrence. Examples of corrective steps include remedial action of employees with poor safety records, elimination or proper identification of trip and fall hazards, safety training, and installation of alarm systems. If a claim was a fluke, explain why.

Red Flags for Property Coverages

Property coverage is essential for today's business owner. Often, when considering insurance for property coverage, buyers unknowingly send red flags to potential insurers. To avoid this red flag problem, be aware of the operations that occur on your property. You can use common sense as you take safety measures to make your property less of a risk to insure.

Rural Properties

Volunteer all the information you can about available fire protection in your area.

Rural properties may be located in areas not protected by fire departments. If you are located in a remote area, volunteer all the information you can about available fire protection in your area. Mention sources of water, pumping systems, and fire suppression systems.

Cooking on the Premises

Cooking on the premises, especially the frying of food, alerts underwriters to the increased chance of fire. Inform both agents and underwriters about your systematic procedures for cleaning the ventilation system. Give them a copy of any flue cleaning contracts. Prove you have an automatic fire extinguishing system in the vents, hood, and over the cooking and fryer system. Advise them of the frequency with which the extinguishers are inspected for charges.

Hazardous Chemicals

Use of potentially hazardous chemicals will raise a red flag. Address any situation where dangerous fumes have a chance of accumulating. Spray painting alerts the underwriters to look for adequate ventilation and fire protection. If sawdust is created, describe your dust collection system to the underwriters. Oily rags can lead to spontaneous combustion, so you will want to inform the underwriters of your acceptable disposal methods. With photographs or tours, prove you properly store and contain chemicals. Show any service contracts you may have for disposing of waste chemicals.

With photographs or tours, prove you properly store and contain chemicals.

Concentrated Values

Susceptibility to major theft losses due to concentrated values is a major concern. Electronic appliances, auto parts, and clothing stores are typical examples. Prove you have adequate alarms and safeguards. Mention iron bars, local gong alarms, central station reporting alarms, and other security services. The use of guard dogs causes more concern than it cures due to increased liability hazards from dog bites.

Red Flags for Commercial General Liability Coverage

Liability coverage is an integral part of any business' risk management program. You will want to take steps to prevent your business from lawsuits. The following commercial general liability coverage red flags will alert underwriters that your business is a risk to insure. You can avoid this negative label with a proactive approach.

Product Liability

The products you manufacture may present a large concern to underwriters. Exposures to serious or even catastrophic loss exist from manufacturing or selling many products — such as aircraft components, auto parts, boat parts, medical equipment, guns and munitions, cutting machines, biotechnical products, and new products not previously produced or tested. The list of questionable products can be very lengthy. Show the product you make or sell is as safe as possible by providing test results or certifications from testing laboratories. Show you are as insulated from lawsuits as possible through the use of hold-harmless agreements and certificates of insurance from subcontractors you have hired.

Hold-harmless agreements are contracts or clauses in contracts, in which one party assumes the liability of another party, and agrees to indemnify (reimburse) you for defense costs or legal judgments you incur. The agreements should be written by an attorney to make them as favorable to you as possible, yet still be honored in your state. Having your suppliers, your subcontractors, and even your customers agree to hold you harmless against liability, creates a line of defense in your risk management strategy. This practice also may make you much more attractive to an insurer.

Certificates of insurance are documents indicating a policy is in force. The certificates usually show the:

- Names and addresses of those insured;
- Insurance company names;
- Effective dates and expiration dates;
- Coverage limits;
- Insurance agency names; and
- Names of certificate holders.

Collect certificates of insurance from anybody providing you with a hold-harmless agreement, because the insurance may provide the money owed you as a result of the agreement. In these cases, you are the certificate holder, so you would be notified should the policy cancel for any reason. When possible, you should also be named "additional insured" by the insurance company on the certificate of insurance. This commits the insurance company to provide you with the benefits of an insured for any applicable loss, including legal defense and liability coverage.

Premises and Operations

The more dangerous your premises and operations, the more you will want to document your safety measures.

The more dangerous your premises and operations, the more you will want to document your safety measures. Contractors involved in excavation, blasting, or the use of cranes raise red flags to underwriters. Major construction projects always require extensive safety precautions.

If you have a swimming pool on the premises, you probably will be required to erect a fence around it. If the pool has a diving board, you may be required to remove it. In fact, diving boards have caused so many losses, many motel and hotel pool owners have removed them altogether.

The use of toxic chemicals, such as pesticides or any substance requiring special care in handling and disposal, must be thoroughly explained. Make your written procedures for handling and disposal available for inspection.

Providing professional services raises red flags. Examples include services provided by doctors, lawyers, engineers, certified public accountants, architects, travel agents, realtors, and insurance agents. If your business renders professional services, show proof that professional liability insurance is currently in force. If you don't have professional liability insurance, keep shopping. Usually, other companies will be available to write your premises and operations anyway.

Red Flags Relating to Vehicles

Just about every business uses some sort of vehicle in its operations. As a result, vehicles and their drivers are often insured. To help you get sound, yet economical coverage for your particular needs, keep the following factors in mind.

Suspicious Records

Suspicious motor vehicle records and department of motor vehicles violations — such as driving under the influence of drugs or alcohol — will certainly need explanation and removal of the driver from driving duties. Indicate if you have a drivers training program or other method to promote safe driving practices.

A bad driver on your driver list can cause an excellent insurance value to slip through your fingers.

Older Vehicles

If your fleet is comprised of older vehicles, prove the road-worthiness of the fleet. Describe your maintenance program for the vehicles. Indicate regular inspections of tires, brakes, and steering systems, along with regularly scheduled maintenance.

Special Use Vehicles

Special use vehicles need additional explanation. Explain any use of cherry-pickers, mobile cranes, or other special equipment. Document the qualifications of the drivers and operators.

The following violations are poison to your rates, and will ruin what could have been a good quote: drinking violations, reckless driving, crossing double lines, and careless driving.

Long-Haul Trucking

Expect underwriters to be concerned if your operation includes oneway trucking over 200 miles. Concern increases when destinations are major metropolitan areas, such as Chicago or Los Angeles. To eliminate this concern, consider the risk management technique of subcontracting your trucking needs.

High-Performance Vehicles

High-performance vehicles or sports cars also cause concern. Often, such automobiles are owned by successful business executives. Unfortunately, these types of cars, combined with young drivers in an executive's household or a poor driving record, can sour an otherwise attractive risk. If this describes your situation, it may pay to separate your personal automobile insurance from your business insurance program.

It may pay to separate your personal automobile insurance from your business insurance program.

Red Flags for Workers' Compensation Coverage

Nearly every state requires employers to provide workers' compensation to their employees. Workers' compensation insurance is typically a state-mandated insurance requirement for most businesses for work-related injuries or illnesses. Check with your state labor department to determine your responsibilities regarding workers' compensation, and when looking for insurance, consider these red flags. For more on workers' compensation, refer to Chapter 6.

Seasonal Workers

Use of seasonal workers or a history of high employee turnover are red flags for workers' compensation insurance. Because of the difficulties of proper screening and training of new employees, describe adequate selection and training procedures.

High Injury Rates

Jobs that include work involving such tasks as heavy lifting, heavy construction, roofing, carpentry, cutting, welding are a major concern. If you are paying high workers' compensation rates, you are familiar with this problem. Describe your complete safety program and welcome review and suggestions.

Poor Inspection Reports

Poorly kept inspection records reveal lack of attention to safety and are seen by underwriters as a morale hazard. Clarify any misconceptions on loss control reports and demonstrate your responsiveness to safety concerns.

Frequent Losses

If losses have occurred, and you have not implemented corrective measures, be prepared for concern by your underwriter. Identify causes of loss and corrective measures. If you cannot comply with insurance company recommendations, show your plan of action to reduce hazards and your implementation schedule.

Correcting workers' compensation red flags involves establishing sound hiring and employment practices, and a commitment to safety, including regular training and safety meetings. Extensive information is available from workers' compensation insurance companies for worker safety.

Solving the Red Flags Problem

Never lie about the existence of your red flags.

What can you do about your red flags? First, never lie about the existence of your red flags. Any short-term gain you may achieve only jeopardizes your continued relationship with your agent and company. Present the red flag with documentation of preventive measures to mitigate the underwriter's concerns. For instance, assume you have a spray booth on your premises, and you spray paint your products. Document the booth as being approved by the local fire marshall and properly installed following factory specifications. Indicate proper ventilation and use nonflammable paints. Also, describe the maintenance procedures for cleaning the booth and vents on a regular basis and indicate how you have conveniently located fire extinguishers near the booth. Obviously, the idea here is to present the red flag in the best possible light. You can apply the principle of this example to any objectionable circumstance your business presents.

Examine your presentation to insurance companies. Look for needless red flags that may alarm and discourage company underwriters. If you are getting ready to print your company brochure, avoid alarming pictures and descriptions of hazardous operations that are not representative of your operations. For example, you would be surprised how many contractors think a picture of an operating crane shows off their expertise, even though they never use one. In fact, crane operations are typically red flags for insurance companies. Thus, your brochure design may needlessly concern insurance companies due to displaying hazards that are misrepresentational. Encourage them to insure your business by providing ample positive information to attract the lowest premium possible.

Indicate if you have a drivers training program or other method to promote safe driving practices.

You now know more about red flags than most insurance buyers. You know how to avoid them, or if they are unavoidable, you have learned the importance of presenting them in their best light. Discuss your red flags with your insurance agent or broker. Make sure your agent is prepared to handle any questions the underwriters may ask.

Use the Underwriting Information Questionnaire

Most insurance buyers are unaware of how they can get the most from their insurance dollars. Additionally, many buyers give control of their insurance purchase to quoting agents or brokers, which leads to buyers purchasing insurance coverages they may not need or paying too much for necessary coverages.

As an informed business insurance buyer, you will want to consider aspects of the insurance purchase that you many have not previously anticipated. Three important considerations are:

- The significance of driving records;
- Your expiration dates; and
- The prequote loss control inspection.

The Significance of Driving Records

Maintain a full awareness of the driving records of your employees and any family members who drive your vehicles. Remember, a prudent risk management practice is to allow only employees — not their family members — to drive company vehicles. Insurance companies will order the records from the department of motor vehicles, in states where permitted, whenever they consider writing the automobile portion of your insurance.

To avoid unnecessary problems, obtain your drivers' records at least once a year. The driving record shows the date and location of any accidents. If the driver was completely innocent in the accident, you will have to prove

Maintain a full awareness of the driving records of your employees and any family members who drive your vehicles.

it by producing a police report or a copy of the settlement check received from the other party's insurance company. You also can stay abreast of your employees and new hires by checking their records. If any of your employees have an unacceptable driving record, the high cost of insurance will probably lead you to eliminate them as drivers. A bad driver on your driver list can cause an excellent insurance value to slip through your fingers. Many good insurance companies have a very low tolerance for bad drivers.

In the states where it is permitted for individuals to obtain other peoples' drivers licenses, you can obtain records if you:

- Ask your current and prospective employees to bring in their records, which they can purchase at a local department of motor vehicles. Remind them to take their driver's license with them, to prove their identification.
- Ask your insurance agent to obtain them for you. Some agencies are willing and able to obtain driving records, and some are not. Your current agency or competing agencies may be receptive to obtaining records for you to examine.
- Subscribe to a service that often obtains the records for you. If you subscribe, the cost per record ranges from two to five dollars. Contact the department of motor vehicles to learn how to best gain access to a subscription service for your situation.

An excellent way to interpret driving records is to keep a copy of your state's motor vehicle code in your office. In some states, you can look up specific citations and understand the exact nature of the codes. The department of motor vehicles sell these for a very modest price. You may prefer to depend on your agency to interpret the records for you; agents are usually experienced and helpful. Further, the drivers themselves can offer understanding about incidents that appear on their records. Make sure the driver's explanations are reliable.

All accidents should be fully explained and documented, and the documentation should become a part of your underwriting information submission.

The driving record is always taken as fact by insurance companies, and you will not win many battles with insurance companies over a bad record. Most companies will tolerate one minor citation in the past three years — such as speeding or stop sign violations — and many will ignore two citations when the vehicle fleet is larger. All accidents should be fully explained and documented, and the documentation should become a part of your underwriting information submission.

Other types of tickets can raise questions and cause problems. Spilled loads and vehicle fix-it tickets indicate to underwriters that the vehicles are not well maintained or they are not being loaded competently. A new driver you hire may have had some of the tickets before joining your business, so be sure to include a note explaining that your business was not involved in the poor management.

The Insurance Assistant is an easy way to gather, store, and update all your driver record information. The automated data storage process makes quoting the automobile portion of your business insurance much easier. For more information, contact:

The Oasis Press
(800) 228-2275

Select Your Expiration Dates

Select your ideal expiration month and day, to save bookkeeping, improve cash flow, and budget your time.

Selecting your ideal expiration dates can be very helpful towards managing cash flow and time resources.

When choosing expiration dates, you:

- Enjoy increased efficiency by arranging for all your policies to expire on the same date. You benefit by only focusing on the insurance renewal issue once per year, instead of having various policies expiring at different times of the year.
- Save bookkeeping expense by having your policy expirations coincide with your fiscal year end, or with the calendar year. Audits conducted to obtain the sales or payroll information are simpler when the policy period coincides with the tax reporting periods.
- Select an expiration date that more adequately suits your cash flow pattern. You may want to position renewal premium payments — and year-end audit billings — to occur during your peak season. Some businesses prefer expiration dates to occur during their slow period, so they can devote more time to concentrate on the insurance issue. The choice is yours.

Agents can help you establish different expiration dates. When your policy next renews, your agent can have the policy issued for a shorter term than usual, so the policy expires when you want. Your agent may have to issue the policy for a longer term than usual. Be sure your agent clarifies the effect the change will have on this year's cash flow, so you aren't surprised by unusual billings needed to align your account.

Expect the Prequote Loss Control Inspection

Before obtaining quotes, be informed about prequote loss control inspections. The following steps may be worth your consideration to prepare your business' premises for the eyes of the inspector. After agents submit your information to insurance companies for quotes, they may casually mention that a loss control representative will stop by for an inspection. Too often, agents underemphasize the potential these inspections can have to either save you money or cost you a fortune.

The on-site eyes of the insurance company are those of the loss control representative. This person inspects your facilities and reports to the insurance company underwriter. How the loss control representative reports your business' appearance directly affects the underwriter's decisions. The underwriter will refer to the loss control inspection in deciding whether to quote your account, and the reasonable price to offer. You can see the potential importance of putting your best foot forward for a loss control inspector — if your business is inspected.

Usually, you will see a loss control inspector two times in the life of an insurance policy. The first inspection is before the policy is written and usually before the quote is given to you. This inspection is the all-important preinspection. Here, the inspector will verify what the agent said about you on the application, and expose issues not disclosed on the application that may concern underwriters. The second inspection can come after the policy is issued — when the company is looking for ways to help you reduce your exposures. This discussion helps you prepare for the first inspection. The discussion in Chapter 10 shows you how to get the most help from the second type of inspection.

You can plan for an inspection. Before a visit, a loss control inspector will look up your type of business in reference manuals, which can alert them to specific loss control issues for your business. While you do not have the manual the loss control inspector uses, the following outline will help you see your business through the eyes of the loss control inspector.

- General housekeeping and cleanup — What does your place look like? Will it pass inspection? Does your business show the signs of neatness that make it fire-proof and trip- and fall-proof? Does it show pride of ownership and professionalism? Sweep, pick up, dust, and put away all extension cords. Throw away oily rags or be sure they are stored in a metal container with a self-closing lid. Clean up any oil spills inside or outside. Take out the trash and if necessary haul it off the premises. Store paint and lacquer in metal containers for which they were designed, and keep all doors closed.
- Life safety gear — Ensure the first aid kits are adequate for your situation.
- Exits and aisles — Clear all exits, fire doors, and aisles. Make sure exits are clearly marked and lights are operational. Repair all stairs and floor coverings if they are not in good condition.
- Vents and hoods — If you work with chemicals, check the ventilation systems to be certain they are operable. If you have a cooking exposure, be sure the hood is clean and the contract for cleaning is up to date.
- Fire extinguishers — No matter what your operation, properly maintain all fire extinguishers with scheduled inspections and current recharging.
- Personnel safety gear — Be certain that everyone who needs safety items has and is using the proper gear. Safety items include: eye goggles, safety glasses, gloves, safety shoes, aprons, hard hats, ear protectors, and seat belts. When the inspectors arrive, give them the same protective gear to wear during the inspection. If you must transport the inspectors in a company vehicle, insist they buckle up.

- Lighting — Good lighting is important for both normal work hours and after hours. Some work sites profit from battery-powered emergency lighting systems that help protect the business during power outages, fires, or other disasters.
- Warning signs and guards — If your operations involve machinery, post signs explaining safety precautions for safe operation of each machine, in language the operators can read fluently, including pictures. Regularly check all safety guards.
- Safety rules — Employees should be well-versed in all safety procedures, and they should follow the rules.

Expect the inspector's visit. Designate a tour guide in advance. Be wise in your selection of a tour guide. This individual should know all operations and should be able to answer almost any question about operations. The tour guide should be a principal of the business, or at least a principal should be available for any questions that may arise. Whoever conducts the tour needs to practice good judgment to answer questions truthfully, but not necessarily overemphasize every negative point about the business. Again, be sure the inspector wears all required safety gear before getting the tour.

Be sure the inspector wears all required safety gear before getting the tour.

Equipped with important preparation facts, you are now ready to complete your questionnaire. This is the final step in preparing your business for action.

Assembling Your Underwriting Information

As discussed in the previous pages, one of the most valuable things an insurance buyer can do is complete the Underwriting Information Questionnaire. As the owner of this book, you are entitled to duplicate the blank form only for your business' insurance purchasing purposes. You should assemble your complete underwriting information as requested on the questionnaire, and keep it current in your permanent insurance shopping file. Prepare a separate questionnaire for each business entity involved. Once the Underwriting Information Questionnaire is completed, it is easy to maintain and becomes the key to managing your insurance program. As you approach future policy expiration dates, simply review your questionnaire to make sure it is current and accurate. This will streamline your renewal process, whether you decide to thoroughly shop the insurance marketplace or just renew your current policies.

Customizing Your Questionnaire

Any requests you get for additional details are clues that those items should be added to your Underwriting Information Questionnaire to become a part of your permanent insurance shopping file. This customizes your presentation based on your business' unique characteristics and experience. Keep adding to your permanent insurance shopping file until all

Once the Underwriting Information Questionnaire is completed, it is easy to maintain, and becomes the key to managing your insurance program.

information needed to accurately quote your account is readily available. The more complete and accurate your presentation, the easier it will be to secure the optimum combination of price, coverage, and service.

The questionnaire is comprised of seven parts. On each left-hand page you are given instructions for completing each corresponding part; the various parts are found on the right-hand pages. The instructions provide explanations, hints, and time-saving suggestions. Refer to the instructions to help you understand what is being requested and the easiest ways to obtain the information.

If you purchased *The Insurance Assistant* software, you save a great deal of time in your renewal preparations. Once your data is loaded into the program, changes are quick, and renewal preparation is extremely easy.

Note, the Underwriting Information Questionnaire on the following pages is not replaced by *The Insurance Assistant*. Rather, the detailed questionnaire is fully automated to assist in your data collection and storage process.

Underwriting Information Questionnaire

Part 1 – General Information

Part 2 – Historical Information

Part 3 – Insurance Policy History

Part 4 – Current Operations

Part 5 – Property Information

Part 6 – Checklist of Enclosures

Part 7 – Vehicle Schedule

Part 1 – General Information Instructions

The Underwriting Information Questionnaire is a list of information about your business that you assemble into a permanent insurance shopping file. Preparation of this information will greatly reduce the time you have to invest with agents in quoting your account. You will be able to hand them the answers to the many questions they would otherwise have to ask.

If you keep adding to your permanent insurance shopping file until it is completed, it will be current and accurate through periodic (at least annual) updates. Once completed and updated, the completed questionnaire makes shopping the market quick and efficient, allowing you to employ as many agents and brokers as you want to work on your account. You will not have to spend your time discussing your business with them because the data speaks for itself.

Be as complete and accurate as you can in presenting your profile. In turn, the whole process of shopping your account will be more efficient. You will be able to thoroughly test the marketplace for improved pricing and coverages.

Complete one separate Underwriting Information Questionnaire for each business operation or entity involved. For instance, the agent/broker wants to know information such as your different exposures and your daily operations. Any requests you get for additional information are clues that those items should be added to your file. The more complete and accurate your presentation, the more responsibility you pass to your agent to present you with adequate and correct insurance.

You may save time by getting copies of your latest insurance applications, which may help you complete the Underwriting Information Questionnaire. Sample Letter I in the Appendix is designed to help you obtain your applications.

The form in this book is a master copy. Photocopy the master and work with your copies.

1. Include the full legal name of the business.
2. Include all owners (active and inactive) and indicate job function and corporate title — such as John Doe, office manager, treasurer. It is important to indicate percentage of ownership. If you are a partnership, note what type of partner — general or limited.

   Note: The first entity or person named is always the one responsible for the premium payment and all audits payments.
3. Where should bills, policies, and other documents be mailed?
4. Include area code, prefix, and four digit extension.
5. Who is responsible for accumulating, coordinating, and communicating information about your business to insurance people? If you are not that person, delegate the remainder of this project to that individual.
6. Identify the person who pays the bills, and the person who has the accounting and finance information.
7. Check one.
8. Include locations of your owned and leased premises, such as buildings, warehouses, offices, and parking areas. Note, if you are a contractor, don't list temporary job sites.

   Note: Attaching photographs of your premises is very helpful to agents and companies.

Part 1 – General Information

1. Our business' legal name (doing business as):

____

2. The owners and/or officers of our business:

Name	Position	Years of Experience	Percentage Ownership

3. Our mailing address:

____

____

____

4. Our telephone numbers:

Primary #: ____________________ Fax #: ____________________

5. The person(s) handling our insurance in the business:

____

____

6. Our accountant's (or bookkeeper's) name and number:

____________________ ____________________

____________________ ____________________

7. The business is operating as a:

☐ Sole proprietorship ☐ Partnership ☐ Limited liability company ☐ Corporation ☐ Other: ____________

8. The addresses of our physical locations:

____________________ ____________________

____________________ ____________________

____________________ ____________________

____________________ ____________________

____________________ ____________________

____________________ ____________________

Part 2 – Historical Information Instructions

9. What is the earliest date operations began?
10. Attach a brochure about your company, if available.

    Mention acquisitions of companies or significant assets. Indicate the start up of operations, expansions into new fields, or major changes in management. Mention dates of incorporation, and dates of ownership changes.
11. Insurance companies are concerned about products that you have previously manufactured and distributed that have been discontinued. The major concern is the products' and services' continued existence and usage by the general public causing current losses under this new policy.
12. Be sure to indicate the type or line of insurance — such as automobile, workers' compensation or package policy. Warning: Failure to disclose this information may expose you to the risks caused by material misrepresentation. See the glossary for this definition.
13. Insurance company loss runs — reports generated by insurance companies displaying losses incurred — can tell the whole story for you. To obtain loss runs, see Sample Letter C in the Appendix. Add any losses not shown on loss runs. Mention the settlement status of the claim. Description should clarify applicable coverage: workers' compensation, auto liability, general liability, property, or auto physical damage and any other coverages that apply. Liability claims should indicate any bodily injury or property damage to other's property. Property losses include fire, vandalism, and theft. Calculate the total amount of any loss you describe.

Part 2 – Historical Information

9. The founding date of our business:

____

10. The major steps in our progress to our current position:

____

____

____

____

11. The following services or products have been discontinued:

Product or Service	Date Discontinued	Reason

12. Our experience with insurance company cancellations or declinations in the past five years:

Company	Type or Line of Insurance	Date	Reason for Cancellation or Declination

13. Claims we have experienced in the past five years:

Date of Loss	Description	Amount of Loss	Settled?

Part 3 – Insurance Policy History Instructions

14. If insurance policy history copies are not easily available for your current policies, have your agent(s) fax the information to you. It may be urgent, because you may not have the coverage you think you have. See the Sample Letter K in the Appendix. The previous year premium history is not always essential, but it can help you in some cases. If you have paid significant premiums over the past three years and had very low losses, attempt to provide the details. The premium history can be used by the underwriters to justify credits to your quotes. Premium history from previous years should be readily available from your loss runs. Sample Letter O in the Appendix solicits help from your current and previous agents in collecting this information.

    If you decide not to disclose what you have been paying, simply omit entries in the premium column. You are usually better served when you disclose your premium history. (See discussion in Chapter 7.) If you are uncomfortable letting quoting agencies know your premium history, ask them to quote "blind," meaning the agents have no knowledge of prior pricing. If you don't want to disclose your premium history, do not hand over your loss runs, because they may indicate the paid premiums. Instead, prepare a list of your losses from your loss runs, showing dates, causes, and amounts of loss. Recognize that you may be considered less cooperative in doing this, and may lose the willing efforts of some agents. Some insurance companies may not quote without the insurance company generated loss runs.

Part 3 – Insurance Policy History

14. Policies we currently hold, and those we have purchased over the past three years:

Description	Insurance Company	Policy #	Expiration Date	Premium
General Liability				
Current year				
Previous year				
Three years previous				
Property				
Current year				
Previous year				
Three years previous				
Auto				
Current year				
Previous year				
Three years previous				
Workers' Compensation				
Current year				
Previous year				
Three years previous				
Equipment Floater				
Current year				
Previous year				
Three years previous				
Other Policies				
Current year				
Previous year				
Three Years previous				

Part 4 – Current Operations Instructions

15. Be specific: Indicate whether you are a retail, manufacturing or service-oriented business. Explain the scope of your business. For instance, if you are a general contractor, describe your focus, such as new construction, repairs, remodel, heating, ventilation, and air conditioning (HVAC), or electrical.
16. Describe what you do, how you do it, where you do it, when you do it, and who your customers are. Your company brochure can help here. Highlight your major activities, especially the general activities that account for significant percentages of sales or receipts.
17. The total number of employees indicates the size of the company, which is used in devising cost, indicating exposure, and determining skill levels.
18. Does your business anticipate growth? Is your business growing or declining? These are important indicators.
19. Hint: A more stable and experienced work force is more attractive to insurance companies.
20. Your payroll and its distribution are some of the most important data on this form, as many premium calculations may start here. To clarify what payroll will not be included for premium calculations, see page Chapter 10. To minimize the risk of costly surprises, list each employee by name, giving job function, work location, and estimated annual payroll. The requested payroll values are your estimates for the coming year. For example, if wages are paid hourly, multiply hourly rate by average hours per week, by number of work weeks in a year to produce a reasonable estimate.

    The payroll presentation is a critical area, and a competent insurance agent should guide you to the best results.

    If you do not have these numbers handy, refer to your accountant, bookkeeper, or the employee who handles your workers' compensation or general liability audits.
21. Itemize major receipts categories or items sold and be sure to indicate sales or receipts from foreign sales or operations. For more information as to what is includable, see Chapter 10.

    Annual gross receipt information is readily available from your accountant or bookkeeper on your income statement.
22. Indicate expected annual costs for subcontractors, broken down by type of work, if applicable.

Part 4 – Current Operations

15. Our business produces the following products and services or both:

____

____

____

16. Our day-to-day operations to produce the products or services:

____

____

____

17. Our current total number of employees:

______ # Full-time ______ # Over age 60 ______ # Temporary

______ # Part-time ______ # Under age 16

18. Our average number of employees:

______ # Full-time

______ # Part-time

______ # Anticipated changes in number of employees: _____ Increase _____ Decrease

19. On the average, our employees stay with our business for ______ years.

20. Annual payroll broken down by job function or general category:

Job Function	Annual Payroll	Average Tenure

21. Annual receipts broken down by general category:

Category	Annual Gross Receipts

22. Subcontracting costs:

Category	Costs

Part 5 – Property Information Instructions

23. Use one property information page for each owned or occupied location.
24. Check one.
25. The insurance company needs to know whether you, or a tenant occupies this location. If there is more than one occupant, describe the occupancy by the type of operations conducted here and the square footage occupied. Examples of types of operations include: retail, restaurant, wholesale, warehouse, manufacturing, processing, office, apartment, motel/hotel, and storage yard. For each occupant, indicate the square footage they lease.
26. a. Describe construction material of floor, walls, and roof. Construction materials include wood frame, concrete, metal, brick facade, and stucco veneer.
    d. Is the roof composed of tar and gravel, composition shingle, tile, or other?
27. e. Is the alarm system a local gong, central station, or guard service?
    f. Measure the exterior perimeter. Hint: old property appraisals do an excellent job.
    h. List height and width of each pane, especially the larger ones.
    l. If so, is the booth UL or fire marshal approved? Is it equipped with extinguishing sprinklers, explosion proof lights, plugs, and switches?
    m. Is there a service contract for cleaning your fire suppression system? If yours is a wood-working operation, do you have a dust collection system?
28. List other occupants at this location, whether you own the building or lease.

Part 5 – Property Information

23. Location:

Street Address: ______________________________

City, State, Zip: ______________________________

24. ☐ **We rent** ☐ **We own this location**

25. General occupancy of this location: ____________________

26. Construction information:

a. Type of construction: ____________

b. Number of stories: ____

c. Year building constructed: ______

d. Type of roof: ____________

e. Year of roof renovation: ______

f. Year of plumbing renovation: ______

g. Year of electrical renovation: ______

h. Year of heating renovation: ______

27. Safety information:

a. Are building sprinklers installed? ☐ Yes ☐ No If partial, describe: ____________

____

b. How many fire extinguishers on premises: ______

c. How many smoke detectors on premises: ______

d. Other fire protection devices provided: ____________

e. Description of alarm system: ____________

f. Square footage of building by floor: ______

g. Total square footage of building: ______

h. Glass dimensions: ______

i. General housekeeping (check one): ☐ Excellent ☐ Good ☐ Fair ☐ Poor

j. Is area free of debris and fire hazards? ☐ Yes ☐ No

k. Any spray painting on site? ☐ Yes ☐ No

l. Approved spray booth? ☐ Yes ☐ No ☐ N/A

m. Cooking area ☐ Yes ☐ No If yes, is a fire suppression system installed? ☐ Yes ☐ No ☐ N/A

28. Occupancy information:

Occupant Name	Own/Rent	Area (sq. ft.)	Operations on Premises

Part 5 – Property Information Instructions (continued)

29. The insurance company is looking for fire hazards presented by your neighbors, such as restaurants, cabinet shops, or fireworks manufacturing. Show the distance from your building to your nearest neighbor to the left, right, and rear of your location. Your neighbors may be adjacent to your building, or they may be thousands of feet away. For example:

	Type of Business	Distance from Us	Type of Construction
Right:	laundromat	adjacent	concrete; tilt up
Left:	restaurant	twelve feet	frame construction
Rear:	none	open land for half a mile	N/A

30. Indicate the name of your closest police/sheriff and fire departments, and approximate distance from your location. Estimate the distance to the nearest fire hydrant. Describe any security systems, including guards and alarms. Include copies of alarm certificates you may have.

31. A friend in the contracting business can be very valuable to assist in this calculation. You can apply a per square foot cost to the size of your building. It is very important not to underestimate the construction cost, as it may become the policy limit. Insurance agents routinely estimate replacement costs, but they are not experts.

    Are there any local building ordinances that would prevent reconstruction of this building, or cause it to be completely destroyed and rebuilt to comply with current construction standards in the event of a fire? Check with the local planning and building authorities.

32. Business personal property includes your inventory, furniture, fixtures, and tenant improvements and betterments. It may include property of others for which you are responsible.

    As a tenant, what would it cost to replace the improvements you have done to your landlord's building? Examples include remodeling, carpeting, shelving, and painting. Your lease may specify improvements for which you are responsible to provide property coverage. Indicate the amount of time before your lease expires.

33. Indicate your construction plans, whether it be a new building, a major remodel, or an addition. If you are a contractor, mention larger projects you anticipate this coming year. Contractors should also estimate the largest job size, average job size, and total number of jobs for the year.

Part 5 – Property Information (continued)

29. Neighborhood information:

Our immediate neighbors are:

	Type of Business	Distance from Us	Type of Construction
Right:	____________	____________	____________
Left:	____________	____________	____________
Rear:	____________		

30. Nearest protection:

Responding police/sheriff department: ____________ distance in miles: _______

Responding fire department: ____________ distance in miles: _______

Nearest fire hydrant: _______ (distance in feet)

Security guard service employed: ____________

Burglar alarm system in building: ☐ Yes ☐ No Type: ____________

Central station: ☐ Yes ☐ No Monitoring company name: ____________

Water flow monitor or fire alarm? ☐ Yes ☐ No

Central station? ☐ Yes ☐ No Monitoring company name: ____________

31. Estimated cost to replace this building in the event of a total loss:

Note to agent: Please provide your best estimate of the replacement cost: $____________

Monthly rental income of property: $____________ Building ordinance coverage needed: ☐ Yes ☐ No

32. Business personal property at this location:

Replacement cost of inventory: $____________

Replacement cost of tenant improvements and betterments: $____________

Replacement cost of furniture and fixtures: $____________

Total business personal property replacement cost: $____________

Loss potential from damage to valuable papers: $____________

Value of receivables that would be uncollectible in event of damage to or destruction of the documents: $_______

33. Planned construction projects:

Completed value of each planned building or project: $____________

Maximum value of materials on site waiting to be installed: $____________

Date construction may begin: ____________ Time to complete: _________

Part 5 – Property Information Instructions (continued)

34. a. Consider the worst case scenario when calculating this timeframe. Omit the end of the world or nuclear blasts, as they are both excluded for coverage anyway.

    b. & c. You may want to ask your accountant or bookkeeper to assist in the computation of these figures. See the glossary for the definition of profit and continuing expenses.

    d. See discussion on business income, extra expense and loss of rents in Chapter 5 for a thorough explanation of this subject.

Part 5 – Property Information (continued)

34. Business interruptions from a fire or other covered peril could cause the following:

a. We would be shut down for ____ ☐ weeks ☐ months.

b. We would lose $______________ per ☐ week ☐ month of profit.

c. We would still have $______________ in continuing expenses.

d. If a fire or other covered peril affected a vendor on whom we rely for supplies, to attract our customers, or to sell our product, the following loss could happen:

____

____

____

____

____

____

____

Part 6 – Checklist of Enclosures Instructions

The checklist on the following page serves as your reminder to include the various enclosures with your Underwriting Information Questionnaire. By providing a quoting agent with all the requested enclosures, you will save time — you will eliminate phone calls from agents who will need this information to quote your business insurance.

35. a. You have heard the adage, "a picture is worth a thousand words." This saying is especially true when describing the physical locations of your business operations to insurance people. Make sure your photographs are good quality, and display your property in a favorable manner.

b. Include a minimum of the last three years of loss runs for the types of insurance for which you are applying, whether it be property, general liability, auto, or workers' compensation.

See Sample Letter C in the Appendix to request loss runs if you do not have them on file.

c. Your lease copies are needed for review, to assure insurance compliance with the terms of the lease and determine your need for items such as fire legal liability insurance and glass coverage.

d. If you have a standard agreement for subcontractors, provide a copy to your insurance company.

e. If you have a standard contract with customers, provide a copy to your agent.

f. The workers' compensation experience modification worksheet is not necessary if you are not applying for workers' compensation insurance now. See Sample Letter F in the Appendix to request the worksheet. (Refer to Chapter 6 for more information on experience modification factors.)

g. Your business plan is helpful, if written. If you have a written plan, note any significant changes you anticipate.

h. Include a list of all self-transporting equipment not licensed for road use, such as forklifts and tractors. Include year, make, model, identification number, purchase price, purchase date, and an estimate of current actual cash value — defined as replacement cost minus depreciation. Also see solving the valuation issue in Chapter 5. Coverage limit is usually actual cash value.

i. List all drivers if you are currently applying for auto insurance. Include names, birthdates, and driver's license numbers. Indicate the states that issued each license. Indicate the hire date for all drivers. If the hire date is less than three years ago and the driver operates a commercial vehicle, explain prior experience of the driver. Attach motor vehicle records, if available.

Usually, nonchargeable accidents are defined as those in which another party was completely at fault, or accidents causing under $500 in property damage with no bodily injury. If the other party was cited and your driver was not, that usually proves the accident was nonchargeable. Provide police reports for non chargeable accidents, as well as copies of checks paid to you by third parties; all are excellent evidence of innocence. Evidence of reimbursement can include copies of claim settlement checks, or settlement agreements. See discussion about driving records in Chapter 4.

j. Computer and electronic equipment information may be readily available from your balance sheet or purchase invoices. Include what you have available in the way of year, make, model, serial number, purchase price, purchase date, and your estimate of current replacement cost.

k. List the names and addresses of all persons who expect to see evidence of your insurance. Be sure to note exactly what their interest is in your insurance, whether they are lenders, lessors, contractors, or other. Also indicate whether they must be named as an additional insured.

l. (See following page.)

Part 6 – Checklist of Enclosures

35. Enclosures for Quoting Agents

a. ☐ Photographs of locations and selected valuable property

b. ☐ Insurance company loss runs from previous years

c. ☐ Copies of leases

d. ☐ Copies of subcontractor agreements

e. ☐ Copies of contracts with customers

f. ☐ Workers' compensation experience modification worksheet

g. ☐ Business plan for coming year

h. ☐ Schedule of mobile equipment — include: year, make, model, identification number, purchase price, purchase date, and current value.

i. ☐ List of all drivers, including:

☐ Names

☐ Birthdates

☐ License numbers

☐ Hire dates

j. ☐ Schedule of computers and other electronic equipment

k. ☐ List of additional insured persons and certificate holders or both — include mailing address and relationship to your business.

l. ☐ Schedule of owned vehicles (see following page)

Part 7 – Vehicle Schedule Instructions

35\. I. Include a schedule of owned vehicles if you are currently applying for auto insurance quotes. A blank schedule is provided to remind you to provide the year, make, model, gross vehicle weight, and estimated cost of the vehicle when new. Your vehicle registration form usually provides all this information except the cost of the vehicle when new, which you must estimate. The gross vehicle weight (see Glossary) may be found on the vehicle's registration. To save time, you may wish to simply provide photocopies of the vehicle registrations.

Do not overestimate the new cost of the vehicle, because it directly affects the rate for any coverage for damage to the vehicle. Indicate any special equipment attached to the vehicle. Mention any special radios, car phones, or custom alterations.

Insurance companies will need information about the company's radius of operation, which is your indication of how far from the garage address the vehicle normally goes in one direction in the course of a business day. For rating purposes, the breaking points for radius, considerations are 0 to 50 miles; 51 to 200 miles; and over 200 miles. Obviously, the higher the radius, the higher the rate. Be sure to mention if one or two vehicles occasionally goes beyond the radius. Use of the vehicle must be indicated. Be specific! If you use the vehicle for deliveries, indicate the typical delivery schedule, and whether the vehicle is driven to homes or businesses. Rates are lower for business delivery and higher for residential delivery.

If the vehicle only transports personnel or material to job sites and then remains parked all day, it qualifies for the lowest rates possible. State if a car is used by salespeople, and whether it goes out of your state. Indicate if the vehicle is used by your service department to go on calls, or if you use it to run errands for the business.

Perhaps a vehicle owned by the company is used as a personal vehicle — for commuting to and from work — and garaged at home. When indicating this type of use, provide driver data for the spouse and children of driving age living in the employee's household.

Agents will interpret your description of vehicle use into one of four classes for each vehicle. Simply describe your vehicle's use, and let agents assign the appropriate class. Their classification choices — from the lowest to the highest rates — are personal, service, commercial, and retail.

- *Personal* suggests no business use.
- *Service* means vehicles are used to transport workers and materials to job sites, and remain parked at the job site.
- *Retail* means running home delivery routes.
- *Commercial* is defined as any use other than service or retail. It may be interesting to see how your vehicles are currently classified to see if improvements are merited.

The following vehicle schedule displays three vehicles. Photocopy enough schedules for your vehicle fleet.

Part 7 – Vehicle Schedule

35. I.

Vehicle # ____________

Vehicle identification number: ________________________

Year: ____ Make: __________ Model: _________

Gross vehicle weight: ____________ lbs.

Used for: ____

Used by: ____

Radius of operation in miles: ☐ Under 50 ☐ 51 to 200 ☐ over 200

Estimated new cost: $__________ Special equipment: $__________

Cost and description of any alterations or customizing: ____

Normally garaged in the following city and state: ____

Vehicle # ____________

Vehicle identification number: ________________________

Year: ____ Make: __________ Model: _________

Gross vehicle weight: ____________ lbs.

Used for: ____

Used by: ____

Radius of operation in miles: ☐ Under 50 ☐ 51 to 200 ☐ over 200

Estimated new cost: $__________ Special equipment: $__________

Cost and description of any alterations or customizing: ____

Normally garaged in the following city and state: ____

Vehicle # ____________

Vehicle identification number: ________________________

Year: ____ Make: __________ Model: _________

Gross vehicle weight: ____________ lbs.

Used for: ____

Used by: ____

Radius of operation in miles: ☐ Under 50 ☐ 51 to 200 ☐ over 200

Estimated new cost: $__________ Special equipment: $__________

Cost and description of any alterations or customizing: ____

Normally garaged in the following city and state: ____

Notes

Chapter 5

Know Your Business Insurance Coverage Options

Introduction to the Many Coverage Options

By now, you have a basic knowledge of the insurance marketplace. You have reevaluated your current service and prepared your business for action. You are well equipped to enter the dark forest of insurance purchasing. However, you may be asking yourself, "How will I ever know all the meanings of my coverage options?"

Being a well-educated and informed insurance buyer puts you in control of your purchase. With even a basic knowledge of the many coverage options, you can intelligently discuss your purchase with insurance professionals. The results are in your favor — you save money, time, and receive the best possible insurance for your business.

Being a well-educated and informed insurance buyer puts you in control of your purchase.

Throughout this chapter, you will learn the specific coverage issues. Some coverages may pertain to your operation; some may not. However, with an understanding of the coverage options, you are ready for the final step in your preparations to approach the marketplace. You are prepared to submit your Business Insurance Coverage Checklist to your current agent and competing agents.

The Business Insurance Coverage Checklist is found at the end of this chapter and the Workers' Compensation Coverage Checklist is found at the end of Chapter 6. Preparation of these checklists is the last step in preparing your business for action. Completion of these checklists is a key element to getting the best out of insurance agents. Before submitting your Business Insurance Coverage Checklist to competing agencies however, it is essential that you understand the key elements of your coverage options.

Before delving into the coverage options, briefly look at the three important ways both of these valuable coverage checklists will serve you and your business.

The Coverage Checklists Allow Easy Comparison

Careful coverage selection is one of the key services you expect from your agent, but is all too often neglected.

The coverage checklists help both you and your agent select the coverages you may need, and compare them to your current coverages. Careful coverage selection is one of the key services you expect from your agent, but it is all too often neglected. The use of a checklist helps make sure important coverages are not overlooked. First, have an agent review your policies — assuming you have some policies in effect — and list your current coverages on your blank coverage checklists. If you are a start-up business, omit this step. Never assume your current coverages are suitable to your needs. Second, have a competent agent recommend coverages by identifying your exposures from your completed Underwriting Information Questionnaire from Chapter 4.

Always refer to insurance professionals when making coverage selections, to minimize the risk of being uninsured in the event of a loss.

In the process of establishing satisfactory specifications on your coverage checklists, questions are likely to arise regarding specific choices. To help clarify key issues, refer to the following pages for straightforward clarifications of confusing subjects. The glossary can add to your understanding of key terms. This coverage reference section serves only to provide background information, and raise points for discussion with your insurance professional. Always refer to insurance professionals when making coverage selections; this will minimize the risk of being uninsured in the event of a loss.

Once a satisfactory analysis of your exposures has been achieved, the coverages and limits you require are selected. With coverages and limits specified, your Business Insurance Coverage Checklist and Workers' Compensation Coverage Checklist become part of your quote specifications, and are used to shop for your coming renewal. Competing agents who quote your account are provided the completed coverage checklists and Underwriting Information Questionnaire. Then the agents are asked to match the coverages in their quotes, or note any variations and recommendations.

Many less prepared buyers resort to digging through their policies, looking for hints about the coverages they want, dangerously assuming their policies are set up correctly. During interviews with quoting agents, the less prepared buyers may lack understanding as to what coverages they have or need. Usually, at this point, the frustrated buyer hands the policies to the agents, asking them to figure it out. This act relinquishes all control of the important coverage selection process to the agents. Use of the coverage checklists avoids much confusion — and leverages the time you spend on insurance — by avoiding repetitive coverage discussions with competing agents.

The Coverage Checklists Save You Time

You save time by using the completed coverage checklists, and your increased efficiency allows you to easily enable agents to quote your insurance. Determining what coverages to quote for you is one of the quoting agents' primary objectives. Providing them with your completed coverage checklists answers many of their questions and eliminates unnecessary discussions. While you are still receptive to quoting agents' coverage recommendations, you will ask the agent to enter the information on your coverage checklists. Following this pattern will help you refine your coverage specifications.

The Coverage Checklists Provide a Standardized Format

The checklists provide you with a standardized format on which to accept competitive quotes, making them easier to compare. Standardization helps you avoid becoming snared in the trap of complicated coverage comparisons, because competing agents are working with identical coverage specifications. You direct the agents to present their coverage quotes on your form, making differences easy to spot.

The checklists provide you with a standardized format on which to accept competitive quotes, making them easier to compare.

A common practice in the industry is for each agency to present quoted coverages on their unique proposal system. The agent hopes to dazzle you, the prospective client, with the many exotic features, bells, and whistles included in their products. Because of the unique proposals, and the complex nature of the coverage subject, you are unlikely to absorb every subtle benefit of each proposal you review. By insisting all coverage presentations include completed coverage checklists, the issues and key points become obvious; thus clarifying comparisons. You can always focus on the more subtle distinctions once you have isolated one or two contending proposals for your business.

By insisting all coverage presentations include completed coverage checklists, the issues and key points become obvious; thus clarifying comparisons.

Using the Business Insurance Coverage Checklist will raise many important coverage questions for you and your agent to discuss. At some point, you must make important coverage purchasing decisions. Unfortunately, insurance language is foreign to most business owners, and insurance concepts are sometimes confusing. To help you better understand the decisions you face, read the applicable coverage options that follow. Throughout this chapter, 39 coverage options are discussed to help you grasp the essential issues, and prepare you for meaningful discussions with your agent. When you are dealing with the Business Insurance Coverage Checklist and need to know more about a specific coverage option, read the appropriate coverage discussion. By understanding each coverage item, you gain control of your insurance purchase.

On the following pages, you will find some common misconceptions many buyers have about what their business insurance policies do and don't cover. Before delving into the nitty-gritty of your coverage options, take this short quiz to test your current knowledge of your insurance coverages.

Test Your Coverage Knowledge

Q. True or False. Your business personal property is covered by your commercial property insurance policy off your premises, just as it is when it is on your premises.

A. False. Your business personal property may be covered off premises, but only for a limited amount of coverage, often as low as $1,000, and only in the United States, its territories, possessions, and Canada.

Q. True or False. Your business personal property is covered by your commercial property insurance policy while at a fair or an exhibit.

A. False. Your business personal property while at a fair or an exhibit is usually excluded from coverage. Coverage can be arranged, but probably will require an additional premium.

Q. True or False. Your business personal property is covered by your commercial property insurance policy while being transported.

A. False. You either have no coverage at all or a very limited amount — $1,000 to $5,000. If your property is transported, make sure insurance coverage arrangements are made for the proper amount to cover the value of your property.

Q. True or False. You are covered for losses you intentionally cause.

A. False. Coverage for intentional losses you cause is never provided by insurance.

Q. True or False. You have no coverage in your commercial property insurance policy for valuable papers.

A. False. Usually commercial property coverage provides some amount of coverage, such as $1,000.

Q. True or False. You have no glass coverage in your commercial property insurance policy.

A. False. In fact, many property policies provide $100 per pane, with a maximum of $500 per occurrence for some perils. Additional glass coverage can be purchased if this is inadequate.

Q. True or False. Your money is fully covered by your commercial property insurance policy.

A. False. Unless money is specifically insured, the property forms exclude it. Also, protection against embezzlement requires special coverage.

Q. True or False. Theft by your employees is covered by your commercial property insurance policy.

A. False. Unless you purchase special coverage — such as employee dishonesty or fidelity bonds — you are not covered for theft committed by your employees, whether they steal your money or your business personal property.

Test Your Coverage Knowledge (continued)

Q. True or False. Your work is guaranteed by your commercial general liability policy.

A. False. Rarely can you purchase coverage for defective or faulty work. For example, if you clean a carpet and cause serious discoloration, the damage to the carpet is not covered! But if you accidentally knock over an expensive vase with your carpet cleaning machine, your general liability will cover the damage to the vase, because you were not working on the vase.

Q. True or False. You have automatic coverage from your commercial automobile insurance policy when you rent a car for business use.

A. Maybe! You may or may not, so be sure to get written confirmation of your coverage from your agent, broker, or insurance company before renting a car.

Q. True or False. It is never a good idea for the principals of a business to be covered by the workers' compensation policy.

A. False. Sometimes it may make very good sense for all or some of the principals to be included in the workers' compensation policy. This will depend on their current health care program, their workers' compensation classification, cost of coverage, and state laws regarding the eligibility for coverage — all of which should be discussed with an insurance professional.

Q. True or False. Your only recourse if you are hit as a pedestrian is to collect from the party that hit you.

A. False. In fact, you may find coverage in your workers' compensation, automobile, or health insurance policies.

Property Insurance Issues

Reading about insurance coverages can be fascinating when you are learning vital information that directly affects you and your insurance purchasing decisions. To help you understand your current coverage issues, the property coverage discussions are organized into four categories:

- Property
- Liability
- Automobile
- Miscellaneous

Property insurance is about protecting yourself from losses to your buildings, furnishings, tools, equipment, and inventory. If you are examining property insurance issues, the following coverage discussions explain essential concepts, so you can initiate meaningful discussions with agents and make informed decisions about what to purchase.

Deductible Versus Self-Insured Retention

You are probably familiar with the term *deductible*, which is the amount you pay of a loss, over which the insurance company pays the rest, up to the limit of the policy. You may encounter the term, *self-insured retention*, which many agents will tell you is the same thing as a deductible because the terms are used interchangeably by many people. Beware, there are important differences. Deductibles are paid after the insurance company does the work, which may include finding adjusters and attorneys, handling paperwork, and paying the part of the claim that exceeds the deductible. In the event the claim is not larger than the deductible, you pay the entire amount.

With a self-insured retention (SIR), if the claim is larger than the SIR the insurance company will become involved and take an active role in all the claim functions mentioned above. If the claim is smaller than the SIR you are responsible for finding claims adjusters, handling paperwork, and paying and settling small claims. Unless you have a staff with plenty of time and expertise to handle small claims, including the availability of legal counsel, SIR may not be your best option.

Fortunately, you can find insurance companies who provide policies with large deductibles, giving you a significant decrease in your insurance premiums. But you don't have to act as the adjuster or defense attorney on claims. You simply pay the deductible if the claim is larger than the deductible, or you pay the entire amount if the claim is smaller than the deductible.

Self-insured retentions are desirable when the savings are significant and the sophistication of your organization enables you to easily assume the duties of defense counsel and claims adjuster, or hire a third party administrator to handle these chores.

Replacement Cost Versus Actual Cash Value

The two main property loss settlement methods are replacement cost and actual cash value. In *replacement cost* settlements, depreciation is not deducted, so you will tend to get more money for your property loss.

In replacement cost settlements, depreciation is not deducted, so you will tend to get more money for your property loss.

For example, assume your ten-year-old roof is destroyed by fire. It will cost $20,000 to replace the roof and settle the loss. The *actual cash value* method would start with the replacement cost value, and deduct a percentage based on the expected life of the roof. If the roof is expected to last 20 years, you may only receive 50 percent of the cost to replace it, as settlement of the loss ($10,000). The rationale for this deduction is that only 50 percent of the usable roof was actually available for future use at the time of the fire. In theory, the rest of the roof had already depreciated, and been used.

In contrast, replacement cost coverage will pay for the replacement of the roof, without deduction for depreciation ($20,000). In practice, with business personal property losses, many actual cash value settlements are paid at the market value of the property. The only time actual cash value coverage is preferable is when replacement cost coverage is not available, such as when a building is in poor repair. The premium will be lower because you are insuring for the lower, depreciated property values. Almost without exception, replacement cost is preferable to actual cash value, so if available, choose replacement cost.

Functional Replacement Cost

The concept of *functional replacement cost* is normally used as a preferred method of loss settlement when insuring machinery, production equipment, and other contents. The idea is to replace destroyed machinery with new, state-of-the-art machinery. This violates one of the basic principles of insurance — indemnity, meaning to be made whole after a loss, exactly as you were before the loss. But it gives the insured an opportunity to have a timely settlement to a loss. For example, suppose your production line equipment is destroyed in a fire and identical equipment is no longer manufactured. New, state-of-the-art equipment is actually an improvement over the destroyed equipment; however, it is functionally replacing the destroyed equipment. This coverage can be very desirable for both the insured and the insurance company.

Coinsurance Versus Agreed Amount

To encourage people to insure their property to value, and to help keep rates stable, insurance companies have put a *coinsurance clause* into most property policies. As a reward for insuring with higher coinsurance limits, you get a small rate reduction that lowers your premium by a small amount. Whenever possible, choose property coverage with no coinsurance clause, because the clause can penalize you for being underinsured. If you must accept a coinsurance clause, be very careful your coverage limits are adequate to meet the coinsurance requirement. For example, if

Whenever possible, choose property coverage with no coinsurance clause, because the clause can penalize you for being underinsured.

you have an 80 percent coinsurance clause and your building's replacement value is $100,000, you must carry at least $80,000 of insurance to avoid a coinsurance penalty. Since the value is determined at the time of loss, you must make sure your values remain current to prevent being underinsured.

How the Coinsurance Clause Works

$$\frac{\text{Amount of insurance carried}}{\text{Amount of insurance required}} \times \text{Loss} = \text{Amount of payment on loss}$$

Example 1

$$\frac{\$80{,}000}{\$80{,}000} \times \$40{,}000 = \$40{,}000$$

Example 2

$$\frac{\$60{,}000}{\$80{,}000} \times \$40{,}000 = \$30{,}000$$

Coinsurance can be applied to both building and business personal property coverages. Take a closer look at how the coinsurance clause works for a loss of $40,000.

Suppose you insure $80,000 on a $100,000 building with an 80 percent coinsurance clause. You are now in compliance with your coinsurance requirement. If you have a loss, you will receive the full amount of the loss with no coinsurance penalty, as seen in Example 1 above.

Assume you only carried $60,000 coverage when the $40,000 loss occurred. The settlement would be $30,000, as seen in Example 2 above.

The coinsurance penalty costs the underinsured policy holder $10,000 — the difference between the $40,000 and the $30,000 settlements.

With coinsurance, the maximum amount you can receive is the limit of the insurance you carry on the property. Carrying the proper amount of insurance is very important to receive an adequate settlement amount if you have a loss.

On the other hand, the purpose of agreed amount is to suspend the coinsurance clause, and avoid the possibility of a coinsurance penalty at the time of loss.

On the other hand, the purpose of agreed amount is to suspend the coinsurance clause, and avoid the possibility of a coinsurance penalty at the time of loss. With agreed amount, you and the insurance company agree on the value and coverage limits on your building at policy inception. All losses are paid in full, up to the amount of the insurance coverage limits you carry. Rates are generally higher, and you still must insure to adequate limits if you are to be fully compensated for any total loss.

Property Coverage Forms

Basic, broad, special, and difference in condition are types of *property coverage forms* that are available in the marketplace. The major difference from one form to the other is the number of perils of loss that are covered by each form.

Basic usually covers the following perils:

- Fire
- Lightning
- Riot and civil commotion attending a riot
- Explosion
- Vehicles (not vehicles owned or operated by you)
- Smoke
- Hail
- Aircraft
- Wind
- Vandalism and malicious mischief
- Sprinkler leakage
- Sinkhole collapse
- Volcanic action (airborne shock waves and ash only)

Broad usually covers all the perils in basic, plus expands several and adds the following:

- Freezing
- Falling objects
- Weight of ice and snow
- Glass breakage ($100 per pane, $500 per occurrence)
- Water damage
- Artificially generated currents

Special form covers everything not excluded by the policy. Special form is the most comprehensive of the standard policies and is your best choice when covering your property. Special form provides a complete change in your posture with the company as it makes all perils covered that are not excluded. In the event of a loss, the insurance company must find an exclusion to deny the claim, instead of you having to find a coverage in the policy that applies. The special form is the one coverage form that provides theft coverage. However, exclusions in this form still exist — such as flood and earthquake.

Special form is the most comprehensive of the standard policies and is your best choice when covering your property.

Difference in condition is sold to cover some of the exclusions of the other forms, most notably flood and earthquake. This form is used with the special property form to provide the most complete coverage available. Other ways to provide flood and earthquake coverage are available and may be less expensive.

Earthquake Coverage

Most property forms exclude damage resulting from the movement of the earth caused by an earthquake. Earthquake insurance covers damage caused by earthquakes. Earthquake coverage can be obtained by purchasing difference in condition coverage or by purchasing a separate earthquake policy. A few companies will add earthquake coverage directly to your property policy. The less likely your area is to have an earthquake, the more likely the insurance companies are to add the coverage. Be concerned with the deductible, as it is a percentage of the amount of the coverage in force at the time of the loss. For example, if you have $500,000 coverage for earthquake on your building at the time of loss, and you have a 5 percent deductible on the policy, you will not get paid until the damage from one quake exceeds $25,000; then you are only paid the damage excess over the $25,000. Keep in mind if an earthquake damages your building, and a fire results, the fire damage is covered.

Flood Coverage

A flood is normally defined as overland traveling water and associated mud flows. The definition of a flood is not when your sink overflows. *Flood coverage* can be obtained as part of the difference in condition coverages, as explained in this chapter, or as a separate flood insurance policy from the federally backed National Flood Insurance Program.

These flood policies can be obtained through any licensed property casualty insurance agent. Flood policies can be written by the government directly, or through an insurance company writing flood insurance on behalf of the government. Both emergency and regular flood programs are available.

Building Ordinance and Law Coverage

The purpose of the building ordinance and law coverage is to cover the increased cost to repair or replace your building because building codes of your city or county require upgrading it to current building code requirements.

To obtain building ordinance and law coverage, it needs to be endorsed onto your property policy. The purpose of the *building ordinance and law coverage* is to cover the increased cost to repair or replace your building because building codes of your city or county require upgrading it to current building code requirements. The building ordinance and law coverage also covers the cost of demolition and the increased cost to reconstruct parts that must be torn down and hauled off. Without the endorsement, you may find you cannot afford to rebuild or repair the property without an additional loan to finance the increased costs. For example, suppose a fire causes $500,000 damage to an older, yet fully serviceable building. The city ordinances and building codes require you to make upgrades to the heating, electric, and plumbing system during repair, costing another $100,000. The additional $100,000 would not be covered without this endorsement. Owners of older buildings, buildings with unusual construction, or buildings located in rezoned areas are wise to investigate their need for the building ordinance and law coverage. To select a realistic limit for building ordinance coverage, consult with a contractor who is familiar with local building codes, your buildings, and can estimate the cost of upgrading your buildings to meet current local codes.

Glass Coverage

Glass coverage is an endorsement that can be added to your property policy to provide coverage for all the glass you wish to insure in your building. The glass in your building is usually covered automatically by your property policy for $100 to $250 per pane, with a per loss maximum of $1,000. If you have significant amounts of glass in your building, this is simply not enough coverage, as is frequently true in retail operations. If you are a renter, check your lease to see whether you are responsible for glass repair and replacement. Glass replacement responsibility is very common in leases of commercial buildings.

Construction or Builder's Risk Coverage

Often, property coverage is needed for buildings during the course of construction. If necessary, make sure items covered include the on-site materials waiting to be used, and the portion of the building that is already completed. Coverage for buildings can be written to cover only the part of the building that has been erected. After that, you are responsible to file a periodic report to update the value and the amount of coverage — as more sections of the building are completed. Alternatively, a *completed value form* can be used, which has the property coverage limit equal to 100 percent of the total estimated construction cost to complete the building project. These forms are more commonly used because they eliminate periodic reports during the building process. The premiums are discounted since the full property coverage limit only exists on the final day of construction. When obtaining *builder's risk coverage,* inform agents of your security measures, such as fencing, lighting, and even security guards. These types of security measures are good loss control methods for theft losses and for safety of the general public.

When obtaining builder's risk coverage, inform agents of your security measures — such as fencing, lighting, and even security guards.

Pollution Coverage

You can count on having *pollution coverage* excluded in every standard policy you buy. Property policies exclude the damage done to your property caused by pollution, and liability policies exclude bodily injury and property damage done to others caused by pollution. All liability policies exclude clean-up costs. However, some property policies have a token amount of clean-up coverage to clean up very small spills — typically those under $10,000. To get any meaningful coverage, get special policies covering pollution, usually sold by companies who specialize in this type of risk. The policy may be designed to cover either your property, bodily injury, property damage to others, or in some cases, all. Either way, you will be required to conduct a site inspection to check for pollution before the policy is issued. The inspection cost is frequently from $2,000 to $6,000, depending on the company doing the inspection. Remember, not all inspection companies are approved by all insurance companies. Ensure the company is approved before you contract the inspection. You don't want to pay for two inspections. A relatively new form of pollution coverage is now available that can protect property buyers, sellers, and lenders from the risk of pollution liability. This form can protect any or all three of the parties involved in the sale of property from prior pollution that occurred before the date of the transfer of ownership. Ask your agent about property transfer insurance.

Reporting Form

Reporting form coverage is an optional property insurance coverage form in which your business personal property coverage limits and associated premiums fluctuate along with your changing coverage needs. If your values for business personal property fluctuate more than 10 percent per month, or you have significant swings in value over the course of the year, check out this option as opposed to buying and paying for a flat limit of coverage. The flat limit will make you over-insured at times, and possibly under-insured at other times — and you will always be paying for the total flat amount. With a reporting form you will submit an actual report of values monthly or quarterly to the insurance company. The reports need to be accurate and on time to insure proper coverage. These reports can be time consuming to complete, so decide if your monthly fluctuations are large enough to justify the increased paperwork.

If your values only increase significantly during one season, such as November and December, then you can satisfy your need for seasonal increase of coverage by having a *peak season endorsement* added to your policy. With this endorsement, you can specify the seasonal period and the amount to increase your coverage during that time.

Property in Transit

Be cautious with property in transit. Your property policy normally offers little or no coverage for your property off your premises.

Be cautious with property in transit. Your property policy normally offers little or no coverage for your property off your premises. Often overlooked, this coverage area needs some definition. Determine:

- Who is responsible for the property?
- How is the property being transported?
- Where is the property going?
- What is the value of the property?

Once you know the answers to these questions, your agent or broker can select the proper coverages. In general, two standard coverage forms are available — *cargo* or *transit*. The right form for you depends on the answers to the above questions. Review your need for the coverage, and determine the proper form for your needs.

Business Income, Extra Expense, and Loss of Rents

Combined business income and extra expense insurance is designed to replace the loss of profit and cover the ongoing expenses of your business after a loss occurs, until you are back in operation. All of the coverages described assume you are moving rapidly to have repairs made so you can return to normal operations.

Calculations for the proper amount of coverage may require some of your bookkeeper's or accountant's time to complete the worksheet, but in the event of a loss, the time spent will be well worth it. Ask your agent or broker if you can get coverage for the amount of loss sustained. This means you won't have to select a coverage limit and your loss will be fully covered.

Be honest with yourself when determining the amount of time it will take to get back in operation after a loss. This is often understated and the amount of work to either relocate, or rebuild and return to pre-loss conditions is much longer than anticipated.

Be honest with yourself when determining the amount of time it will take to get back in operation after a loss. This is often understated and the amount of work to either relocate, or rebuild and return to pre-loss conditions is much longer than anticipated.

Your business may be such that you must resume operations within 24 hours to prevent the loss of market share. Examples of these types of businesses are printers or manufacturers who do a high percentage of their work for only one customer. If this is necessary, you need *extra expense coverage* to supply the temporary location and equipment to get your business immediately operational. Extra expense coverage pays the expenses necessary to continue operations during the recovery period after a property loss. A common example is the extra expense of renting temporary space or equipment after a serious property loss.

Another coverage you may need to look into is *loss of rents coverage.* If you derive all or part of your income from renting part or all of a building to others, and the building is damaged from a covered peril, you may not be able to collect the rent, due to the damage. Rental coverage will reimburse you for the loss of rents until you get the property repaired.

Blanket Coverage

Blanket coverage is generally preferable to separate property limits. Sometimes it can be very difficult to get the proper amount of coverage on the buildings and contents of your business. In the normal course of business, adequate coverage becomes more unlikely without blanket coverage, when inventory and equipment move from building to building. To simplify the issue, you can purchase *blanket coverage,* and lump the buildings and contents together. You can also just blanket the business personal property at all locations, and leave the buildings on a separate blanket or schedule. Through use of blanket coverage, you remove the problem of frequent changes of values on buildings as repairs are made or additions are built and as contents are shifted from location to location. Blanket coverage is particularly useful in a manufacturing operation where the product moves between locations as part of the production pro-

Blanket coverage is generally preferable to separate property limits.

cess. Blanket coverage is often available for the asking, and the insurance company's main concern will be that the blanket limit is adequate to provide enough coverage for all of the items that are insured by the blanket coverage. For example, if the items covered are three buildings you own, the insurance companies want the blanket coverage for them to be equal to the total value of the three buildings added together. So, if one building's replacement cost is $1 million and the second and third buildings are valued at $500,000 each, the blanket coverage limit must be $2 million.

A Generous Coverage Package — The BOP

If you qualify, a Business Owner's Policy (BOP) is your best bet for very broad coverage, because the policy forms are easy to read and understand. The BOP can include coverage for your building, business personal property, and property of others. Generally included are generous business interruption coverages — loss of income, extra expense, and loss of rents — with no dollar limit, but paying for your entire actual loss for up to twelve months. Peak season coverage is normally included, which typically provides an increase of 25 percent in your business personal property coverage if you have a predictable three-month period when your property values surge due to high sales. If peak season coverage appeals to you, be sure to discuss your fluctuating property values in depth with your insurance agent, so you buy coverage limits that are adequate, but not excessive. The liability coverage is very similar to commercial general liability and contains most of the same coverages, plus nonowned and hired auto coverage is available as an option. Optional coverages can be added for glass, signs, machinery, and employee dishonesty.

The BOP is normally for small retail businesses, but some companies have expanded the BOP to include some larger accounts. Also, a number of carriers have modified the program to include service businesses, including small contractors, wholesalers, and some restaurants.

The BOP is usually available as a named peril or special form policy, with replacement cost on the buildings and business personal property with no coinsurance clause in the policy. Further, the general liability is often not subject to audit. You need to shop to find a company offering this program with eligibility parameters you can meet. Keep in mind, price varies by as much as 100 percent from company to company.

Coverage Territory

Most insurance policies provide coverage for losses occurring only in the coverage territory. *Coverage territory* is usually defined as the United States, its territories and possessions, Puerto Rico, and Canada.

Commercial general liability policies provide a slightly broader definition of coverage territory if the loss is from a product the insured business sells or manufactures. Coverage will normally be provided if the suit was filed in the coverage territory, even if the loss actually took place outside of the territory. If your business currently has operations outside the coverage territory, even temporarily, notify your agent or broker — if possible before operations begin to allow your agent necessary time to arrange for foreign operations coverage. Normally, you don't have coverage for Mexico in commercial and personal insurance policies. This is especially true for auto insurance policies.

Liability Insurance Considerations

Liability insurance is about defending your business against civil lawsuits and legal liabilities for damages caused to others. The following coverage discussions explain vital insurance concepts and practices to help you avoid unintentional gaps and understand the basic limitations of your liability insurance protection. Know the following liability coverage options to avoid confusion about when liability coverage begins and ends for your business. After reading this section, you will know what to look for when discussing your purchases with your agent or broker.

Be proactive about defending your business against civil lawsuits and legal liabilities for damages caused to others.

General Liability Forms

When referring to general liability forms, you might have heard talk about old occurrence (pre-1986) versus new occurrence (post-1986). Before 1986, the *comprehensive general liability* insurance policy was available. Unfortunately, the policy was not all-inclusive, as the word comprehensive would lead you to believe. At least eleven areas of coverage were lacking, and adding the broadening endorsement was the only convenient way to plug the coverage gaps. The old policy made it necessary for agents to attach a large number of endorsements to the basic policy. You may encounter an old policy form if you purchase your policy from a nonadmitted insurance company, normally because of a highly hazardous operation or product. Otherwise, you will almost certainly have the new policy form. If you find yourself purchasing the old form, be sure to add the broadening endorsements that you and your agent decide are necessary. If you are a contractor, be sure to include coverage for collapse, underground damage, and explosion, which are normally excluded on the old policy form.

In 1986, the *new commercial general liability* policy was introduced with the broadening endorsement coverages built into the policy. With the broadening endorsement coverages included, coverage for the following items are written into the policy.

- Personal injury — This coverage is now built into the post-1986 policy form and has its own limit of coverage per occurrence available for losses caused by libel, slander, false arrest, wrongful eviction, invasion of privacy, malicious prosecution, and other similar coverages.
- Advertising liability — This is also included in the post-1986 policy and provides coverage for copyright infringement and misappropriation

of advertising ideas. Of course, if your business is an advertising agency, publisher, or broadcaster, you cannot usually get this coverage included in the policy and must purchase a professional liability policy to cover this exposure.

- Medical payments — This is usually a small amount of coverage ($1,000) for minor injuries suffered by the general public — not your employees or tenants — while on your premises. For instance, this will normally cover emergency room expenses for someone who tripped and fell in your premises. If this occurs, you should assist and encourage the injured person in getting medical treatment. This is a good gesture of friendship and may keep the person from suing you and, subsequently, your insurance company. The coverage does not have a deductible.
- Fire legal liability — This is usually $50,000 of fire, smoke, and explosion property coverage for the building you lease or rent if you are legally liable for the damage. This is necessary because the general liability policy has an exclusion for property in your care, custody, and control. If you have a subrogation clause — an agreement with your landlord where each party assumes responsibility for their own property — in your lease, you probably won't need more of this coverage. If not, discuss the need for increased coverage with your agent.
- Broad form contractual liability — This covers the liability you assume for insured contracts. Insured contracts usually include: lease of premises, sidetrack agreements with railroads, easements, elevator maintenance agreements, naming municipalities as additional insureds, and, finally, any contract directly involved in your business.
- Broad form property damage liability — This covers the property damage you cause to property you have in your care, custody, and control except that part of it on which you are actually working. The part you are actually working on is your responsibility and is usually not covered while you are working on it.
- Host liquor liability — This is liquor liability coverage for those businesses who do not manufacture, distribute, sell, or serve alcohol. This covers losses from the occasional serving of liquor and the subsequent bodily injury and property damage losses caused by the intoxication of the persons served.
- Limited worldwide products liability — This is an expansion of the geographic territory where the insurance policy's coverage applies. It does not provide coverage everywhere in the entire world, but it does provide coverage for certain products exposures in places outside the normal policy territory, which is the United States, its territories and possessions, and Canada. Read the territory definition in your policy for further information.
- Incidental medical malpractice liability — This covers the exposure for giving emergency first aid on your premises to an injured person and being sued for the resultant injuries caused by improper first aid efforts.

- Nonowned watercraft liability — This is coverage for the use of nonowned boats in the course of your business. For example, the rental of a fishing boat for a business trip can result in a suit if someone is injured while on the boat.
- Employees as additional insureds — This gives employees coverage under their employer's liability policy for any bodily injury or property damage the employees cause while in their course of employment. Employees might have no way of getting coverage for this exposure unless their employer provides this coverage. If this is an issue, you will also want to consider adding employees as insureds under the commercial auto policy.

Significant changes were made in the way some businesses were rated, and the post-1986 policy was simplified, so the need for endorsements was greatly reduced. Now, many of the most wanted coverages are built into the post-1986 policy, and if for some reason you do not want the coverages, they can be excluded.

The pre-1986 policy did not have an aggregate limit for the entire policy. The post-1986 policy does have an aggregate limit, which means the policy has a maximum limit it will pay in one year from all coverages it provides. Thus, each loss you suffer depletes your coverage limit, and lowers the amount of coverage available to cover future losses during the remaining portion of the policy year. If your aggregate liability insurance limits are being depleted due to losses in your current policy year, you must consider purchasing increased aggregate limits of liability. If you don't, you run the risk of running out of coverage if you suffer more losses this year. Consult your agent or broker to arrange additional coverage if you think your limits are being depleted.

If your aggregate liability insurance limits are being depleted due to losses in your current policy year, you must consider purchasing increased aggregate limits of liability.

The general liability post-1986 policy usually pays all sums for which you become legally liable as a result of bodily injury and property damage, which occurs during the policy period and in the policy territory. In addition, the supplemental coverages provide for your complete defense and all court costs. The sums for which you can be legally liable are special, general, and punitive damages. The types of damages the policy pays include special or specific damages and general damages. Special or specific damages are for such things as medical bills and the costs of repairing or replacing damaged property. *General damages* include such things as pain and suffering and the loss of companionship. *Punitive damages* are sometimes assessed against the liable party by a court as a form of punishment and to deter anyone else in society from doing the same act as the negligent party. In some states, insurance is not permitted to pay punitive damages on behalf of the insured, and you must pay these sums out of your own pocket.

The general liability policy usually does not provide coverage for wrongful termination and discrimination. If you want this coverage, you need to discuss it with your agent and see if an endorsement is available for your policy. Sometimes an umbrella policy may cover these two coverages; but, make certain you are covered by getting confirmation in writing from your agent.

Other types of liability exist that the general liability policy is not designed to cover without an endorsement. Several of these coverages result from federal legislation regarding the treatment of employees and their benefits and retirement plans.

Employee benefits liability coverage will need to be endorsed onto your policy. You will want this coverage if you provide any benefits to your employees, since failure to add your employees to employee benefits coverage could expose them to uninsured losses. Your employees' uninsured losses could result in a suit against you and your business for failure to provide coverage.

The Employee Retirement Income Security Act of 1974 (ERISA) makes pension fund trustees liable to comply with specific guidelines. If you have employees covered by a pension plan and you or your business is the trustee for the plan, you will need ERISA liability coverage.

Owner's and contractor's protective is coverage for bodily injury and property damage caused to a third party by independent contractors working under contract for you. This is usually covered by the general liability policy as added protection. However, contractors or property owners may have independent contractors purchase an owner's and contractor's protective liability policy. This provides the owners or contractors an additional layer of protection. Discuss this further with your agent.

Occurrence Versus Claims Made

Occurrence versus claims made is the classic confrontation over the two types of liability policies that exist. *Claims made* policies are primarily written for hazardous exposures, such as professional liability, malpractice, errors and omissions, and volatile risks like pollution and hazardous products liability. For commercial general liability insurance, the occurrence form is preferable when available. The *occurrence* form covers losses that occurred during the policy period, even if the claim is presented years after the policy expired.

If claims made coverage is all you can get, you will have a retroactive date in the policy. The claims made type of policy states claims arising out of incidents occurring before the retroactive date will not be covered by the policy. Further, any claims that occur from incidents arising during the time the policy is in force will be covered only if they are made — reported to the insurance company or agent — during the time the policy is in force.

Claims reported more than 60 days after the policy expires will not be covered, which is especially important since many liability claims take considerable time before they manifest themselves. An occurrence policy will not cover any incidents occurring before its inception date. But any incidents that occur during the time the policy is in force will be covered by the policy, whenever the claim is made to the insurance company — even several years in the future.

If you can only get a claims made policy, consider adding endorsements that provide an extended reporting period to allow claims to be made and honored after the expiration of the policy, just as the occurrence policy would. Of course, this will increase your costs as much as 200 percent of your last year's premium. Exercise special caution whenever switching between claims made and occurrence forms to make sure no gaps in coverage are being created. Get second opinions!

If you can only get a claims made policy, consider adding endorsements that provide an extended reporting period to allow claims to be made and honored after the expiration of the policy.

Deductibles – Per Claim Versus Per Occurrence

Liability insurance sometimes comes with a deductible, an amount you must pay before the coverage takes over and pays the rest. The amount of deductible you may have to pay can range from zero to $5,000 or more. Be sure to check whether any deductible you are considering is per occurrence or per claim. Deductible per occurrence is always preferable to deductible per claim, because any single occurrence may give rise to multiple claims. For example, suppose a contractor's crane falls off a building, causing damage to eight vehicles. With the deductible per occurrence, only one deductible would have to be paid by the insured. The per claim deductible costs the contractor eight separate deductibles.

Deductible per occurrence is always preferable to deductible per claim, because any single occurrence may give rise to multiple claims.

Defense Costs

One of the most important benefits of liability insurance is in having the cost of defending yourself paid by the insurance company when you are sued. Defense costs can be provided by a policy in two ways. First and most frequently, the defense costs are included in the policy for an unlimited amount paid in addition to any settlement. For example, suppose you are sued for selling candy to someone who became ill after eating it. The court finds you guilty and you must pay $300,000, which is also the policy limit of your products liability policy. The defense costs are paid by the insurance company in addition to the amount paid by the policy for the claim settlement. Defense costs are usually paid from the first dollar by the insurance company, but a new movement within the industry is wanting to put a deductible on the cost of defense to help control costs and hold down the costs to you for the coverage.

Second, the policy provides defense costs coverage, but the costs are subtracted from the amount of the coverage you have available for claim payments — referred to as an inside limit. In the above example, assume defense costs were $50,000, and you had a $300,000 policy limit with a $300,000 judgment against you. The company would pay $250,000 of the loss and $50,000 for defense costs, leaving you responsible for the remaining $50,000 of the judgment. Whenever possible, choose the policy that provides full defense costs and does not subtract from the policy

Whenever possible, choose the policy that provides full defense costs and does not subtract from the policy limit.

limit. Some liability policies that omit burdening the insurance company with the duty to defend the insured have been especially written for hazardous risks. Expect your agent to advise you if such limitations exist in a policy under consideration. Check with your agent and read your liability insurance policy to make sure your insurance company has the duty to defend you against legal actions.

Pay-on-Behalf-of Versus Indemnify

Some excess liability or umbrella policies differ in their approach to payment of the claim. If the policy is a *pay-on-behalf-of* type, the insurance company will pay all sums the insured becomes legally obligated to pay. You, the insured, will not have to pay the claim nor ask the insurance company to reimburse you for the payment, as may be necessary with the *indemnity* contract. Read your contract very carefully, since there is no standard policy for umbrella and excess policies. A policy that pays-on-behalf-of is usually the best, if it is available.

Umbrella Versus Excess Liability

The umbrella will cover over the underlying liability insurance policy, and in certain cases, provide coverage where no underlying coverage exists.

Suppose you have already purchased general liability, auto liability and miscellaneous liability insurance coverages. What if the claim exceeds your liability limit? For instance, suppose you have a $1 million auto liability policy and a $1.5 million judgment against you as the result of a serious automobile accident. You can protect yourself from this type of occurrence by buying an umbrella or excess liability policy. An *excess liability* policy is designed to only cover directly over the underlying (already existing) liability policies, such as an auto liability policy. The *umbrella* will cover over the underlying liability insurance policy, and in certain cases, provide coverage where no underlying coverage exists. With an umbrella policy, you must first pay a self-insured retention, which is typically $10,000.

If you have the option, take an umbrella policy instead of an excess liability policy.

Review the policy with your agent or broker to determine the exclusions in your policy, since no standardized umbrella form is used in the insurance industry. Some insurers will include your personal liability exposures — such as homeowners, automobile, and hobbies — as part of the commercial umbrella policy. If not, purchase a separate personal umbrella policy. If you have the option, take an umbrella policy instead of an excess liability policy. The coverage is broader and the price difference between the two is usually reasonable.

Professional Liability and Errors and Omissions

Professionals — including doctors, lawyers, engineers, architects, dentists, computer programmers, insurance agents or brokers, veterinarians, barbers, and morticians — have a professional duty to perform their services without causing financial loss to their clients or the general public. When a professional makes an error, the resultant action is frequently a lawsuit seeking restitution for the damages. This restitution is specifically excluded under the general liability policy for coverage and requires the purchase of an additional *professional liability* policy that is designed to cover the exposures of providing a professional service.

Director's and Officer's Liability

Whenever you serve as a director or officer of a corporation or a nonprofit entity, you expose yourself to legal actions from those you serve. You may be liable for damages caused by your negligence in the performance of your duties. Commercial general liability forms exclude this type of exposure, so you need to obtain special *director's and officer's liability coverage*. If this exposure exists in your situation, be sure to include it in your coverage specifications, and obtain quotes. The board of directors of your company needs this coverage too, even if it is a closely held company, as claims can arise between close associates.

Whenever you serve as a director or officer of a corporation or a nonprofit entity, you expose yourself to legal actions from those you serve.

Underground Storage Tanks

Underground storage tanks normally are used to store gasoline, diesel fuel, or chemicals. If you have one or more of these on your property, you are responsible for any leakage that may occur and the subsequent damage and pollution it causes. Assuming the tank is used for a purpose other than storing heating fuel for your personal residence, you must show proof of financial responsibility to a federal Environmental Protection Agency (EPA) inspector, or an Occupational and Safety Health Administration (OSHA) inspector. Contact your insurance agent and your state water resources board to discuss various options. Keep in mind no standard insurance policy covers the pollution damage from one of these types of tanks. To obtain coverage, you will need a special policy from a company specializing in this kind of insurance. See the discussion on pollution coverage in this chapter.

If you have any underground storage tanks on your property, you are responsible for any leakage that may occur and the subsequent damage and pollution they cause.

Automobile Insurance Issues

Today's business owner cannot ignore the many facets of automobile insurance, even those businesses that don't own vehicles. Don't wait to become a victim of an automobile accident to learn whether your coverage is good enough. Be sure you are informed about the following automobile insurance issues, so you and your agent address these important issues for your business.

Business Automobile Coverage Symbols

For each coverage listed on your policy declarations page of your business automobile policy, you will find numeric coverage symbols ranging from 1 through 9 that are very important, because they specify exactly which vehicles will be insured for each coverage. The following list explains which vehicles are defined by each symbol, so that you can better understand your business automobile coverage proposals and policies. The Business Insurance Coverage Checklist, located at the end of this chapter, includes the use of these industry standard symbols also. Be sure to inspect these symbols when you examine any business automobile insurance proposal. If the symbols are not provided, request them.

- Symbol 1 — Covers any automobile, which includes private passenger autos and business-use pickups, vans, trucks, nonowned, and hired autos.
- Symbol 2 — Covers any owned auto.
- Symbol 3 — Covers any owned private passenger auto. Coverage for business semi-trailers or trucks does not exist.
- Symbol 4 — Covers owned autos other than private passenger autos.
- Symbols 5 and 6 — Only used to refer to no-fault and compulsory uninsured motorist coverage. Check whether your state requires either of these coverages.
- Symbol 7 — A commonly used symbol, providing coverage only for those autos specifically described in the vehicle schedule listed in the policy and showing a premium charge for the coverage on each specific auto. If no premium charge, no coverage is provided.
- Symbol 8 — Provides coverage for autos you lease, rent, hire, or borrow, as long as they do not belong to your employees.
- Symbol 9 — Covers autos you do not own, lease, hire, rent, or borrow, which are used in your business, including those owned or operated by your employees.

Ideally, you would see symbol 1 for liability coverages. The next most liberal combination would be 2, 8, and 9. The third most common choice for liability symbols is 7, 8, and 9. Because of the potential for serious uninsured losses, thoroughly discuss this issue with your agent or broker, and read your business auto insurance policy.

If you own a garage operation, you will have coverage symbols using the numbers 21 through 31, instead of 1 through 9, on your commercial auto declarations page. Symbols 30 and 31 deal with customers' autos left in your care, custody, and control and dealers' autos held for sale. Symbols 21 through 29 are the same as 1 through 9 in usage.

If you have a trucking company that only hauls goods for others, you will have symbols 41 through 50. Symbols 48 and 49 apply to trailers you might pull on a trailer interchange agreement, in which truckers might haul each other's trailers.

Uninsured and Underinsured Motorist Coverage

In some geographical areas the number of drivers on the road without insurance is higher than one in four drivers.

In some geographical areas, the number of drivers on the road without insurance is higher than one in four. This means your odds of being hit by a person without insurance are very good. Anyone in your vehicles injured by an uninsured motorist will be covered by workers' compensation if they are riding in your vehicle as a part of their work-related activity. If not, your *uninsured motorist coverage* will cover their bodily injuries. In some states, you can purchase an optional uninsured motorist coverage to provide a limited amount of coverage for damage to your vehicle caused by uninsured drivers.

Underinsured motorist coverage is the companion coverage to uninsured motorist coverage. Underinsured motorist coverage also applies only to bodily injury and not to vehicle damage. The coverage takes effect if the person who hits you has less coverage than the amount of underinsured motorist coverage you have chosen to carry. For example, suppose you carry $300,000 of underinsured motorist coverage and are hit by a driver carrying only $25,000 of coverage, and you sustain $100,000 of injuries. You will be paid $25,000 by the other driver and $75,000 by your insurance to complete the coverage on this claim.

Rented Vehicles Coverage

Never assume you have coverage for use of rented vehicles without getting written confirmation from your insurance agent. Your existing commercial auto or business package policy may provide coverage for hired autos, which includes rented vehicles. If not, purchase the maximum coverages offered by the rental agency.

Never assume you have coverage for use of rented vehicles without getting written confirmation from your insurance agent.

If your commercial auto or business insurance policy includes hired autos coverage for liability, then you have coverage for vehicles your business rents when they are used for business purposes only. Caution should be used when vehicles are rented for nonbusiness purposes and when a driver does not have his or her own personal auto insurance policy. To get the necessary coverage, you need to add *drive-other-car coverage.* You can add this with an endorsement to your business auto policy. Make sure you name the drivers to be covered — especially those employees who are furnished with cars as part of their jobs or who are given a car as a company perk, such as a company president.

When renting an automobile, you are confronted with a choice — whether to purchase or waive the insurance coverage offered by the rental agency. While the coverage is usually quite expensive, some situations advocate purchasing the rental insurance as the only sensible option, particularly if you are renting for only a day or two. Declining the coverage without knowing your commercial auto or business insurance will cover you is generally a poor choice. This choice leaves you exposed to paying for any damage to the car, including a total loss. Coverage may already be included in your commercial auto or business insurance, but get written confirmation showing your policy protects you. Sample Letter Q, found in the Appendix, is designed for this purpose.

Coverage is also commonly included as a benefit for using certain credit cards for the vehicle rental transaction. Before depending on this resource, carefully read the rental car coverage material provided by the credit card company to make sure the vehicle you are renting is covered. Also, call the toll-free customer service number provided on the back of your credit card, and discuss your specific rental.

If you rent or lease a car for a period of more than six consecutive months, it may be necessary to add the vehicle to your existing insurance policy. Be sure to advise your agent whenever renting a vehicle for an extended period of time.

Garage Liability

Garage liability provides bodily injury and property damage liability for garage operations — such as engine repair shops, body shops, and brake shops. Garage liability provides bodily injury and property damage liability for your garage, plus coverage for claims from defective work and products. For example, suppose a mechanic improperly installs the brakes on a car and the owner drives away and the brakes fail to stop. The resultant accident causes damage to the car and injuries to the driver of the car. When the mechanic's shop is sued for faulty work, the bodily injury or property damage claim is covered under its garage liability. The faulty work itself is not covered, only the resultant bodily injury and property damage.

Garage Keeper's Liability

The *garage keeper's liability* is liability for physical damage to customers' vehicles in the care, custody, and control of you or your employees. The garage keeper's liability is an important coverage for any business owners who find themselves in possession of customers' vehicles. Coverage limits are usually stated in a per vehicle limit and maximum per loss limit. When comparing coverage quotes, find out whether coverage is direct or legal, and whether coverage is primary or excess.

- *Direct* coverage pays with no regard to your legal liability for damage.
- *Legal* coverage only pays if you are negligent.
- *Primary* coverage pays regardless of a customer's insurance coverages.
- *Excess* only pays after the customer's insurance is exhausted.

The most coverage is provided by direct primary, and the least is provided by legal excess. Prices and availability vary greatly. The more coverage you have, the happier your customer is in the event of loss.

Actual Cash Value Versus Stated Amount

A specific valuation clause in auto physical damage and inland marine policies is available. *Actual cash value* is defined as replacement cost minus depreciation. In actual practice, claims settlements are frequently based on the market value of the item. *Stated amount* coverage is used to establish a higher than normal value due to some unique characteristics of the item. For example, if you have a vehicle valued above the actual cash value due to its outstanding condition — you have negated the effect of depreciation — you would use a stated amount coverage to establish the maximum value of the vehicle. At the time of a loss, it is possible the vehicle could be repaired or replaced for less than the stated amount, and you would not receive the maximum coverage limit. Even with stated amount coverage, you will never be paid more than the amount for which the item can be repaired or replaced with like kind and quality or the stated amount — whichever is smaller.

Car Phones, Radios, Special Stereos, and Vehicle Accessories

Special vehicle accessories are usually not insured unless they are originally factory installed. To investigate the cost of purchasing coverage, provide an estimated value of these items to your agent, and ask for a quote. Coverage is generally not very expensive, but you will need to provide the make, model, and serial numbers of the items you wish to insure. Your receipts may help specify this information. Always get written confirmation from your agent to be sure these items are covered.

Miscellaneous Insurance Coverages

Miscellaneous coverages don't fit neatly into the previously discussed categories, yet are important topics for you as a business insurance buyer. Because the miscellaneous insurance options are out of the mainstream, they are easily overlooked until a loss occurs that is not properly insured. Understand the following miscellaneous coverage issues and become an informed buyer who ensures these matters are considered for your business.

Crime Coverage

Crime coverage takes many different coverage forms and policy types. Basically, crime coverage insures the loss of money and property through the illegal acts of others. It can cover the acts of your employees or the general public, depending on which policy form. Three main areas of coverage are available.

First, various types of theft coverages are available based on the definition of these criminal acts.

- Burglary is defined as someone breaking into your business premises.
- Robbery is defined as placing you or your employees in fear of bodily harm.
- Theft is a very broad definition of stealing by almost any means, including burglary and robbery.

Various forms of coverage are available for losses resulting from the various criminal acts covered. For example, safe burglary and robbery cover only your personal property if the items are stolen from the safe or if your premises are burglarized. Loss of money and securities are not covered by the form — only loss of business personal property. For coverage of money and securities, you need to purchase the *theft, disappearance, and destruction crime* form, which provides extremely broad coverage, but only applies to cash and securities. Discuss which theft coverage is best suited for your needs with your insurance professional.

Some of the largest losses paid out by bond companies every year are due to the ingenious methods long-term, loyal employees have devised to swindle and skim large amounts of money from their employers.

Second, employee dishonesty will cover the loss of money or business personal property through the dishonest acts of one for more of your employees. You can buy this coverage for certain named individual employees or to cover certain positions held by your employees, such as your treasurer or bookkeeper. In addition, a blanket coverage can cover all your employees for theft of your money or your business personal property. Further, fidelity bonds are another way to deal with the dishonesty of your employees. The fidelity bond can allow you to blanket all your employees for one sum of coverage, or to cover only various positions or employees. Many business owners decide they don't need any coverage for their employees, since all the employees have been with the business for a long time and are very loyal. Remember, however, some of the largest losses paid out by bond companies every year are due to the ingenious methods long-term, loyal employees have devised to swindle and skim large amounts of money from their employers.

Third, you can opt for miscellaneous coverage forms for things like forgery, alteration, extortion, and all sorts of lesser used coverages. Ask your agents and brokers to suggest any additional crime coverages they think are necessary for your business to be completely covered. Then assess value of the coverages by using the mandatory, important, and optional method discussed near the end of Chapter 2.

Boiler and Machinery Coverage

Boilers can explode and all subsequent damage is excluded under your property policy. To solve this problem, purchase boiler coverage.

Boilers can explode and all subsequent damage is excluded under your property policy. To solve this problem, purchase *boiler coverage*. The few companies that write the coverage give some of the best and most needed service in the insurance industry. These companies inspect boilers and machinery and offer maintenance and operation information. The price of the insurance is usually very reasonable, and the inspection, which is a valuable and useful service, is usually provided at no additional cost. The policy covers the damage to your property, the damage to the property of others, and the increased cost to expedite parts to repair the boiler.

With the decrease in the use of boilers in industry, a *machinery coverage* policy will cover mechanical and electrical apparatuses and equipment for damage from mechanical and electrical breakdown. Thus, machinery coverage is valuable for the business that depends on the operation of apparatuses and equipment to conduct the business. The types of equipment that can be insured are very broad, and allow the average business to insure everything from the air conditioner to the electrical distribution panel.

Business interruption and extra expense coverage is also available for these losses, since your building and business personal policy excludes this from coverage when caused by boilers and machinery losses.

Inland Marine Insurance

Inland marine insurance is a physical damage coverage for items that are usually considered easily transportable. Inland marine forms can also insure items of the transportation and communication industries, such as bridges and radio or television transmission towers. These policies are frequently called *floaters* or *floater policies*. The list of items that can be insured is quite broad and the forms used are often not standard forms. This means the insurance company has a great deal of latitude in its coverages and pricing. Ask any quoting agents or brokers if they feel you need any other coverages or forms that are available. Remember coverage is usually provided on a worldwide basis and the perils covered are the special perils sometimes still referred to as all risk, except as excluded. This brief description of inland marine coverages only touches on some of the most common coverage forms.

- Cameras and musical equipment coverage provides coverage for dealers' stock and property of others that is in their care.
- Equipment or tool floaters are frequently used by contractors, or anyone else whose equipment is highly movable, and is used on job sites.
- Fine arts and antiques coverages are used at the insured's location or at exhibits and fairs for protecting your fine arts. This coverage is frequently not worldwide in its territory of coverage. If you intend to cover fine arts overseas, or south of the United States' border, check your policy for coverage and contact your agent to get the required coverage.
- Dies, patterns, and molds coverages are used for these items as though they were art works on special perils basis.
- Floor plan coverage is for items held for sale by a dealer, which can cover the dealer's interest and the interest of a lender.
- Bailee's or customer's goods covers property of others in your care, custody, and control. Various types are available, such as a warehouseman's form.
- Jeweler's/furrier's block covers the merchandise held for sale or storage and your customer's goods.
- Mail insurance forms cover valuable documents shipped by mail for loss caused by the mail service.
- Parcel post coverage is used for business personal property you ship via the U.S. mail, United Parcel Service (UPS), or other carriers.
- Livestock mortality coverage is similar to life insurance, but for animals. It covers animals that die from accidental causes, usually not from sickness.

- Communication equipment coverage includes radio and television antennas and satellite dishes plus towers, transmitters, and receiving equipment. It covers both mobile and stationary equipment.
- Installation floaters provide coverage for material and equipment that contractors possess for installations at job sites. Installation floaters can cover items contractors own or for which they are responsible.
- Motor truck cargo and transportation floaters cover property that is being transported. Business personal property policies, like the ones most businesses have, frequently exclude coverage for property in transit. You can tailor cargo and transit policies to provide coverage for each trip or for the entire year, and include all of your loads. Coverage can be written to cover the interests of the owner, buyer, or the cargo carrier.

Ocean Marine Coverage

Ocean marine coverage is another form of coverage for items in transit, usually when they are being shipped overseas. The coverage can apply both to shipments by sea and air. It is possible to arrange the coverage to be effective from your dock to the recipient's dock, and all points in between, or the reverse. To obtain this coverage, document:

- What is being shipped;
- The value per shipment or container;
- The route of the shipment;
- The vessel transporting the items; and
- The length of time for the trip.

If you own a ship, you can also arrange coverage for the hull with this policy form too. If you own vessels, get quotes from agencies who specialize in this type of business, as it is a fairly small market and requires an agency which understands the business and can arrange the proper coverage for you.

Electronic Equipment Coverage

Many companies have developed policies to insure electronic equipment, including computers, peripherals, even telephone systems, as well as the data stored on the various forms of disks and tapes (media). The main advantages to insuring your computer and its accessories under one of these forms is the very broad coverage it provides, and the ability to choose the exact amount of coverage you need for your systems. You can also add coverage for extra expense that will provide funds to rent a replacement until yours can be repaired or replaced. It may be necessary to add business interruption coverages to your electronic equipment coverage form to make sure loss of earnings and extra expense will apply to losses to this property. Some of these policy forms have added various coverages, such as electrical breakdown and replacement of lost data.

Many companies have developed policies to insure electronic equipment, including computers, peripherals, even telephone systems, as well as the data stored on the various forms of disks and tapes (media).

Now that You Know Your Coverage Options

You now have a useful overview of essential coverage issues and a basic understanding of the "foreign language" of insurance. You are also better prepared to use the following Business Insurance Coverage Checklist to your fullest advantage. As coverage issues and questions arise in working with the checklist, the corresponding instruction pages will assist you in referencing the applicable coverage discussions throughout this chapter. Take advantage of this standardized format for selecting the right coverages for your business. By understanding each coverage item, you take control of your insurance purchase.

A Quick Guide to Using the Business Insurance Coverage Checklist

- Copy the blank Business Insurance Coverage Checklist, located at the end of this chapter. As the owner of this book, copy this checklist for your business' insurance purchasing purposes only. Remember the checklist in this book is your only copy — so make enough photocopies for your use.
- Have your current agent specify your current coverages on the Business Insurance Coverage Checklist. Use Sample Letter B in the Appendix. Also, have your current agent specify coverage recommendations, based on your completed Underwriting Information Questionnaire.
- If you prefer, ask a competing agency to review your current policies and indicate your current coverages on the checklist. Have the agency specify coverage recommendations, based on your completed Underwriting Information Questionnaire. You can use Sample Letter A in the Appendix.
- Refer to the discussions on the coverage options discussed throughout this chapter to clarify any coverage issues. This background information prepares you for meaningful discussions with agents, and helps you make informed decisions.
- Provide competing agents with your completed Business Insurance Coverage Checklist for them to use in preparing your quote. Ask the agency to indicate the coverages they are quoting on the checklist, and to highlight any coverage differences or additions from your original checklist.
- When quotes arrive, compare the coverages presented on the quoting agent's completed checklist with your quote specifications.

Have your current agent specify your current coverages on the Business Insurance Coverage Checklist.

Notes

Business Insurance Coverage Checklist

Part 1 – Building Coverage

Part 2 – Business Personal Property Coverage

Part 3 – Miscellaneous Property Coverage

Part 4 – Business Income, Extra Expense, and Loss of Rents Coverage

Part 5 – Commercial General Liability Coverage

Part 6 – Umbrella/Excess Liability Coverage

Part 7 – Automobile Coverage

Part 8 – Miscellaneous Insurance Coverage

Part 1 – Building Coverage Instructions

Now that you have a basic understanding of your coverage options, you are ready to receive and more easily compare proposals. Your current agent should complete this form to show the coverages you currently have. This checklist is designed to give competing agents or brokers the opportunity to quote your account and gives your current agent an opportunity to review coverages that your business may need.

General information

To effectively analyze your building coverage, have quoting agents complete this section. Your quoting agents can give you a "building coverage limit" based on the information you present on your Underwriting Information Questionnaire. You will want to know or choose your building coverage deductible — the amount of money you will pay for each loss before the building insurance kicks in.

Available options and endorsements

Ask the agents to indicate which options and endorsements can be added to your building coverage. For instance, in determining the right coverage for your building, you will need to identify the replacement cost of the building.

Also, in this area, your agents should indicate which coverages are available to your business by checking the "yes" or "no" boxes. You will want to be concerned with certain aspects of these coverages that your agents will indicate in the far right columns. For example, you will want to know the percentage of coinsurance you will have in your policy.

Coverages like flood and earthquake will have separate premium figures and will help you decide if the coverages are affordable or if you will need to retain these risks.

Keep in mind, your agents will not itemize a quote for you because the current marketplace is not set up for such an ideal system, as discussed in Chapter 1. However, a quoting agent can provide you with total the premium for the applicable building coverage and endorsements. This dollar figure will help you compare other proposals with the same coverages.

You may need to review the coverage options in Chapter 5 to brush up on the important issues you need to understand to make informed buying decisions.

Part 1 – Building Coverage

General information

(Use one page for each location)

Street address: ______________________________

Building coverage limit: $__________

Deductible: $__________

Forms, options and endorsements

Yes	No				
☐	☐	Blanket coverage			
☐	☐	Replacement cost			
☐	☐	Coinsurance	Percentage: __________		
☐	☐	Agreed amount			
☐	☐	Special form			
☐	☐	Broad form only			
☐	☐	Basic form only			
☐	☐	Signs included		Limit: $__________	
☐	☐	Antennas included		Limit: $__________	
☐	☐	Earthquake	Deductible: $__________	Limit: $__________	Premium: $__________
☐	☐	Flood	Deductible: $__________	Limit: $__________	Premium: $__________
☐	☐	Difference in conditions form			
☐	☐	Course of construction/builder's risk		Limit: $__________	
☐	☐	On-site building materials covered			
☐	☐	Building ordinance coverage		Limit: $__________	
☐	☐	Glass schedule		Limit: $__________	
☐	☐	Glass	Deductible: $__________		
☐	☐	Pollution — First party site cleanup		Limit: $__________	

Total premium for building coverage: $__________

Part 2 – Business Personal Property Coverage Instructions

General information

This part of the coverage checklist is vital to your business because it addresses coverages for your business personal property. In selecting the limit for business personal property, include the cost to replace your furniture and fixtures, machinery and equipment, stock, tenant improvements for which you are responsible, and leased personal property for which you are responsible. Make a separate special note of any property of others that is in your care, custody, and control.

Review the property coverage discussions to brush up on the important issues you need to understand to make informed decisions. If you need help with some of these terms, refer to the glossary.

Available options and endorsements

Your quoting agents will need your guidance in setting the necessary values of coverage and deductibles. Remember, you pay the deductible on each loss before insurance kicks in, to cover the rest of the loss.

If the coinsurance clause is in your policy, you will want to be certain you are insuring for the proper dollar amount of coverage to comply with the clause. (See the discussion in Chapter 5.)

Part 2 – Business Personal Property Coverage

General information

(Use one page per location)

Address: ______________________________

Owned business personal property (contents) limit: $__________

Business personal property of others limit: $__________

Deductible: $__________

Forms, options, and endorsements

Yes	No				
☐	☐	Replacement cost			
☐	☐	Functional replacement cost			
☐	☐	Coinsurance		Percentage: __________	
☐	☐	Reporting form		Max. limit: $__________	
☐	☐	Peak season		Max. limit: $__________	
☐	☐	Special form			
☐	☐	Broad form			
☐	☐	Basic form			
☐	☐	Property in transit		Limit: $__________	
		Own vehicle:		Limit: $__________	
		Nonowned vehicle:		Limit: $__________	
☐	☐	Loss of refrigeration		Limit: $__________	
☐	☐	Off-premises power failure		Limit: $__________	
☐	☐	Earthquake	Deductible: $__________	Limit: $__________	Premium: $__________
☐	☐	Flood	Deductible: $__________	Limit: $__________	Premium: $__________

Total premium for business personal property coverage: $__________

Part 3 – Miscellaneous Property Coverage Instructions

This miscellaneous property coverage section helps you inspect your needs for computer and electronic equipment coverages. Provide the costs to replace your electronic equipment, and provide separate values for your computer software. Review the discussions on inland marine, ocean marine, and electronic equipment in Chapter 5 to provide you with the necessary background information to have informed discussions with your agent about insuring special property situations. This will help you make sure you are actually insured for the types of property addressed on following page.

You will want to discuss the exclusions on the various electronic equipment forms with your agents. The various insurance companys' forms vary significantly and some forms don't cover magnetic damage, or electronics or electrical breakdown.

Set your limits of coverage to insure the replacement of your property. Be sure to consider business interruption and extra expense. These coverages will help you get back in business when your computer system is inoperable due to a covered peril causing the loss.

The coverages under the electronic equipment category are each separate coverages. Your business may never need most of these coverages, but don't overlook valuable papers or accounts receivable. Your agents should be very helpful in suggesting limits for you to consider and showing premiums to help you decide.

Part 3 – Miscellaneous Property Coverage

Electronic equipment coverage

Yes	No		
☐	☐	Replacement cost valuation	
☐	☐	Functional replacement cost	
☐	☐	Hardware/equipment	Limit: $__________
☐	☐	Media coverage	Limit: $__________
☐	☐	Business interruption	Limit: $__________
☐	☐	Extra expense	Limit: $__________

Total premium for electronic equipment coverage: $__________

Miscellaneous property coverage

Yes	No			
☐	☐	Accounts receivable	Limit: $__________	Premium: $__________
☐	☐	Valuable papers	Limit: $__________	Premium: $__________
☐	☐	Installation floater	Limit: $__________	Premium: $__________
☐	☐	Scheduled equipment	Limit: $__________	Premium: $__________
☐	☐	Rented equipment	Limit: $__________	Premium: $__________
☐	☐	Transportation	Limit: $__________	Premium: $__________
☐	☐	Motor truck	Limit: $__________	Premium: $__________
☐	☐	Fine arts	Limit: $__________	Premium: $__________
☐	☐	Bailees	Limit: $__________	Premium: $__________
☐	☐	Dies, patterns, and molds	Limit: $__________	Premium: $__________
☐	☐	Ocean marine	Limit: $__________	Premium: $__________

Total premium for miscellaneous property coverage: $__________

Part 4 – Business Income, Extra Expense, and Loss of Rents Coverage Instructions

Pay close attention to this part of the checklist because this coverage is often set up incorrectly. Perhaps you can get coverage to reimburse you for your actual business interruption loss sustained for twelve months with no dollar limit. If so, you will have very little work to do on this subject. Otherwise, you will need to estimate your gross profit and continuing expenses from your income statements. Further, estimate how long it will take you to restart your business in the event of loss, and estimate how much extra expenses you will pay to keep the business operating, if it is possible. Review the discussion on business income, extra expense, and loss of rents to brush up on this important topic, then review it in depth with your insurance agent or broker.

Part 4 – Business Income, Extra Expense, and Loss of Rents Coverage

(Use one page per location)

Address: ____

Business income

Yes No

☐ ☐ Will I get actual loss sustained for twelve months for business income?

If no, please specify coverage provided and all limits: ______________________

____

____

____

____

Extra expense

Yes No

☐ ☐ Will I get actual loss coverage for twelve months for extra expense?

If no, please specify coverage provided and all limits: ______________________

____

____

____

____

Loss of rents

Yes No

☐ ☐ Will I get actual loss coverage for twelve months for loss of rents?

If no, please specify coverage provided and all limits: ______________________

____

____

____

____

Total premium for business interruption coverage: $__________

Part 5 – Commercial General Liability Coverage Instructions

Coverage limits

The key elements to Part 5 of this checklist are the coverage limits, forms and endorsements, rating basis, and deductibles. Refer to the discussions on general liability forms, defense costs, professional liability, errors and omissions, director's and officer's liability and pollution coverage to provide you with the vital background information to help you have meaningful discussions with your insurance agent. Some technical terms are carefully defined in the Glossary.

Forms and endorsements

Purchase a per occurrence limit that is as high as you can afford, based on your situation. Limits sometimes go as low as $100,000 per occurrence, but $1 million is much more common. Many leases and contracts require $1 million in coverage.

If you are able to purchase the occurrence form, the rest of the claims made items will not apply to you, so they can remain blank. Move on to the rating basis section. Review the discussion on occurrence versus claims made in Chapter 5 to help you better understand this topic.

Rating basis

The rating basis is very important to understanding how much your liability insurance will cost you. Your rating basis may be payroll, sales, or square feet, depending on your type of business and your insurance company. Make sure your policy is based on correct estimates of your applicable values. If you use artificially low figures now, you will pay for it at audit time.

Deductibles

Understand per claim versus per occurrence deductibles that will apply to your liability insurance. Read the discussion on deductibles in Chapter 5, and make sure quoting agents disclose any deductibles included in their quotes, by asking them to complete this section for you.

It is uncommon to see bodily injury deductibles, but property damage deductibles are used rather frequently in some types of business, such as with contractors.

Remember, per occurrence deductibles are favorable over per claim deductibles, because you pay only once per occurrence, which can cause multiple claims. For example, if you cause an explosion it will be considered an occurrence, so you will pay one deductible for all property damage — even if you damage five different individual properties. With per claim, you will pay five deductibles, one for each property based on the claims the property owners submit.

Part 5 – Commercial General Liability Coverage

Coverage limits

Policy aggregate: $____________

Products and completed operations aggregate: $____________

Personal and advertising injury: $____________

Per occurrence limit: $____________

Fire legal liability: $____________

Medical payments: $____________

Forms and endorsements

Check one:

☐ Occurrence ☐ Claims made

If claims made: Retro date: ____________

Is extend discovery reporting offered: ☐ Yes ☐ No

Length at no cost: ____________ Maximum length and cost: ________________________

Special liability exclusions: ____

Rating basis

Payroll:	Amount: $_______	Classification _______	Rate: _______	Premium: $_______
Sales:	Amount: $_______	Classification: _______	Rate: _______	Premium: $_______
Area:	Sq. ft.: _______	Classification: _______	Rate: _______	Premium: $_______

Yes	No			
☐	☐	Minimum earned premium	Amount: $_________	
☐	☐	Additional insureds		Premium: $_______

Deductibles

Yes	No		
☐	☐	Bodily injury deductible	Amount: $_________
☐	☐	Property damage deductible	Amount: $_________
☐	☐	Per claim	
☐	☐	Per occurrence	
☐	☐	Self-insured retention (SIR)	Amount: $_________

Part 5 – Commercial General Liability Coverage Instructions (continued)

This page of the checklist provides more important detail about your liability coverages. Pay careful attention to the boxes checked "no" and inspect to see if you have exposures to losses in these areas. Review the chapter discussions on pollution coverage, general liability forms, defense costs, professional liability, errors and omissions, and director's and officer's liability for the background information you need.

If you are in the business of selling alcohol, you need liquor liability. If not, host liquor liability is probably still necessary as part of your liability insurance program.

Employer's stop gap coverage only applies to employers operating in the six monopolistic states — Nevada, North Dakota, Ohio, Washington, West Virginia, and Wyoming. If you operate in any of these states, get a quote for this coverage; otherwise, ignore the coverage.

Review the discussion on defense costs in Chapter 5. Pay attention to whether the defense costs are inside or outside your limits of coverage and if the costs are limited. Normally, the costs are outside with no limit, but be certain to carefully check this coverage option.

If you have employees, get employee benefits errors and omissions, and ERISA liability coverage. These coverages will protect your business from errors in handling benefits and failing to enroll your employees for coverage.

If you have officers and directors, the officer's and director's coverage merits attention. Be sure your agents explain the defense costs and coverage for each individual officer and director, as well as for your organization.

Part 5 – Commercial General Liability Coverage (continued)

Liability coverages included

Yes	No		
☐	☐	Discrimination/wrongful termination	
☐	☐	Owner's and contractor's protective	
☐	☐	Defense costs inside limit	
☐	☐	Defense costs outside limit	Limit: $________
☐	☐	Broad form property damage	
☐	☐	Contractual liability	
☐	☐	Host liquor liability	
☐	☐	Incidental medical malpractice	
☐	☐	Nonowned watercraft coverage	
☐	☐	Limited worldwide products coverage	
☐	☐	Employer's stop gap coverage	

Total premium for commercial general liability: $________

Miscellaneous Liability

Yes	No			
☐	☐	Director's and officer's liability	Limit: $________	Premium: $________
☐	☐	Professional liability	Limit: $________	Premium: $________
☐	☐	Punitive damage coverage	Limit: $________	Premium: $________
☐	☐	Employee benefits errors & omissions	Limit: $________	Premium: $________
☐	☐	ERISA fiduciary liability	Limit: $________	Premium: $________
☐	☐	Liquor liability	Limit: $________	Premium: $________
☐	☐	Pollution coverage	Limit: $________	Premium: $________

Total premium for miscellaneous liability: $________

Part 6 – Umbrella/Excess Liability Coverage Instructions

Umbrella or excess liability can save you if you suffer a major liability loss that exceeds your coverage limits of your general liability or auto liability insurance. Many businesses overlook the purchase of umbrella or excess liability insurance, so this part of the checklist is designed to help you address this issue. You will find the background information you need in the chapter discussions on deductible versus self-insured retention, occurrence versus claims made, defense costs, and umbrella versus excess liability.

These umbrella/excess policies spell out requirements for you to carry underlying liability insurance, with which your agent should make sure you comply. Insist that your policy dates for both your underlying policies and your umbrella/excess liability policies are concurrent — meaning the policy periods are the same. This practice helps avoid unintended coverage gaps.

If you consistently purchase the occurrence form of umbrella/excess liability, the claims made issues will not apply to you.

No standard umbrella or excess liability coverage is available, so be sure to discuss each item on Part 6 with quoting agents to ensure coverage is provided.

Ideally, you will want an occurrence form, umbrella with worldwide coverage, and defense cost outside your policy limits, with no defense cost limits. Refer to Chapter 5 for details.

Pay on behalf is a desired coverage, and a "yes" in all the remaining boxes is also desirable. Only a few companies will insure the remaining items, however, so expect some boxes that may be checked "no."

Part 6 – Umbrella/Excess Liability Coverage

Limit of coverage: $__________

Self-insured retention (SIR): $__________

Yes	No		
☐	☐	Concurrent expiration	Expiration Dates: __________

If claims made liability form:

Retro date: __________

Yes	No		
☐	☐	Extended discovery: ________	Length at no cost: ________ Max length and cost: ________
☐	☐	Umbrella form	
☐	☐	Excess only	
☐	☐	Following form	
☐	☐	Worldwide coverage	
☐	☐	First dollar defense	
☐	☐	Defense cost inside limit	
☐	☐	Defense cost outside limit	Limit: $__________
☐	☐	Premium subject to audit:	
		If subject to audit, what are the terms: ____________________	

Yes	No	
☐	☐	Premium subject to a flat charge
☐	☐	Pay-on-behalf-of
☐	☐	Indemnify
☐	☐	Coverage for acquisitions
☐	☐	Discrimination
☐	☐	Aircraft or watercraft owned, nonowned
☐	☐	Professional liability covered
☐	☐	Personal umbrella/excess included
☐	☐	Punitive damages

Total premium for umbrella/excess liability: $__________

Part 7 – Automobile Coverage Instructions

This part of the checklist helps you understand your automobile insurance. A most important factor in getting an accurate quote is to provide quoting agents with an accurate vehicle list and driver list with your Underwriting Information Questionnaire. Refer to Chapter 4.

Refer to the Glossary if you need any help understanding the terms; most are defined for you there. The important coverage discussions are found in the automobile insurance issues section of Chapter 5. Make sure you understand which vehicles will be insured for which coverages, by inspecting the coverage symbols next to each coverage. Below are some quick hints for each area of coverage.

Liability

Liability pays other people for bodily injury or property damage you caused to them, when you are legally liable to pay them. In addition, liability will provide your legal defense, normally without a dollar limit and outside your policy limits. Combined single limits are most common.

Uninsured/underinsured motorist

Uninsured/underinsured motorist covers all persons in your vehicle for injuries to their bodies caused by someone with no insurance, or coverage limits too low to cover the damage they caused.

Physical damage coverages

Comprehensive is the broadest coverage and the one you will most likely want for all your private passenger vehicles. Pricing may be best on specified perils for trucks, but comprehensive coverage is always your best choice.

Miscellaneous automobile coverages

Ideally, you will have a "yes" in all the miscellaneous auto coverage boxes on this page. Hired auto physical damage may be cost prohibitive, but all others should be reasonable.

Part 7 – Automobile Coverage

Liability	Coverage symbol	Coverage limit
Bodily injury – each person	________	$________
Bodily injury – each accident	________	$________
Property damage liability	________	$________
Combined single limit	________	$________
Medical payments limit (PIP if no-fault state)	________	$________
Uninsured motorist		
Bodily injury – each person	________	$________
Bodily injury – each accident	________	$________
Uninsured property damage/waiver of deducible	________	$________
Underinsured motorist		
Bodily injury – each person	________	$________
Bodily injury – each accident	________	$________

Physical damage coverages			Coverage symbol	Deductible
Yes	No			
☐	☐	Specified causes of loss:	________	$________
☐	☐	Comprehensive (OTC)	________	$________
☐	☐	Collision	________	$________
☐	☐	Actual cash value		
☐	☐	Stated amount		Limit: $________

Miscellaneous automobile coverages			
Yes	No		
☐	☐	Employer's nonowned auto liability	
☐	☐	Employees as additional insureds	
☐	☐	Hired auto liability	
☐	☐	Hired auto physical damage	Limit: $________
☐	☐	Drive other car coverage	

Drivers: ____

____

____

Part 7 – Automobile Coverage Instructions (continued)

Miscellaneous automobile insurance coverages are often overlooked, particularly regarding rental cars, and special auto coverages. Refer to automobile discussions in Chapter 5 to brush up on insurance for rented vehicles and vehicles with special auto equipment. If Mexico is in your driving radius, be sure you read the coverage territory discussion in Chapter 5.

Garage coverage applies to businesses that involve automobiles owned by customers or the public, including repair shops, parking, and even valet services. Inspect the coverage limits and symbols, as well as the garage keeper's liability coverages. If you need these coverages, carefully review the automobile insurance issues section in Chapter 5 and insist that your agent completes this part of the checklist for you.

Part 7 – Automobile Coverage (continued)

Miscellaneous automobile coverages (continued)

Yes	No		
☐	☐	Rental car's liability	
☐	☐	Rental car's physical damage	Limit: $________
☐	☐	Rental reimbursement	Limit: $________/day Max: $________
☐	☐	Phones, radios, stereos, electronic equipment	Limit: $________
☐	☐	Towing	Limit: $________
☐	☐	Coverage for customized vehicles	Limit: $________
☐	☐	Mexico coverage	Limit: $________

Total premium automobile coverage: $________

Garage liability

	Coverage symbol	Coverage limit
Bodily injury – each person	________	$________
Bodily injury – each accident	________	$________
Property damage liability	________	$________

Total premium for garage liability coverage: $________

Garage keeper's liability

Yes	No	
☐	☐	Direct
☐	☐	Legal
☐	☐	Primary
☐	☐	Excess

Maximum coverage per vehicle Limit: $________

Maximum coverage per occurrence Limit: $________

Yes	No		
☐	☐	Collision	Deductible: $________
☐	☐	Comprehensive (OTC)	Deductible: $________
☐	☐	Specified causes of loss	Deductible: $________
☐	☐	Coverage for cars held for sale	Limit: $________

Total premium for garage keeper's liability coverage: $________

Part 8 – Miscellaneous Insurance Coverage Instructions

Boiler and machinery

Make sure you explore this issue with your agent if you have any pressurized equipment. If your business operates expensive machinery, inform agents in your Underwriting Information Questionnaire. This part of the checklist reminds agents to consider using boiler and machinery coverage, which may be a better way of insuring you. Review the boiler and machinery discussion in Chapter 5 for background information in preparation to discuss this with your agent.

Boiler and machinery is replacement cost coverage and has no coinsurance in it. This replacement cost coverage does require that you pick a coverage limit. It also has expediting expense coverage to help you get repairs done quickly.

Crime coverages

Crime coverages are often overlooked, so be sure to review the crime coverage in Chapter 5 and examine your potential for loss in this area. Consider obtaining quotes for at least employee dishonesty coverage; this is where many employers are most vulnerable. A wide variety of specialized crime coverages is available; so if you have concentrated values of property, be sure to discuss the best way to insure them with your agent.

Employee dishonesty is usually written on a *blanket* basis — meaning it pays only the limit shown for a loss, regardless of the number of employees involved. If five employees conspire and cause a $100,000 loss and you have $100,000 of coverage, the loss is paid in full. But, if two employees conspire and each employee causes you a $100,000 loss, you will only be paid a total of $100,000.

Other coverages

Finally, encourage agents to suggest other coverages you may need. This Business Insurance Coverage Checklist cannot possibly be completely ideal for all businesses, nor can it replace the professional services of a competent insurance professional. This checklist can help you make sure adequate attention is devoted to investigating your coverage needs, to increase the chances of you being properly insured in the event of loss.

Part 8 – Miscellaneous Insurance Coverage

Boiler and machinery

Yes	No		
☐	☐	Boiler and machinery	Limit: $________

Objects covered: ____

____

____

Yes	No		
☐	☐	Business interruption/extra expense	Limit: $________

Total premium for boiler and machinery coverage: $________

Crime coverages

Yes	No		
☐	☐	Employee dishonesty	Limit: $________
☐	☐	Forgery or alteration	Limit: $________
☐	☐	Theft, disappearance, and destruction	Limit: $________
☐	☐	Computer fraud	Limit: $________
☐	☐	Other crime coverages	Limit: $________

Total premium for crime coverage: $________

Other coverages

Other coverages recommended by agent or broker: ____

____

____

Total premium for other recommend coverages: $________

Notes

Chapter 6

Know Your Workers' Compensation Issues

How Workers' Compensation Affects You

You, like many other business owners, probably pay more for workers' compensation insurance than you would like. One way to reduce workers' compensation costs is to purchase policies called *participating policies*, which have the possibility of returning dividends to you if your loss experience is favorable. The lower your losses, the higher the dividend you may receive. *Dividends* are technically defined as refunds of overpaid premiums due to your favorable loss history, but they come in the form of checks you can take to the bank. If your annual premium is in excess of $10,000, be certain you attend to each issue covered in this chapter. All workers' compensation policyholders should try to make sure their policy has the potential to return dividends, no matter what size the premium.

If your annual premium is under $10,000, you will probably find time spent working on this subject less profitable than if you are paying over $10,000. Seeking out group plans for which you qualify is worthwhile, since that may be the only way you can participate in a dividend program. A *group plan* is one that pools a group of smaller buyers, collects all the premiums and loss experiences, then evenly distributes the dividends to the group members. Group plans are often located through trade associations, or through insurance brokers and agents, and are sometimes referred to as safety groups.

Workers' compensation coverage pays the benefits for covered employees mandated by state law for job-related illnesses, injuries, and deaths. Benefits include medical expenses, death benefits, lost wages, and vocational rehabilitation. Failure to carry workers' compensation coverage leaves an employer out of compliance with the law, and vulnerable to paying all the benefits, in addition to possible fines. Always check with your state workers' compensation office for laws specific to your state.

The insurance marketplace for workers' compensation varies greatly, depending on the state in which you reside. In some states, only the state is allowed to sell workers' compensation insurance. These states are referred to as monopolistic fund states. In some states, private insurers compete with state workers' compensation insurance providers. In other states, coverage is sold by private insurers only. In these states, when private insurers refuse to insure a business, the business can purchase coverage from government-mandated *assigned risk plans* — also called *pools*. Private insurers in the state must participate in the pool in proportion to the amount of business they do in the state.

To better understand your overall workers' compensation coverage, you need to understand ten important issues. These ten issues are:

- How premiums are calculated;
- Applying correct payroll classifications;
- Effects of experience modification factors;
- Dividend programs;
- The question of insuring owners;
- Cash flow considerations;
- Recordkeeping practices to avoid trouble at audits;
- Working relationships that require special attention;
- How workers' compensation premiums are reduced; and
- Proper handling of claims.

Each of these ten issues is discussed in greater detail in the following sections.

Issue 1 – How Premiums Are Calculated

Workers' compensation premiums are determined by the type of work your employees perform.

Workers' compensation premiums are determined by the type of work your employees perform. Hundreds of occupations are classified by the workers' compensation rating bureaus. Sometimes, a specific class for your type of work will not exist, so your workers will be grouped in the class that most nearly fits the work they do. A specific rate is established for each occupational class by studying the loss history for that specific occupation. These rates are then used by your insurance company to calculate your annual premium.

Your annual premium is calculated by multiplying the defined rate by the number of hundreds of dollars of remuneration — usually payroll paid annually to each employee in a given class. For example, suppose you had an administrative employee work for you for 1,500 hours last year. You paid $5 an hour for a total annual payroll of $7,500. Assuming the state rate for administrative employees — referred to as clerical employees by insurance rating bureaus — in your state is $0.50 (50 cents) per hundred dollars of payroll, your annual premium would be $37.50 as seen in Example 1 below.

Because different occupations involve greater risk for bodily injury, the class rates will vary significantly. For example, suppose you employ a roofer for the same amount of hours as the clerical or administrative person (1,500). You pay the roofer the same hourly wage of $5 per hour. Assuming the state rate for roofers in your state is $30 per hundred dollars of payroll, your annual premium would be $2,250 as seen in Example 2.

How the Workers' Compensation Premium Calculation Works

Total hours x Hourly wage = Total wages

$$\frac{\text{Total wages}}{\text{\# of hundreds of payroll paid}} \times \text{Occupational classification rate} = \text{Total premium}$$

Example 1

1500 x $5 = $7,500

$$\frac{\$7{,}500}{\$100} \times \$0.50 = \$37.50$$

Example 2

1500 x $5 = $7,500

$$\frac{\$7{,}500}{\$100} \times \$30 = \$2{,}250$$

Take note that the annual premiums will be multiplied and may be reduced or increased by an experience modification factor, if you pay enough payroll to qualify for one. This factor is explained in detail later on in this chapter.

Issue 2 – Applying Correct Payroll Classifications

Your payroll classifications must be established correctly. From the previous rating examples, you can see the difference an error can make. Failure to get your employees' payroll properly classified can ruin your business, through a devastating final audit billing from your workers' compensation insurance company. If your insurance company discovers an error in classification, it can adjust your premium and retroactively collect — or refund — for the past three years. To protect your business from this danger, keep track of your payroll information in detail — itemize each position with a job description and allotted payroll. Thoroughly discuss the work performed by your employees with your agent or broker to make sure the classification assignments match the job descriptions.

To help avoid a reclassification nightmare, an informed buyer will document important personnel changes and the reasoning behind the changes. If problems do arise, turn to your agent or broker for help. With the exception of court appeals, your state's workers' compensation insurance rating bureau has the ultimate authority for classification assignments. Once the bureau has inspected your operation, and ruled as to the appropriate classifications, insurance companies will generally accept those guidelines. Employers are often reluctant to invite the bureau to inspect their job classifications, fearing they could open a can of worms. If you are paying the higher rate, and think you deserve to use a lower-rated classification, you have nothing to lose in asking for a bureau inspection.

Issue 3 – The Effects of the Experience Modification Factors

The experience modification factor is a multiplier applied to standard workers' compensation rates, serving to either discount or surcharge your premium.

Standard workers' compensation rates are published by the workers' compensation insurance rating bureaus and are frequently referred to as the *manual rates*. The manual rates cover a large number of occupational classifications, and are the basis for your policy's premium. The rates are designed for the average risk, to which your business and all other business in the same category are compared. The *experience modification factor* is a multiplier applied to standard workers' compensation rates, serving to either discount or surcharge your premium. The calculation is based on your history of losses versus premium size, as it attempts to measure whether your experience falls in the average risk range contemplated in the manual rates, or if you are above or below average in losses.

Any business subject to an experience modification will obviously want to minimize the modification factor to reduce workers' compensation premiums.

Businesses paying more than the current minimum threshold over a three-year period are generally subject to experience modification factoring. For instance, a factor of 1.0 means you will pay the manual rates for the coming year. In like manner, a factor of 0.80 means you pay 80 percent of the manual rates, and a factor of 1.35 means you pay 135 percent of the manual rates. Any business subject to an experience modification will obviously want to minimize the modification factor to reduce workers' compensation premiums.

Consider the example of the roofer from the beginning of this chapter. With an experience modification factor of 1.0 the premium was $2,250. If your roofer suffered an increase in losses, and received an experience modification factor of 1.35, the premium would rise to $3,038. However, if the roofer enjoyed a favorable claim experience and received an experience modification factor of 0.80, the premium would fall to $1,800. The lower the experience modification factor earned by an employer, the lower the premium paid. This reduced overhead allows the employer to be more competitive in pricing goods and services.

The experience modification factor is calculated once per year, thus locking in your workers' compensation insurance premium overhead for the full year. To determine the anniversary of your experience modification effective date, look at your latest experience modification worksheet. If you do not have your experience modification worksheet, Sample Letter F —located in the Appendix — can help you obtain it. The calculation process generally begins six months prior to your anniversary date, which is usually the same as your expiration date. This is an important fact if you want to know how to influence your experience modification factor to reduce your workers' compensation premium cost for the coming year.

The calculation will take into account three years of loss history — skipping the most recent 18 months — because recent claims have not had time to clearly establish the amount of loss. So, a claim you suffer today will not impact your experience modification for at least 18 months, which allows you time to take the corrective measures suggested on the following page and exercise some control over your factor. Remember, the result of this year's calculation will apply to your premiums for all of next year, beginning with your renewal date.

Control Your Factor

You can take several steps to minimize your experience modification factor. The following procedures will establish the groundwork for exercising control over your modification calculations.

Depending on the size of the premium you pay, make sure you are getting loss runs regularly — either on a monthly, quarterly, semiannual, or annual basis. Obtain all your loss runs for the previous five years. Sample Letter C, located in the Appendix, assists you in ordering these insurance company-generated reports. The reports display losses incurred, including dates, category of loss, cause of loss, and amounts paid or reserved. Review these with either your agent or your prospective agent, and look for:

- Claims that don't belong to you or your business. Insurance companies are not infallible so losses that don't belong to you may end up on your loss run report and impact your account completely by accident.
- Claims that don't make sense as they relate to the way you understand the claim to exist. Mistakes such as entering too many zeros or transposing numbers are easy to make.
- Claims that should be closed, but are not. If an injured employee is back to work and the claim is still open, check it out. A document may need your signature to close the claim.

Check these details to make sure the values used to establish your modification factor are valid. If you find errors or have questions, your agent should contact the insurance carrier and get an explanation, correction, or both. If the losses you need reviewed are not from the time period in which your agent handled your account, appoint your current agency as your consultant, so it can work with the insurance company to resolve your difficulties. Because your current agency is earning commissions on your current policy, you probably will not be charged an additional fee for this service.

No less than 90 days before the next calculation date you should obtain open claim status reports for the three policy years that will affect your factor. See Sample Letter P in the Appendix. Each open claim should be reviewed with the claims department to determine if the reserves are overstated, and how the claim can be closed. Claims are often held open through unintentional neglect. An open claim tends to be reserved for amounts higher than the final payment amount will be when closing it. If the claim is still open, the reserve amount is used in your modification calculation. By monitoring open claims, you may expedite their closing, and argue for lower reserves. Working closely with your agent and claims adjusters is one of the most important things you can do to help open claims promptly get closed, and for the correct amount.

Loss Control Services

In selecting a workers' compensation insurance company and agent, ask what you can expect in the way of loss control services. These services can be very valuable in helping you avoid claims and minimize their impact. Loss control services deal in two areas: loss prevention and loss reduction. Assistance comes in various forms, that include:

- Free published materials
- Guidance
- Evaluation
- Problem solving

For example, a company may evaluate air quality, identify a pollutant in the air, and offer potential solutions for removing the pollutant, then conduct follow-up inspections. These services can be expensive to purchase, but are provided free to many policyholders. For a further discussion of loss control assistance with safety programs, see Chapter 10.

The preventive approach starts with a commitment to safety, beginning with upper management and subsequent education of all employees.

To attack the root cause of a high experience modification factor, you must decide to invest resources in loss control and prevention. This long-term, preventive approach works toward reducing the number and severity of workers' injuries via loss control. The preventive approach starts with a commitment to safety, beginning with upper management and subsequent education of all employees. A good motto is: "Safety is our number one concern."

Implement a progressive discipline system to reward good safety habits and deter unsafe acts. You can:

- Purchase safety equipment;
- Provide training;
- Inspect to make sure established procedures are followed;

- Enforce the use of seat belts; and
- Improve lighting, or anything that will help avoid or minimize injuries.

Good hiring practices must be established to help reduce employee turnover. With a decreased turnover rate, you reduce the risks associated with hiring new employees who may be looking for a place to file a workers' compensation claim. Get assistance to start or improve your loss control program from the loss control department of your insurance company or agency.

Get assistance to start or improve your loss control program from the loss control department of your insurance company or agency.

Alternatively, you may decide to do nothing about your high experience modification, and continue to pay excess money to the insurance company. Because workers' compensation is federally mandated, someone will always have to insure you, though the premium may continue to rise unless you cure the root cause of your losses.

Stay Informed about Your Factor

To remain informed about your experience modification factor, obtain a copy of your current experience modification worksheet — the worksheet on which the coming year's factor is calculated. See Sample Letter F in the Appendix to have your agent obtain a copy for you. The worksheet will show you when the calculation was made, so mark your calendar for the next anniversary to remember when the next one is due. Ninety days before the anniversary date, launch your open claims status review. Sample Letter P in the Appendix can be used to start the review. Knowing next year's factor can be a useful fact for budgeting purposes.

Many agencies have computer systems that notify them when your modification changes. If this service is not available, simply send the letter requesting the worksheet once each year, to remind your agency you are concerned about your modification factor.

If you currently have a high modification factor, you may not be able to change it. The only grounds for having a current modification altered is a mathematical error found in the *Unit Statistical Report* — the report of premiums and loss data, including reserves, provided to the rating bureaus. Persuading an insurance company to revise its reserves for an open claim will not help your current modification, though it can help future calculations.

Issue 4 – Dividend Programs

Whenever you purchase a workers' compensation policy, ask for a written explanation of your potential for dividends. This practice will help prevent you from unknowingly purchasing a *nonparticipating policy* — the kind of policy that never pays you a dividend. Only *participating policies* have the potential to pay you dividends. The nature of a dividend program should be explained to you in a dividend disclosure statement by your

Whenever you purchase a workers' compensation policy, ask for a written explanation of your potential for dividends.

selling agent or broker. After reading this section, you will have a firm grasp on the vital issues surrounding dividends. Then you will be able to make informed decisions about which dividend proposal is most attractive.

First, you must understand the concept of safety group programs, which pool groups of policyholders into a common dividend program. These programs are usually attractive to business owners paying under $10,000 per year in premiums. Second, you must understand the concept of individual dividend plans, which are attractive to business owners paying over $10,000 per year and have good loss experience.

As you discover the variations in plans, you will learn not to expect a check for your dividends the day your policy expires. Usually, dividends are not paid for 6 to 18 months after your policy expires, allowing time for your claims to mature. You will learn that dividends can never be guaranteed, because it is against the law for a company or agent to promise or guarantee dividends. You will understand exactly what you need to know to compare dividend programs, and how to use the Workers' Compensation Coverage Checklist at the end of this chapter to help you collect essential information. The following information will help you acquire a basic knowledge of dividend programs.

Types of Dividend Programs

One common type of dividend program is called a *safety group program*, which is generally used for smaller, homogeneous accounts. For example, your policy is placed with a group of similar businesses, and the loss experience of the entire group dictates what percentage of each member's premium will be paid as a dividend. If the group performs profitably, you may receive a dividend, even if your particular business suffers serious losses. If your company has no losses, yet the group suffers serious losses, you might not receive a dividend — because you have pooled your loss experience with that of the group.

When enrolling in a group program, first consider whether you would be better served in an individual dividend program.

When enrolling in a group program, first consider whether you would be better served in an individual dividend program. If the group program makes the most sense, then select the best available program relative to its dividend history. To make an informed decision about whether to enter a group program, obtain an individual dividend proposal based on your situation and the dividend history of the groups available to you. With a prior knowledge of the potential dividends and the timing of the possible dividend distributions, you can then make an informed decision.

Proposals that illustrate *individual dividend plans* — also called *retention plans* — are usually presentations of what a particular company would have paid you based on past histories for businesses like yours. Usually, you are shown what you would have received if you had varying amounts of losses against the estimated premium level you will pay this year.

Typically, a dividend formula is provided by a quoting insurance company that discloses how the dividends are currently calculated. Comparing individual dividend plans can seem very complicated; but it can be simple by analyzing the basic issues.

How to Compare Dividend Proposals

Comparing individual dividend plans can seem very complicated; but it can be simple by analyzing the basic issues.

Imagine you have three competitive dividend proposals on your desk and you want to identify the most attractive proposal from a dividend standpoint. You can make a quick comparison if you know what to look for.

First, you must be familiar with the basic terminology. Then you can apply some very basic math to make your comparison. The Workers' Compensation Coverage Checklist, located at the end of this chapter, asks agents to provide you with the values you need to perform your comparison. The values you need are described with the following terms.

- Retention — This value represents the percentage of your premium the company will keep, even if you have no losses.
- Loss conversion factor (LCF) and loss development factor (LDF) — These values are multiplied by your claims dollar amounts to magnify the losses to allow for their potential increases prior to final settlement.
- Incurred but not reported (IBNR) — This is a percentage multiplied by your premium to allow for possible claims that have occurred, but have not yet been reported.

The first step in comparing dividend proposals is to identify the values for each of the above terms. The Workers' Compensation Coverage Checklist provides spaces for you to enter these values, if your agents have not already done so for you.

With the values entered in the form, only simple math is needed to add the retention plus the IBNR for each proposal. The proposal with the lowest total of retention, plus IBNR, is probably the most attractive from a potential dividend standpoint.

In addition to the above simple comparison, five additional considerations are explained below.

- One-, two-, and three-year plan comparison — When making your decision, remember that valid comparisons can only apply between plans with similar terms. The long-term plans tend to have more favorable retention numbers, because they demand a longer commitment from you to remain insured with the insurance company. However, beware when entering into a long-term plan, because you will usually lose future dividends if you change insurance companies before the end of the plan.

  If your dividend proposal is for more than one calculation and payout, look for and understand the recapture clause. The *recapture clause* means the dividends already paid to you in the first payout may be reclaimed by the insurance company if future calculations show losses larger than projected in previous calculations. Avoid this clause whenever possible. Usually a proposal with a recapture provision is less desirable than a proposal without one.

To simplify your decision, primarily focus on the retention plus IBNR percentages, comparing among plans that are for the same term.

- The potential to lose dividends — Keep in mind you can completely lose any potential dividend by allowing your policy to lapse for nonpayment of premium. You jeopardize your right to receive your dividend by failing to keep your policy in force during the policy year. Failure to respond to audit requests or to pay audit premiums can also deprive you of your dividends. In some cases, it makes sense to borrow money to honor your agreement with the insurance company, to preserve your right to receive coming dividends.
- Dividend check payouts — The timing of dividend checks can vary widely, so compare this issue among your various dividend proposals. The company may have all of the dividend released 18 months after the policy expiration. On the other hand, the company may release half of the dividend 12 months after the expiration, and release the other half 24 months after the expiration. The variations in dividend payout dates can be confusing. Don't attempt to base your decision solely on the timing issue; rather, use it when deciding between two close proposals.

  Mark your calendar for the payout dates indicated in the dividend disclosures. Dividend checks are usually mailed to insurance agencies for delivery to you. Some checks get lost, or worse, misappropriated. A dividend check can be inadvertently deposited into the agency's general account, or a dishonest person could deposit the check. You should not depend on the insurance company to notify you if a check is not cashed or misappropriated. Sample Letter E, located in the Appendix, is designed to help you get a report of when you can expect future dividend checks. If you suspect you did not receive a check that was due you, call your workers' compensation insurance company. Have the applicable policy numbers and effective dates handy and ask if any dividend checks were issued for the period in question. If checks were issued that you did not receive, the company should help you investigate where the money went.

Ask each agent to provide a table showing exactly what dividend will result from various assumed loss amounts.

- LCF and LDF considerations — The loss conversion factors (LCF) and loss development factors (LDF) are applied to magnify losses you incur, thus reducing your dividend. The closer these numbers are to 1.0, the less effect they have. For example, if you have no losses, the LCF and LDF values won't matter anyway. But but if you have a $10,000 loss and the factors total 1.15 you will be charged $11,500 for the loss. The two factors previously discussed generally have less impact than the retention number. The greater your losses, the greater the impact; the lower your losses, the less the impact. If you want to get very specific in your proposal comparisons, ask each agent to provide a table showing exactly what dividend will result from various assumed loss amounts.
- The insurance company's dividend history — Unfortunately, what you see in your dividend proposal is not necessarily what you will get. You

should investigate the history of a company in terms of its consistency in honoring dividend projections. A company that has consistently paid its projected amounts demonstrates a commitment to its customers. Financial strength is a factor in the likelihood a company will honor its projections.

It is illegal for insurance companies to guarantee the payment of dividends. Dividend proposals are based upon historical payment practices to policies with premiums relatively the same size as yours. One reason dividend payments cannot be guaranteed is because the issuance of dividends involves a subjective evaluation process. The dividends are actually authorized by an insurance company's board of directors. Further, the dividends you actually receive for your current policy will not be approved and paid until usually one year has passed so that claims can get settled. Sometimes an insurance company's financial strength erodes to the point when it cannot afford to pay the full amount of the dividends. So, you may receive a reduced amount of your dividends — a practice known as *factoring* in the insurance industry.

A Word on Agents' Commissions

Agents' commissions for workers' compensation policies are usually a maximum of 10 percent. Buyers with larger workers' compensation premiums — over $50,000 annual premium — should be aware dividend retention plans can sometimes be improved when the agent is willing to accept a lower commission than the common 10 percent. Should the agent decide to accept only 5 percent commission, the insurance company will sometimes match with 5 percent, thus lowering the retention, and increasing your potential dividend by 10 percent. State plans do not pay commissions to agents, so they don't manipulate dividends this way.

Issue 5 – The Question of Insuring Owners

To insure owners or not? This question confronts both large and small businesses. The answer is up to the needs and wants of the business and its owners. You can opt to exclude coverage for owners or stockholding corporate officers. However, excluding coverage for these individuals may not be the wisest option. The owners' and officers' payrolls are often assigned to the low-cost clerical or sales class. If owners and officers want to be covered, this is usually not a problem.

You may have trouble finding coverages, however, if you are the owner of a sole proprietorship, partnership, or a one-person corporation. Because it is difficult to determine when you are not at work, insurance companies feel they are providing 24-hour coverage, when their intent is to only cover the 8-hour workday. You can see the reason for the insurance company's reluctance, since the coverage includes all medical expenses from work-related injuries and illness with no dollar limit. Coverage for loss of wages if the person is disabled is also included.

Many insurance companies will not want to provide coverage on the owners of small businesses since they are literally at work 24 hours a day.

If the owners have a good medical plan and some disability insurance in place, the workers' compensation coverage may be redundant and need not be purchased. You can still get a premium quote, which includes owners, so you can make an informed decision.

Usually, the state insurance fund or the assigned risk plan will be the only markets available for this coverage on one-person operations, depending on the state laws where you live and work.

Issue 6 – Cash Flow Considerations

Variations in cash flow include the required deposit amount, and the frequency of payroll reporting and payments. Deposits are typically 10 to 20 percent of the estimated annual premium — you may find companies asking for a deposit greater than 20 percent. Generally, sizable accounts should opt for monthly reporting of actual payroll, and pay their premium as the payroll occurs. As payroll fluctuates, so do the premium payments.

Monthly reporting allows maximum control of cash flow, and seems to work better for businesses with fluctuating payrolls. You can get quarterly, semiannual, and annual reporting of payroll, and pay premiums based on these cycles.

Sometimes insurance companies will want to use *stipulated billings*. A stipulated billing entails an estimate of the premium at the beginning of the year, a collection of fixed installments during the year, and then a one-time adjustment at the year-end audit. Stipulated billings are generally less preferable, because they become a fixed cost during the year, which doesn't go down if you reduce payroll. If payroll goes up, you can be adversely affected by the year-end adjustment. Some companies will check during the policy year, to make sure the stipulated billings are adequate. If the billings are going to fall short of equaling the necessary payments based on the mid-term estimates, you will get an endorsement to the policy increasing your payments.

Alternative Risk Financing Techniques

As your company grows, you will reach a point where the standard insurance programs may not be the best financial alternative for you. The exact point when you become able to use alternative financing will vary for each insured.

You should consider looking into alternatives when your annual premium is in excess of $300,000. This level may not be large enough for you to begin to actually use an alternative method, but you can at least look at the options and prepare for the move to it. Retrospectively rated polices and self-insurance programs offer you opportunities to use more of your money in your business by having less of it in the insurance company's hands during the policy period. These plans can save you money if your claims experience is good, but can cost you more than you estimate if your claims experience is higher than you anticipate.

Some agents do specialize in these types of programs, so request several proposals to see if your business qualifies for one of these plans. Normally, the large insurance brokerage houses have persons specializing in these programs; however, many smaller specialty consultants offer a variety of programs too.

Many financing options are available. Have your accountant review these proposals before you reach any final decisions.

Issue 7 – Recordkeeping Practices to Avoid Trouble at Audits

All workers' compensation policies are auditable. Usually, you will receive either a voluntary audit request by mail or a visit from a company auditor — called a *physical audit* — at least once a year. A voluntary audit asks you to provide your actual payroll information for the policy year, broken down by workers' compensation classification. The physical audit entails an auditor visiting your office and inspecting your records for the purpose of verifying your payroll and workers' job classifications. The auditor may inspect your payroll tax returns, financial reports, time cards, and certificates of insurance from subcontractors. These records must agree, so the auditor can satisfactorily reconcile your records to the payroll estimates on which your premium was calculated.

Be sure to keep certificates of insurance from all subcontractors, proving they carried workers' compensation insurance.

Common problems with audits include getting charged for amounts paid to subcontractors and disputes about classification assignments for specific employees. To protect yourself, be sure to keep certificates of insurance from all subcontractors, proving they carried workers' compensation insurance. Keep daily time cards on employees, recording which hours apply to different classifications. This is particularly important when more than one classification may be applied to a single employee. The time cards will serve as your evidence of the exact nature of the work performed.

Issue 8 – Special Working Relationships

You should be aware of special working relationships that need examination from a workers' compensation coverage perspective. You may be surprised to learn there are employees who are not necessarily covered by your policy. These include illegal immigrants, independent contractors, owners and officers, voluntary workers, and those individuals who work outside your coverage territory.

Illegal Immigrants

Workers' compensation policies exclude illegal immigrants when their employer has knowledge of their immigration status. Since, as an employer, you are now required by federal law to check the status of all your potential employees, you should not have any problems in this area of your policy. However, if you knowingly hire an illegal worker and that worker is injured, you will be personally liable for any claims. Make sure you follow all the legal guidelines for checking the status of your employees.

Owners and Officers

Depending on the state you live in, you may or may not be able to include sole proprietors, partners, owners, and stock-owning corporate officers for coverage. See page 141 in this chapter for more information on this topic.

Independent Contractors Versus Employees

What if you replaced your employees with independent contractors? Would you still need workers' compensation insurance? Numerous tests can be applied by a workers' compensation rating bureau to determine whether someone is your employee or an independent contractor. Before replacing employees with independent contractors, contact a business consultant, your workers' compensation rating bureau, and your tax adviser. The IRS may have some impact on your decision to change to independent contractors and the workers' compensation rating bureau may challenge you as well.

Voluntary Workers' Compensation Coverage

Two different situations involving voluntary workers may apply in which you need to obtain an endorsement to provide coverage.

- First, when you employ workers for whom your state's laws do not require you to provide coverage, you may wish to voluntarily do so.
- Second, if you ever are lucky enough to have donated labor, the workers will be covered just as anyone else you employ. Unfortunately, you are supposed to report an honest estimate of the payroll you would have to pay to get equivalent service. Your workers' compensation carrier will charge a premium to cover the exposure of the volunteer laborers.

If there is anyone working for you other than employees on payroll, be sure to discuss your exposures in depth with your workers' compensation agent or insurance company underwriter.

People Working Outside of Your Coverage Territory

You can face paying the difference in benefit levels between the home state and the state in which an employee is injured.

Whenever you have an employee working outside your own state, immediately notify your workers' compensation insurance company. When you have employees working in other states, you must add an endorsement including those states — commonly called an *other states endorsement*. If your employee works in one of the six monopolistic states, you must purchase coverage directly from that state's workers' compensation fund. An employee injured in a state other than the employer's is eligible to collect either the benefits of the state in which the injury occurred, or those of the state where the employer is domiciled. Without the special coverage, as an employer, you can face paying the difference in benefit levels between the home state and the state in which an employee is injured.

When employees work outside the United States, investigate the purchase of a foreign endorsement coverage. The *foreign endorsement coverage* can:

- Provide coverage for 24 hours a day;
- Include endemic diseases as work-related; and
- Offer an option to provide money for repatriation.

Workers Subject to Special Laws

Over the years, various laws have been passed to provide benefits to workers subject to federal jurisdiction. If your employees work on or near waterways, boats, ships, docks, or wharves, be sure your workers' compensation coverage provides benefits stipulated by the United States Longshoremens' and Harbor Workers' (USL&H) Compensation Act or the Jones Act. Further, employees working in or near mines may be subject to the Federal Black Lung Compensation Insurance Act. Contact your agent or workers' compensation insurer to arrange this coverage. If you fail to do so, you may end up paying the difference in benefits between your state's workers' compensation benefits and these more generous federal benefits.

Issue 9 – Reducing Workers' Compensation Expenses

For a large number of businesses that are incorporated, an immediate reduction can be taken for their current and ongoing expenses for workers' compensation coverage, general liability, and employers contribution to FICA, while at the same time giving pay increases to employees. Section 125 of the Internal Revenue Code is the gift that makes this work.

A Section 125 Plan is a payroll diversion plan that enables employees to divert portions of their payroll into a designated fund to purchase certain benefits with pretax dollars, which they currently purchase with after-tax dollars. The effect of the plan is to increase the after-tax spendable income to the employee, which pleases most employees. In addition, employers in many states are pleased because all payroll diverted into the plan is excluded when calculating the premium for workers' compensation — and the employer does not have to pay the FICA contribution. Most states allow exclusion of Section 125 payroll from workers' compensation premium calculation.

What expenses can employees pay with pretax dollars by diverting payroll into the Section 125 plan? The simplest expense to divert is the portion of medical insurance now paid, including dependent medical insurance. Other insurance premiums can also be included, such as dental and vision. Employees may also fund deductibles and other uninsured medical expenses through the plan. They can pay for home day care expenses for their dependent children through the plan. The more the employees use the plan, the greater their tax savings, and the greater the benefit to the employer.

Types of Business that Benefit from Section 125

The more employees a business has, the more profitable it can expect the plan to be. Even businesses with under ten employees can enjoy significant profit, if the circumstances are right. Any corporation with a group medical plan, with significant amounts of money being paid by the employees for the dependent coverage, is a good prospect for Section 125. Look at your latest group health insurance billing and determine the amount your employees are currently contributing to pay medical premiums with their after-tax dollars. Typically, they might be paying 100 percent of the dependent medical premiums, which you have been deducting from their paychecks after taxes. If total employee contributions exceed $10,000 per year, seriously consider implementing at least the simplest application of Section 125, the premium-only plan.

The premium-only plan only affects employee's contributions to your business' group health insurance, and makes no provision for the flexible spending account described below. The advantages of the premium-only plan are minimal employee involvement, and relatively simple and inexpensive setup and administration.

For some businesses, expansion of the premium-only plan to include a flexible spending account for employees makes most sense. With the flexible spending account, employees elect fixed monthly deductions for insurance premiums, health care costs, and dependent care costs. These dollars are deducted from payroll and reimbursed to employees as costs are incurred. Employees must use all the amount they deduct during the plan year, or the money is forfeited. The employer benefits because all dollars diverted to the flexible spending account qualify for Section 125 treatment.

Making a Section 125 Plan Profitable

A motivated employer will make sure the employees understand how the plan serves them, and sees that they use it.

Profitable application of the concept calls for competent administration of the plan, and effective enrollment of the employees. Fortunately today, due to improving computer programs, a number of inexpensive, competent administrators can manage the mechanics of the plan and keep it in compliance with the law. Enrollment is a matter of the employer making sure the benefits of the plan are communicated to the employees, and that they use it to its full value. Enrollment materials are often provided by the administrator, who will assist you in making the plan successful. A motivated employer will make sure the employees understand how the plan serves them, and sees that they use it.

To set up and administer a Section 125 plan can cost between $500 and $1,000 and about $5 per month, per employee. You can pay more for deluxe programs. Additionally, soft costs are involved — such as the time employers spend in the enrollment process. You must reach the break-even point, which is calculated by simple mathematics. Then, all payroll diverted beyond the break-even point translates to pure profit.

Information about the Section 125 plan is not widely distributed because few insurance agents make money from it. A few firms make money selling life insurance to employees while they do the enrollments, but generally, insurance agencies feel they can't make commissions by working to help employers reduce their workers' compensation premiums. Many agencies do not realize the Section 125 qualifies payroll for exclusion from workers' compensation premiums as well as FICA contributions.

Many agencies do not realize the Section 125 qualifies payroll for exclusion from workers' compensation premiums as well as FICA contributions.

If you suspect you can profit from the Section 125 plan, conduct an informal feasibility study to get an idea of how much payroll your employees might divert into the plan. Ask them to estimate their annual expenditures for:

- Insurance — health, dental, term life, disability, vision;
- Health care — predictable medical expenses, dental, vision, prescriptions; and
- Dependent care — children in nursery schools or daycare, and parent care.

If these dollars are diverted out of payroll and your workers' compensation costs, how worthy is it to you and your employees? If the answer is significant, the next step is to seek professional assistance by talking to several employee benefits advisers.

Your local Yellow Pages may list a heading called "Employee Benefits and Compensation Plans." Firms listed here should be able to help you locate qualified specialists in Section 125 enrollment and administration. Larger employers in your community can probably recommend competent specialists in employee benefits. Their controller or personnel department managers may tell you who handles their benefits.

When interviewing prospective employee benefit's specialists, carefully check their experience and referrals. Make sure they have handled enough prior enrollments to know what they are doing. Seek an enroller who will really sell your employees on participating to their full benefit, to maximize the value of the plan installation.

Make sure the administration of the plan will be flawless. Your payroll staff must be completely comfortable with the mechanics of the plan — which will require effective training. Explore the option of using a third party administrator to handle all the disbursements versus handling them internally. Handled properly, many companies can dramatically save through implementation of this plan.

Issue 10 – Proper Handling of Claims

When your employees report injuries, assist them in getting immediate medical attention, and immediately give them claim forms to report the incidents. Provide the insurance company with a *first notice of loss* within 24 hours of the injury.

You may ask why the rush of paperwork? Various state laws impose weighty penalties for delay. An insurance company has a limited number of days to provide an initial payment to an injured worker, or deny the claim. If you are the cause of a slowly reported claim, expect to pay the accruing penalties.

Check with your insurance company or your state workers' compensation office for details on handling claims.

Use the Workers' Compensation Coverage Checklist

You now have a solid understanding of the important issues surrounding the purchase and maintenance of workers' compensation insurance policies. Your completed Underwriting Information Questionnaire provides agents with all they need to provide you with sales proposals for your workers' compensation insurance. You know what information is essential to making informed decisions. To help you make sure agents provide you with the essential information, ask them to complete the following Workers' Compensation Coverage Checklist when presenting you with proposals.

Workers' Compensation Coverage Checklist

Instructions

Checklist

Workers' Compensation Coverage Checklist

Make sure insurance agents and brokers complete the checklist on the opposite page to collect information you will need in your standardized format. This will help you make informed workers' compensation purchasing decisions. You will save time because you won't need to dig through proposals for needed information to complete the Workers' Compensation Quote Comparison Worksheet, a part of your buying decision as outlined in Chapter 9. For a firm understanding of the important background information, read Chapter 6 in its entirety. Below are brief reminders of some of the important workers' compensation issues.

1. Employer's liability protects an employer against liability for damages resulting from injuries to employees who are not subject to the workers' compensation laws, subject to exclusions. As with other liability insurance, a good rule of thumb is to buy all you can afford. Most insurance companies include preestablished limits for employer's liability, and additional limits must be negotiated. Determining the limits you are quoted is a sound purchasing practice.
2. Owners and officers can be excluded from coverage, so it is important to be clear about who is and is not covered, as well as the expected cost of such coverage.
3. The discussion regarding dividend programs explains the dividend terms, which you should review to understand the significance of these items. You need to know for how many years the dividend plan is because you must compare plans of the same duration. The retention percentage and other factors will be used in the Workers' Compensation Quote Comparison Worksheet in Chapter 9. The calculation dates and payout dates help you understand when to look for dividend checks.
4. Inspect to make sure all quotes are based on the actual experience modification factor that will apply to you for the coming policy year.
5. It is wise to inspect the estimated annual premium to make sure all quotes are based on the same payroll and classification assumptions.
6. Audit and billing frequencies will help you understand your cash flow. Audit frequency is how often you will report your actual payroll, and billing frequency helps you understand when you will pay your premiums. The deposit premium is the amount you must pay to get a policy started, which will be credited at the final year end audit.
7. The endorsements for special working relationships are discussed in Chapter 6. All states endorsement is necessary when you have employees working out of state. Voluntary labor may be necessary if there is any possibility of donated labor, or uncompensated workers. USL&H and Jones Act endorsements may be necessary if there is any chance of your employees working on or near the water.
8. In the unlikely event you are examining retrospectively rated plans, which adjusts the final premium after the end of the policy year, be sure to inspect the minimum and the maximum premiums, as well as the stop loss. This will provide a starting point for in depth discussion with the quoting agent.

Workers' Compensation Coverage Checklist

1. Employer's liability limit

Bodily injury by accident — Each accident: $__________

Bodily injury by disease — Each employee: $__________

Bodily injury by disease — Policy limit: $__________

2. Owners and officers that are covered: — **Estimated premium (each owner):**

____________________ — ____________________

____________________ — ____________________

____________________ — ____________________

____________________ — ____________________

3. Participating policy

Yes No

☐ ☐ Dividend potential

(Check one) ☐ One-year plan ☐ Two-year plan ☐ Three-year plan

☐ ☐ Safety group used (Note to agent: If so, please provide group's dividend history.)

Retention percentage: ________ Loss development factor: ________

Loss conversion factor: ________ Incurred but not reported factor: ________

Recapture provision: ______________________________

____

Dividend calculation dates: ________________

Payout dates: ________________ Payout percentage: ________________

4. Experience modification used: ________________

5. Estimated annual premium: $________________

6. Audit frequency: ☐ Monthly ☐ Quarterly ☐ Semiannual ☐ Annual

Billing frequency: ☐ Monthly ☐ Quarterly ☐ Semiannual ☐ Annual

Deposit premium: $__________

7. Yes No

☐ ☐ Other states endorsement

☐ ☐ Voluntary labor coverage

Yes No

☐ ☐ USL&H coverage provided on if any basis

☐ ☐ Jones Act coverage provided on if any basis

8. Yes No

☐ ☐ Retrospectively rated plan

Basic premium: $__________ Minimum premium: $__________

Maximum premium: $__________ Stop loss: $__________

Notes

The Purchase

Section II

Chapter 7

Motivate Insurance People

Earn Willing Cooperation

To effectively approach the marketplace, you must practice some general human relations skills. The assistance of insurance people can be extremely valuable to you — you will save premium dollars and solve difficult problems. To earn willing cooperation, get people to focus on your situation as if it were their own. When you have properly encouraged insurance people to help you, they can produce a wealth of surprising solutions, ideas, and innovative suggestions. The willing cooperation of insurance people can make dramatic differences in the prices you pay. Getting insurance people to work wholeheartedly for you improves the values you receive, and leads to extraordinary service at basement prices.

The more you practice sound human relations and win wholehearted cooperation, the more you move towards your goal of reduced prices and increased service.

You can build sound human relations if you:

- Make an effort to see the world from the other person's point of view;
- Are kind, gentle, and understanding with insurance people;
- Are considerate of their feelings;
- Are friendly and courteous;
- Present the information they need openly and honestly; and
- Deal fairly with them.

Although it never pays to take out your aggravation on an insurance person, buyers complain every day. Habitual complaints mark you as one of the dreaded customers, and the only work you will get accomplished is the bare minimum. If you are a complainer and threaten to take your business elsewhere, the typical insurance person will silently hope you go elsewhere. Your complaints have a way of shutting down service after the

Although it never pays to take out your aggravation on an insurance person, buyers complain everyday.

phone call or visit is over. Your file will get passed around from one person to another, and the last thing you will get is meaningful service.

Friendly relationships with insurance people tend to be far more productive than antagonistic relationships.

The lack of willing assistance from insurance personnel can be expensive, and can cost you dearly when your agent is handling your file with a bad attitude. Try not to antagonize insurance people, because their actions or inactions directly affect your insurance costs. You can, however, be very effective at staying on top of work that needs to be done. You can be the nicest pain-in-the-neck and people will help you in spite of what they would rather be doing. Through diplomatic communication, appeal to higher causes like fair play, professionalism, reasonableness, and the fine human relationship you have established to get all kinds of things done. For example, you can say:

- It is only fair to ask for written follow-up, just to make sure things get done, isn't it?
- Isn't it reasonable to hear from the claims adjuster by now?
- It is only professional to help me select the best values by quoting those alternative coverages, isn't it?
- Of course, our friendship will outlast any insurance problem, but doesn't the price seem too high?
- You don't object to me collecting quotes from other agents, to help make sure our price is right, do you?

Appeals such as those listed above keep people working for you and willing to help you.

Building a Favorable Rapport: Nine Proven Techniques

Consider using the following specific human relations techniques to keep insurance people working for you. The following ideas seem to win favorable attention and are the result of years of trial-and-error situations. Do not apply each suggestion every time you deal with an insurance person. Instead, use the ideas as insights when you feel they are needed. These insights, when added to your human relations skills, will help achieve the results you desire.

Empathize

If you recognize that an insurance person is probably having a difficult day, you will establish a slight bond of friendship that can make a big difference. Taking a little time to establish rapport can be a valuable step in getting better service.

Recognize They Are Busy

Tell them you recognize they have many responsibilities and that you hope your timing is good. Typical insurance people will shift their attention from whatever they were doing and will ask how they can help you.

Blame the System, Not the Individual

Whenever discussing apparent disservice you have received, it is usually futile and counterproductive to blame individuals personally. Customer service failures are usually rooted in poorly designed systems — and the insurance industry has many of these systems. Instead of attacking your customer service representative personally, if you must, take your anger out on the system. Customer service people will tend to agree with your criticisms of their industry, and not feel the need to become personally defensive. This directs their energy much more effectively toward finding solutions to your problem, not raising defenses against personal criticisms.

Assure Them of the Confidence You Have in Their Service

Even if you have your doubts about their integrity, people will rise to your praise, and try to help you even if they neglect everybody else during a workday. If you wish to question the quality of service you have received, assure them you are confident they did not intentionally cause your trouble. Tell them you are confident they can fix the problem.

Offer to Save Them Time or Effort

When possible, try to avoid calling at the busy times of the day and week.

Saving people time and effort is a wonderful way to make them happy to hear from you again. Fax them information to save them from taking detailed notes. Avoid unnecessary phone calls, and when possible, handle business via fax or mail. Insurance people will appreciate the efficiency of your actions. The completed Underwriting Information Questionnaire is the ultimate time saver. Handing the completed questionnaire to agents saves them substantial time and effort in collecting this information about your business.

Be Responsive to Requests for Information

When you are asked for specific information, it is usually because a memo or phone call came from a company underwriter. Promptly respond with the requested information — agents are more responsive to the underwriter with whom they are maintaining a relationship. Your quick response keeps the process of serving you moving at a rapid pace, and everyone involved remembers the situation because it is still fresh in their minds. Customers who drag their feet in producing requested information do not endear themselves to the people who are trying to serve them. The more responsive you are in compiling complete information, the easier it will be for insurance people to serve you.

Consider the Timing of Your Phone Calls

Call at the best possible times of the day and week. Monday mornings are usually busy and stressful, because clients have had all weekend to think of valid reasons to call. On late Friday afternoons, people are focused on getting their week's promises kept and starting their weekends. A Friday afternoon promise to do something will likely be deferred to a Monday. This change increases the risk that the task will be forgotten, or that its purpose will lose clarity after the weekend. Also, calling just before lunch or just before closing time tends to be less effective than calling earlier in the day. You can call any time, but considering the insurance person's point of view, you will understand some timeframes are better than others to call.

Be Sparing with Urgencies

Many insurance clients think every request is urgent. If a request can wait a few days, offer the extra time as a gift to your insurance person. Offering less important tasks as items that can wait may endear you to the overcommitted insurance professional. Later, should you declare a task is truly urgent, you will be taken more seriously than a client who thinks everything is urgent.

Be Candid and Frank

Nothing wastes more time for an agent than working to resolve a situation, only to learn the insurance buyer misrepresented a key fact. If you misrepresent information on your account, don't expect to receive special attention. In fact, you may be treated much differently. It is outside the scope of this book to define the difference between right and wrong, but your relationship with an insurance person can be much more productive if you trust one another.

If your service person responds too slowly for your needs, ask to be reassigned.

If you feel your reasonable efforts at communicating with your customer service person are failing, talk with your agent. You may be able to have your account transferred to another service person in the office. While changing service people may be unusual — but an extremely valuable step — your agent should be able to make the change for you. To be reassigned, you may have to remind the agency that you are the customer.

Strategies to Approach New Agencies

Congratulations — with your completed Underwriting Information Questionnaire and Business Insurance and Workers' Compensation Coverage Checklists you are considered a sophisticated insurance shopper. Now you must temper this image with friendliness and encouragement, if you want to establish relationships with competent agents to quote your insurance. You want the quoting agents to think you are a well-organized and efficient businessperson, who needs assistance with your business insurance program. Keep in mind some simple strategies for effective dealings in the marketplace.

Let Quoting Agents Know if You Were Referred

Every agent knows the odds of doing business with a referral are much greater than with a caller motivated by an agency's direct advertisement. Be sure to let them know if you were referred by a satisfied client, and you will tend to get better treatment from the beginning.

Identify yourself as a referral, and you are immediately separated from the Yellow Page callers, and will tend to receive better attention.

Express the Possibility of Doing Business with Them

Agents don't make a dime unless you purchase their products, and some will fear they are wasting their time when they see how prepared you are. You can reduce that fear by promising to be reasonable and fair with any quoting agents. Communicate your reasonable objective: you seek the best possible insurance value relative to price, coverage, and service. Getting other opinions and quotes is perfectly reasonable, and no sensible agent or broker will fault you for testing the marketplace. You communicate fairness by making sure all agents are working with the same information. You hope to establish a lasting relationship with the right vendor, who must meet your reasonable objective. Projecting this attitude assures quoting agents they are entering a level playing field, and have a reasonable chance of earning your business.

Let Quoting Agents Know Who Else Is Working on Your Account

Brokers need to know what other brokers are doing with your account, so they don't approach the same insurance companies for you. Once a broker submits your information to a specific insurance company, avoid letting other brokers approach that company. Ask brokers with which companies they will be working, and pass this along to the other quoting brokers. Further, apply competitive pressure on brokers quote by letting them know direct writers are quoting also. Brokers fear the pricing that direct writers offer, and often cannot predict their quotes, so they lower their prices as much as possible.

Once a broker submits your information to a specific insurance company, avoid letting other brokers approach that company.

Have at Least Two People Attend Agent Interviews

Avoid attending agent sales presentations alone, including the information collection interviews and the quote presentations. At an interview, two people will learn much more than one because both can ask questions and absorb answers. If an important dispute arises about what was said during the interview, you will have a witness to confirm your account of the meeting. This practice encourages a higher level of professionalism from your insurance people.

Pass on Information about Your Insurance History

Agents are likely to ask you about your insurance history. When describing your insurance history, it helps to speak in terms that make changing agents a strong possibility. They would like to hear that you have been with the same agent for years, but you feel it is time for a change. Ideally, they would like to hear you are dissatisfied with your current agency and definitely plan to change to another one. Dissatisfaction typically arises from unjustified price increases, a mishandled claim, or poor policy service.

Show Quoting Agents Your Current Policies

If a quoting agent asks about your current policy, disclose your policies and the premiums you have paid. This cooperative approach is more effective when dealing with agents and insurance company underwriters. Some buyers imagine they will get lower quotes by not disclosing their premium history. However, your premium history does not dictate what your renewal premium will be, because you have made it known others are quoting your business.

Make Your Account More Profitable

It makes sense to try to be more profitable to your agency, especially when you pay under $25,000 in annual premium. A profitable account is one that does not require an inordinate amount of service for the premium paid. As you learn to demand more service and pay less premium, your account may become unprofitable. Your effort and consideration toward your agency costs you almost nothing, and benefits you tremendously.

Agencies have widely differing attitudes about the definition of a profitable account. Newer agents and agencies tend to write every policy they can. As they mature, many become more selective in the accounts they will accept. They try to select clients that create more commission income and require less service labor. It is difficult to predict at what point your account might be perceived as a money loser for your agency, because of the many variables in commissions and agency attitudes. If you feel you may be losing your agency money, below are some specific actions to counteract this concern.

Reward Your Agents by Sending Them a Referral

Most agents find prospecting — the digging up of new accounts to quote — to be a very difficult part of their job. Yet getting new business is one of their most important responsibilities. Once your agency identifies you as a source of referrals, they will continue to provide you with superior service. If your agent serves you well, you should feel comfortable referring your friends and acquaintances.

Make the Referrals Productive

Agents will appreciate any referral, even if they do not write the business. When communicating with friends or associates, take time to explain why you are referring them to your agent. For example, inform referrals that your agency is very competitive, or their service is outstanding and reliable. Also, help set up the initial interview. Get them on the phone together, or arrange a meeting that suits everybody. If you do this with a worthwhile account, you greatly increase your odds of superior treatment in the months and years ahead. Opening doors for agents endears them to you, which encourages them to keep working for you when it comes time to negotiate your program.

Opening doors for agents endears them to you, which encourages them to keep working for you when it comes time to negotiate your program.

Perform Acts of Loyalty

Be sure your agent knows about your loyalty. It doesn't hurt to show your current agents you have a lower quote, even if you are going to stay loyal. Agents work more for customers who show some sense of loyalty, because they will have a greater tendency to renew. The agents hope to depend on that loyalty while on vacations and during retirement because they will collect renewal commissions.

Agents work more for customers who show some sense of loyalty, because they will have a greater tendency to renew.

Offer Them a Letter of Recommendation

Agents will see value in a letter of this nature, as it is helpful for selling purposes. Use Sample Letter J in the Appendix, printed on your letterhead to recommend your agent. If the letter is shown to various prospective clients, the last thing agents will want is for you to become unhappy about some disservice. This assistance qualifies you for the preferred treatment, at a minuscule cost.

Offer to Travel to the Agent's Office When Appropriate

Agents consider their time to be their most valuable commodity, and welcome saving travel time and expense. In the long run, it may not be profitable for you to have your agent running all over town when it is not absolutely necessary.

Deal with Other Staff Members on Routine Matters

Usually, the agency's staff — customer service representatives and administrative support — can better handle your daily questions anyway. Save the agents' time for the issues they can really help you with — such as problem solving with insurance company underwriters and claims adjusters, and guidance toward effective and profitable insurance programs.

Allow Your Agency to Quote All Aspects of Your Insurance

Rather than just getting quotes on the policy with which you are most concerned, offer the workers' compensation, health, life, or disability policies. Consider all your insurance expenditures to identify those that may be used as incentives to get superior attention.

Pay Your Bills Like Clockwork

Timely payments make you a more valued account, and work to your advantage when you need help. The late payer causes extra paperwork and concern about whether coverage is in force. Late payers are considered worse insurance risks, because they appear to be under financial strains. (See moral hazards discussion in Chapter 4.) Should you find you have to make a late payment, let the agent know. Send Sample Letter R in the Appendix, which will be appreciated. You may save your agent considerable concern by communicating your situation.

Twelve Rules to Avoid Problems

The best solution to a problem is to prevent it from happening.

The best solution to a problem is to prevent it from happening. Preventing insurance problems is accomplished by practicing effective communication. Because poor communication is the cause of most insurance problems, effective communication tends to solve the problems. Admittedly, the best prepared correspondence can be ignored, but by applying the rules below, you experience smoother transactions with insurance matters.

Rule 1 – Always Check to Make Sure Things Get Done

A fundamental business practice is to set up procedures to make sure things actually get done. The procedures do not necessarily entail calling the insurance company every month to make sure they received your check. Following smart procedures does mean checking your bank account at least once a month to make sure the checks you wrote actually cleared. As you send requests, look for responses. If there is no response, follow up with a call or other appropriate method of communication.

Rule 2 – Follow Up All Requests for Action

Failure to follow up can result in your business being uninsured. For example, suppose you take your newly purchased car to your insurance agent or broker. You carefully discuss the changes you need to your insurance policy, and the agent inspects your car. You ask for written confirmation of the changes, however, you are assured the changes will be mailed. Typically, you should insist on getting written acknowledgment of the changes immediately. Imagine the impact if the endorsement is completely wrong. If your new car is totally destroyed in the meantime, settlement of the claim could be unnecessarily complicated.

Rule 3 – Read Your Insurance-Related Mail Regularly

When insurance-related mail arrives, open and read it. You will be surprised how many people think problems go away if the envelope isn't opened. The fact is: surprises come in the mail. Your insurance company may have decided to cancel you, because they tried to pull your driving record and accidentally received your son's record instead. The problem may be easily resolved, but only if you open the envelope. If an accident occurs after you tossed an unopened envelope containing a cancellation notice into the bill pile, the problem may be much more difficult to resolve.

Rule 4 – Correspond in Writing

When it comes to insurance transactions, nothing is as valuable as written correspondence. A memo summarizes changes and possible errors. When correcting any error, written confirmation of policy changes gives you proof of your policy specifics — so losses can be covered with little difficulty. Sample letters L, M, and N in the Appendix provide examples of such written correspondence. Letter L asks for billing clarification. Letter M asks for verification of vehicle or equipment's schedules, and letter N requests written problem solving. These letters can be easily adapted for your immediate situation, to get service moving in your direction.

Rule 5 – Document Phone Calls

Jot down calls as they occur. Keep a separate log, or record discussions on your calendar. Be sure to write down the name of the person with whom you spoke, the date and time, and the highlights of the discussion. Your log can become extremely helpful. If things go wrong and you start quoting dates, times, and names from your log, all concerned will realize you have been keeping good records. When people realize you are logging details of conversations, they become more professional and businesslike in dealing with you.

When people realize you are logging details of conversations, they become more professional and businesslike in dealing with you.

Rule 6 – Keep Orderly Files for Quick Reference

Your insurance agency keeps a file on you, so it makes sense for you to keep one on them. An organized filing method includes one file for each insurance policy. Label the files with policy descriptions and numbers. Attach the policy to the right inside folder, and as you receive endorsements attach them to the policy. Bills, correspondence, and notes you record can be attached to the left inside folder. Good file keeping puts information you may need at your fingertips. Many disputes can be resolved quickly by referring to well-maintained files.

Rule 7 – Write Your Account Number on Checks

Sometimes a payment is applied to the wrong account or policy, resulting in a policy lapse for nonpayment. Habitually writing these numbers on your checks may save you this aggravation.

Rule 8 – Get Binders Sent to You When Adding Coverage

Binders are written evidence of insurance, issued in lieu of a pending policy or endorsement. Requests for coverage are important, and it is very reasonable to request written verification for each change or addition. Waiting for policy changes from insurance companies can take a long time, so get a written acknowledgment from the agent to document your change immediately. It helps to order coverage changes in writing. First, always discuss the changes with your agent; a follow-up letter from you creates excellent documentation. Sample Letter W in the Appendix provides an example.

Rule 9 – Ask for Premium Quotes Before Authorizing Coverage Changes

Get an estimate of what the coverage changes will cost you — because it may take months for the endorsement to be issued and the bill to arrive. While the accuracy of an agent's quotes will vary, an estimate provides you some protection from a surprisingly high premium. If the premium dramatically differs from the agent's estimate, it is reasonable for you to expect the agent to correct the situation. The agent may either get the premium reduced or have the transaction reversed due to the surprisingly high cost.

Rule 10 – Understand How Your Policy Premium Is Developed

Make sure you understand if your policies are auditable and their corresponding rating basis.

You can correctly assess your costs of doing business with an understanding of what your premium is based on. Insurance people call this the *rating basis*. Without knowing your true overhead, you may make serious errors in pricing the goods or services you sell. Make sure you understand if your policies are auditable and their corresponding rating basis. You can then factor the rates into your costs and cash flow projections. Sample Letter U located in the Appendix requests this information for general liability, and can be altered to request the premium base for any other auditable policies, such as reporting forms for property policies.

Rule 11 – Avoid Paying too Much Premium in Advance

You gain leverage by not paying too much premium in advance, because you have more freedom to change policies.

Some insurance buyers like to pay their full annual premiums at the beginning of the year, which can be a sound business practice under the right conditions. You usually save on installment charges or interest, and avoid the risk of missing a payment while you are on vacation. The downside to payment in advance is that refunds can be very slow, should you cancel or reduce the policy during the policy year. Also, if the insurance company becomes insolvent, you have no recourse for the return of those funds. You gain leverage by not paying too much premium in advance, because you have more freedom to change policies. Also, withholding an installment payment may put pressure on your agent to get a problem resolved. Remember, however, withholding payments will cause your policy to be canceled, so you must arrange replacement coverage should this occur.

Rule 12 – Never Plan on Canceling a Policy in the Middle of a Term

Sometimes people will purchase a policy knowing they are going to cancel after a short period of time. If you plan to cancel after a short period of time, obtain an estimate of a short-rate cancellation charge. You can always pay the minimum deposit premium, rather than the full premium, because you can allow the policy to cancel for nonpayment. Cancellation caused by nonpayment avoids the short-rate cancellation charge, usually with no unfavorable side effects to you. Consult with your agent when considering this strategy.

Specific Problem-Solving Actions

Earlier in this chapter, we reviewed some general human relations techniques that can motivate insurance people to help you. But what about when a problem arises? Keep the following problem-solving actions in mind. Take caution, however, since being more aggressive than the situation merits can result in aggravating the only people who can help you.

Being more aggressive than the situation merits can result in aggravating the only people who can help you.

Make Yourself Heard

To prevent people from forgetting about you and the problem you want solved, the telephone call can be most productive. A friendly phone call to the right person can get your problem solved today. If that person is not available, be sure and leave a detailed message. The return call may be just to inform you that your problem has been solved, or to give you some other productive message. Always document these phone calls in your log.

Faithfully Place Friendly, Follow-up Phone Calls

After the first few calls, your insurance person will accept the fact you are a persistent customer who demands satisfaction. Your systematic contacts will have earned a sense of importance and urgency to make you satisfied.

Use Your Facsimile Machine

Faxed correspondence can be more effective than phone conversations in certain situations. If you want to communicate detailed written information, you save time and effort by faxing. You avoid reciting details over the phone. You save the other person from writing details, and you avoid the risk of transposed numbers or other errors. The magic of the fax machine is that it combines the urgency of the telephone call with the power of the written word.

The magic of the FAX machine is that it combines the urgency of the telephone call with the power of the written word.

Write a Letter

Letters requesting services are helpful in getting the results you want. Most people don't go to the trouble to write a letter. So when you write a letter, you make it clear you are serious about your request. Fortunately, many special-purpose sample letters are prepared for you, located in the Appendix. You can easily customize the letters, so you and your staff can send useful communications with little effort. The letter you send becomes a permanent part of your insurance agent's file — as well as documentation for your file — and a professional response can reasonably be expected. If the agency fails to respond, you can document the poor service you endured to the agency's top management. A record of these letters also helps you remember this sluggish service when the policy comes up for renewal.

Clarify with a Letter

Suppose you have been advised you will have to pay more than you expected, due to some obscure company rule applied to your policy. The insurance people have given you the news over the phone, and you are not very happy. Sending a letter asking for written clarification of the entire situation can be very useful. The person responding to your letter has to think through the situation well enough to write down what happened, and why it happened. Sometimes in doing so, insurance people discover potential solutions they did not initially consider. Also, another person may be brought into the situation to help respond to your letter. This person may see the problem in a whole new light. Further, your letter may be read by the management of the company, which escalates your problem to a higher level. In fact, the correspondence can ultimately end up being scrutinized through a judge's bifocals. Sending a letter asking for clarification of an unresolved problem affords you silent power to motivate insurance people to help you. See Sample Letter N in the Appendix.

Follow Up with a Phone Call

When faxing or mailing important correspondence, assure your correspondence arrives by following up with a phone call. It pays to phone and let the recipient know your correspondence is on its way. Phoning can avoid aggravation and delay, should your correspondence become misfiled, because the person expecting it will inform you if the correspondence doesn't arrive. While both mail and faxes are quite dependable, they are not 100 percent reliable. Faxes can get misdirected, or fax machines can fail. Until you get confirmation your correspondence has been received, be aware of the possibility it fell into the black hole of lost paper. The phone call helps eliminate mishaps, and helps confirm your correspondence ended up in the right hands.

Send a Registered Letter

When you feel you are really being ignored, or if you are taking a very decisive action — like canceling your policy to get a refund — send a registered letter. With a return receipt requested, a registered letter is a powerful move to get attention. The return receipt eliminates the response, "I never received your letter!"

Call the Upper Management of the Insurance Agency

People in top management tend to be very easy to get along with, and they look for swift solutions to problems. Be pleasant and friendly when you make this call, and apologize for the interruption. Explain your dilemma, and be prepared to tell the manager the name of the person with whom you have been dealing and what has transpired. This preparation will usually lead to much more thoughtful and resourceful handling of your problem.

Contact the Insurance Company's Upper Management

When you feel your agency is ignoring you, call the insurance company's management. Your call will usually result in the company calling the agency — usually the president of the agency — and discussing the complaint. No agency wants its relationship with an insurance company ruffled over one unhappy client. To appease the situation, you may be rewarded with satisfaction greater than your situation merits. Generally, this strategy should be reserved for agencies you intend to leave when your policies expire.

Have Another Agent Call Your Agent on Your Behalf

Suppose you have been told some astounding story about your insurance, which another agent has trouble comprehending. Two peers communicating in insurance jargon may clarify the problem and identify the next step towards a solution. By taking this step you have put your agency on notice that its work is being scrutinized by its peers.

Assign Your Business to a Different Agent or Broker, but Keep the Same Insurance Company

A letter to your insurance company that authorizes your newly selected professional to serve as your new agent or broker is a swift and decisive action. Your new agent will provide you with the assignment letter to sign and mail to the insurance company. The letter simply states, "I hereby assign XYZ insurance agency as my agent (or broker) of record." This letter is known as an *agent-broker of record letter*. Use this letter only with the assistance of your new agent, to make sure the assignment is valid. Your former agent is notified by the insurance company, and is typically given ten days to obtain a rescinding letter from you, to revoke the assignment. Assuming you don't revoke the assignment, your new agent is empowered to act on your behalf to resolve problems, obtain information, and order coverage changes. Naturally, this action deprives your old agency of commission income on your future renewal business.

Mention Your Attorney

Insurance people would rather settle issues without attorneys getting involved.

Insurance people know from experience that bringing an attorney into a dispute may not result in you getting what you want, but it will certainly create additional work and expense to respond to the attorney's inquiries. Avoid directly threatening insurance people with the use of an attorney. Instead, refer to the need for such action as a dismal failure for all concerned.

Have Your Attorney Call Your Agency

Assuming you feel abused enough to seek legal counsel, and have spent the time to explain your dilemma, encourage your attorney to call the person at the center of the problem. Even if the attorney happens to be a friend of yours, who is not charging you the hourly rate, the communication will be clearly received — you mean business!

File a Complaint with Your State's Department of Insurance

Insurance professionals want to avoid complaints with the department of insurance, and this is particularly true in today's political environment. A complaint results in an inquiry by mail or phone, and can lead to a personal visit by an inspector and court hearings. Ultimately, the department has the power to subpoena and audit records, and to revoke licenses. While most insurance people do not usually commit acts that warrant losing their licenses, who wants to spend time explaining the events leading to the complaint? Use of the complaint applies when you feel you have been unfairly abused, and nobody is attempting to correct the situation.

In preparing your written complaint, describe your experience in detail, dating the events and correspondence that led to your situation. Any log of transactions is most valuable here. With these tasks completed, you can approach the person with whom you have had trouble. You will be delighted at how well this works at capturing undivided attention. Don't be surprised if your agent calls a meeting after all.

If the agency fails to respond, go ahead and send your complaint. Look in your telephone book under state government listings to find the number. Or, a call to a local librarian should help you obtain the name, phone number, and address of your state's insurance complaint department.

Offer to Take Your Business Elsewhere

Keep in mind, if you have been more trouble than you are worth, they may love the idea of getting rid of you.

Stating you may take your business to another agency may be fairly impotent, unless your account is a meaningful size to the agent or firm. If you compound the threat to include taking all your referred friends with you, this may result in some desired action. If you can specifically name accounts the agency has written, you will have more impact. Remember, bringing in referrals quietly empowers you and your friends to receive better than average service. Voluntary cancellation of your policies declares your dissatisfaction with the service or pricing, and is an unhappy event in any agent's life. You will usually get better results from discussing the possibility of cancellation, because you allow room for the situation to be corrected. Keep in mind, if you have been more trouble than you are worth, they may love the idea of getting rid of you.

A Quick Guide for Solving Insurance Problems

- Define the problem. Be very clear about the results you desire and why you are not getting these results. To clarify the problem, write it down.
- Find out who is responsible for taking the next step. Call people until you determine who is blocking progress.
- Call that person. Communicate your defined problem with the person. Make sure the person acknowledges responsibility for taking the next step, and he or she understands the problem. Make sure he or she knows the next step, and you both agree upon the timeframe in which to act.
- Make sure the person has all the information he or she needs to act on the problem. If you have information he or she lacks, provide it. If you know someone else has the missing information, let him or her know who has it.
- Get a commitment of the specific actions the individual will take, and when he or she will contact you next. Reasonably expect regular status reports. Write down this information.
- If the individual does not follow through on his or her commitment — such as failure to return a call or mail important correspondence — engage in the increasingly intense actions described in the previous section until satisfied.

Now that you have learned the basic techniques to motivate insurance people, apply your human relations skills to get the best purchase. Your next step is to evaluate your proposals and negotiate your price, as discussed in the next two chapters.

Notes

Chapter 8

Effective Negotiation Tactics

You Can Negotiate Your Price!

Buying business insurance presents many fertile opportunities for practicing your negotiating skills. By now, you should have some interesting quotes from a reasonable sampling of the marketplace. You are nearing your final buying decision — a choice you will probably live with for the coming year. Before you make your move, recognize that negotiating your insurance is a neverending process. You will negotiate before, during, and after your purchase for better prices, coverages, and service. This chapter will help you apply some well-known negotiating principles in the insurance marketplace.

You Have More Power than You Realize

If you have followed the suggestions in the previous chapters, you have developed astonishing strength for negotiating in the insurance industry. You are armed with a superb presentation of your account and a thorough understanding of the insurance industry. Now you must wield your power with great confidence. No insurance agent, broker, or company can control you, and you can use your power to win stunning negotiating victories. Remember, the agents who have invested time and effort working on your account will be paid only if you buy from them. So you are in an excellent position to ask for concessions.

Aim High

Set high aspirations for your purchasing efforts. Resolve to achieve price reductions of 25 to 50 percent below what you have been paying — except for rates that are set by law. Don't make the mistake of going into the buying process thinking your insurance won't improve. If you begin your purchasing efforts with high expectations, you are more likely to realize them. Remember, you will encounter resistance and discouragement from quoting agents and brokers, so you will need to continually remind yourself your efforts will be rewarded.

When agents feel you want to do business with them, but price is the real obstacle, they often become very resourceful in finding ways to save you money.

When agents feel you want to do business with them, but price is the only real obstacle, they often become very resourceful in finding ways to save you money. The agent who wants your business may call the underwriter and earnestly request a reduced premium. For instance, an agreement may be made with the underwriter in which the agent's commission is reduced by 5 percent and the underwriter matches that with a 5 percent credit — so your price is reduced by 10 percent. The quoting agent may come up with a last minute quote from another company with the satisfactory price. The larger your premium, the more likely an agent will put this kind of effort into reducing your price.

Negotiating Is Worth Your Effort

Your negotiating efforts can be worth a great deal when buying business insurance. It is not unusual to realize cost reductions from $100 to more than $1,000 per hour invested in following these methods. For example, if you spend ten hours putting together your information and interviewing agents, you have saved $1,000. With the amount of money businesses spend on insurance today and the nature of the insurance marketplace, saving $100 per hour of effort is no great feat.

Deflating Agents' Expectations

The last thing you want is for agents to consider you an easy sale. When they feel confident they have your business, prices tend to rise, and services and coverages diminish. Sometimes, it pays to deflate your agents' expectations as to whether you will buy and how much you will spend. Whenever you feel the need, use the following specific disheartening actions to create a low-pressure system around agents' expectations.

- Inform agents you have been talking with their competitors.
- Tell the agents that their proposals are out of the ballpark.
- Question the strength of the insurance company or agency, especially if you have any negative information.
- Ask agents to explain when they say they have shopped the market — specifically noting what companies from whom they have received quotes.

- Cancel an appointment. Delay communication for two or three weeks.
- Inform agents of any bad experiences you have had with their agency. For example, let them know if you got stuck in their voice mail, or left on hold, or if a call wasn't returned.
- Mention that you are the one writing the checks, and you expect excellent service.
- Let your expiration date come and go — by making temporary arrangements with your current agent. Tell the quoting agent you are still open to change, if improvements can be made.
- Ask agents to translate their commission into an estimated hourly rate. For instance, suppose your policy costs $50,000 per year and your agents' commission is 15 percent or $7,500. If your agent only works ten hours on your account, that translates into $750 per hour. The point is: make sure your agent is working hard for you.
- Let your agents know that they are not on top of your priority list by allowing incoming phone calls and interruptions during interviews with them. This will communicate to the agents that they must work for your attention and your business.
- Advise agents that you won't be able to make the decision without getting approval from somebody else.
- Tell them you feel insurance products are all about the same.
- Inform the agents that you aren't concerned about your expiration date, and that any changes will be made only when you are ready.
- Let the agents know you are perfectly satisfied with your current agent.
- Leave proposals from the agent's competitors in plain view, but out of reach, at the sales interview.
- Show the agent a more competitive proposal from a competitor.

In addition, you can keep a copy of this book on your desk during interviews. When agents see the book, they will know that you are a serious, informed insurance buyer.

Be sure not to overuse these deflating tactics, but apply them whenever you sense an agent is attempting to control you or take your power.

Many issues surround your insurance purchase. Issues can be valuable for controlling the direction and impact of your negotiations. Sometimes you can run out of ideas, so here is a collection of issues you can raise to keep the negotiations moving your way.

Realistic Concessions for which to Ask

- Ask for an extension of time in which to pay. Agents can sometimes accept smaller downpayments than what was initially quoted.
- Ask for specific audit procedures in writing. If you will be audited at year end for a final premium calculation, you can also request that the

auditors visit your office early in the policy year to make sure your recordkeeping is adequate. See the discussion in Chapter 10 for more information.

- Get promises in writing. During the sale, the agents tend to make many promises. Ask the agent to summarize the promises in a letter for you. To ensure the agents keep these promises, you may need written confirmation.
- Insist on cost-breakdowns. Agents are sometimes reluctant to disclose the pricing formulas used to develop your premium quotes, because power is shifted to the buyer. As the buyer, you can use this information to challenge assumptions, delete nonessentials, and give to other agents for better pricing. The Business Insurance Coverage Checklist requests this information, but you may have to insist agents provide it.
- Ask your agent to discuss your coverages in depth with you to help decrease your coverages to only those you really want. Identify the coverages you can live without as distinguished from those you must have to satisfy leases, mortgages, laws and live within your comfort level. Determine the cash savings that will result from deleting the nonessential coverages. Make your decision as to what to insure or not insure. Sample Letter G in the Appendix shows one way of requesting this exceptional service concession in more detail. Also refer to the risk management discussion in Chapter 2.
- Ask agents to commit in writing what services they will provide particularly in the area of help with loss control measures. See Chapter 10 for the Service Schedule Checklist to help define excellent service.
- Request your quote by your stated deadline, not your expiration date.
- Insist on completion of your coverage checklist. Sometimes agents resist completing the coverage checklist because it involves extra work. Stand your ground and demand the checklist completion.
- Ask for a risk analysis and coverage recommendations. With all the information you provide, agents should be willing to make coverage recommendations in writing.
- Split your account. Just buy part of the agency's proposal, and buy the remaining coverages from its competitor.
- Compare rebates from agency to agency. See the discussion later in this chapter on commission rebates.
- Ask for a three-year price guarantee from the agent. These guarantees have become very rare, but requesting the rates be locked in for three years will start an interesting discussion. Such a guarantee is worthless unless put in writing by an insurance company employee with the authority to do so.
- Suggest the agent takes a lower commission on the workers' compensation portion, so your dividend potential increases. Or offer to grant the workers' compensation policy in exchange for discounted premiums on other policies or extra services.
- Expect the agency to buy your goods or services. Let the agency know you expect their business.

In today's business world, it is not uncommon to employ tactics such as expecting your agency to introduce you to a valuable contact you want to meet. In many cases, you can realistically expect your agent to take you to lunches and dinners and provide other forms of entertainment. Because you are paying a large sum to the agency, you should expect special treatment.

Premium Payment Alternatives

Have you considered the terms of your premium payment? You will normally have several options. Before you decide, check with your accountant to determine the tax consequences of your various choices. Frequently, business owners enter into payments on an insurance program only to find out from a tax standpoint it might have been better to pay for the premium all at once, or at least to get the premium paid before the end of the fiscal year.

If you are using premium financing, have your accountant advise you if you can take the entire premium as a deduction this year, though your payments may continue into the following tax year.

If it is not advisable or feasible to pay the entire premium in a lump sum, ask the agent or broker to arrange a monthly or quarterly payment plan with no interest charges and only nominal handling charges. If you followed the checklists and comparison forms from the previous chapters, you have already discussed this issue. Agents may not volunteer these plans as options because they can slow payment of commissions, but they will usually use them when asked. The small handling charges should range anywhere from $3 to $15 per payment. The installments may be billed by the agency, or directly by the insurance company. The insurance company direct billing method tends to be less lenient, and quicker to issue cancellations, if the premiums are late. Your average independent agency can offer more flexibility in the timing of its payments, so an agency billing installment program may be the best from the buyer's point of view.

If no installment plans are available from the insurance company, your agent should be able to arrange premium financing for you. Normally, a company specializing in premium financing is available to finance the premium for most insurance companies. The quoting agency will typically require a down payment of 10 to 25 percent depending on the size of your account and the quality of your insurance company.

The quoting agency will typically require a down payment of 10 to 25 percent depending on the size of your account and the quality of your insurance company.

Compare the rate of interest charged by the premium finance company to make sure you cannot do better by borrowing the money from your banker, or other cash resources, such as a life insurance policy. Usually, for smaller premiums, the finance company's interest rates seem relatively high, while on larger premiums, they reduce to the point of being very competitive with ordinary financial institutions. Attending to the issue of installment terms helps you control your cash flow to your best advantage. Most insurance agencies prefer to keep their cash available for operating capital by using low-cost installment programs when available.

Commission Rebates

Asking for a rebate is playing hardball. A rebate involves agents or brokers giving you a cash refund from the commission they receive on the sale. For many years, this has been illegal. In recent years, however, California and Florida have changed the laws to legalize this practice. Be sure to have alternatives ready as you could make the agent or broker angry by suggesting this tactic. Long-time agents and brokers still feel this practice is taboo. If the rebate idea is met with complete indignation, consider asking other agents. If another agent already offered a rebate to you, let it be known. Obviously, the rebate tactic's effectiveness is directly proportionate to the size of your account.

Agency Commissions

The larger the commission, the better your chances the agent or broker will share some of the money with you to get your business.

The larger the commission, the better your chances the agent or broker will share some of the money with you to get your business. As insurance companies try to cut costs, commissions paid to independent insurance agencies continue to fall. Current commission levels top out at 20 percent —15 percent is the average. Less desirable lines of insurance — such as commercial auto — may pay 10 percent or less. Workers' compensation commission is usually 5 to 10 percent.

The commission figures noted above are what the agency receives. But the agency has significant operating expenses, which means the agent or broker you are dealing with may get less than half of the full agency commission. Some agents are on salary with a year-end bonus arrangement, so they would have to win their agency's cooperation in offering you any cash refund from the big commission check. If you are bold enough to ask for a rebate, you may get a pleasant surprise.

Broker's or Agent's Fees

Brokers are permitted to charge a fee when they place business with insurance companies for which they are not appointed as an agent. No clear guidelines exist for brokers' fees; however, the general rule in practice seems to be whatever the market will bear.

A broker's fee is typically charged at the inception of the policy if:

- The markets available are limited.
- The previous agency was much higher in premium.
- The broker believes the insured will pay more than the premium quote received from the company.
- The work involved was disproportionately large as compared to the small premium involved.

Sometimes at renewal date, when the premium is lower than last year, your broker may feel there is room to negotiate. Your broker may describe how he or she thoroughly searched the marketplace and finally obtained an exceptional value. You may hear your broker had to go outside his or her own firm to an *excess/surplus lines broker,* and "agency policy" mandates a broker's fee be charged. Because the sum of the premium charges and the broker's fee is still lower than last year, you are expected to go along with the additional fee.

In some cases, you are charged a broker's fee, and not told about the fee. Most states' laws dictate that brokers' fees be fully disclosed before a client billing. Unfortunately, not all brokers are informed or diligent in following the law.

Informed clients almost never pay brokers' fees, and if they do, they usually pay less than originally requested. To protect yourself from paying a broker's fee, consider these three steps.

Informed clients almost never pay brokers' fees, and if they do, they usually pay less than originally requested.

Step 1 – Listen Carefully to Everything Your Brokers Say

Let them make their entire presentation. Allow them to assume you will accept their program, and ask from which insurance company they are quoting. Some veteran brokers will respond, "Our policy is not to disclose the carrier; but, we can assure you the carrier has a Best rating of A+XV, so you can be confident the company will meet your requirements in the way of service and financial strength." With this type of response, they skillfully avoid opening themselves up to competition on the brokers' fees, and they make it very clear their own interests are very high on their priority list. Other brokers will disclose which company they are quoting. Thank them for their efforts, and allow them to leave their coverage proposal and premium quotation for review and consideration.

Step 2 – Contact the Brokers' Competitors and Complain about the Concept of a Broker's Fee

Tell them you have a quote from a competitor, who has added a fee. Disclose the name of the company if you were able to get it, and ask if they would be able to do the same transaction without the fee. You are now using the free enterprise system as it was designed to function. At this point, the competitor is likely to respond positively and tell you they can handle the job. Chances are, any broker can get to the same market, and with the use of a agent-broker letter of record — an authorization form that assigns an individual the right to act as your broker — you avoid the fee with a different brokerage. With minimal effort, the competitor can assemble, and profitably write your business without the fee. They will need to obtain your signature on a broker of record assignment letter, which they provide.

Step 3 – Call the Initial Quoting Agency if You Don't Get a Better Deal

Chances are good you will win your policy without the broker's fee. Only in an exceptional situation, where you want to reward the broker for outstanding effort, would you voluntarily pay such a fee.

Tell the agent you really like the agency's professionalism, but you cannot accept the broker's fee. Tell the agent you will buy the policy, if the agency will remove the broker's fee; otherwise, you will be forced to take another deal. In the rare case where your agent calls your bluff, offer your thanks for their effort, and compliment their agency on its professionalism. Tell your agent that you would like to do business with the agency, but they must understand the difficult position you are in.

If they do not call back within the week and reverse their position, you can always call back and buy the policy. You can save face by blaming the other agency for failing to honor the quote they had given you — noting that the new quoted premium was more expensive than what they had quoted. Shake hands and the entire ordeal will be forgotten, because you were always careful to treat the broker with respect throughout the negotiations.

Chances are good you will win your policy without the broker's fee. Only in an exceptional situation, where you want to reward the broker for outstanding effort, would you voluntarily pay such a fee.

Chapter 9

The Buying Decision

Know Your Motivation for the Purchase

Have you asked yourself why you are buying business insurance? The better you understand your purpose for buying insurance, the easier the decision-making process is when you receive proposals.

People buy insurance for different reasons. You may buy insurance because you are required to by an outsider's request. You may need to satisfy the requirements of a law, a landlord, a bank, or a customer. You may be purchasing insurance only to obtain vehicle registrations and meet state insurance requirements. If this describes you, your dominant motive is to provide the required evidence of insurance, so you can effectively operate your business. You may be like many buyers — you want to keep insurance costs low. So you are willing to stay exposed to many of the risks that can be insured so you can conserve cash flow. If the evidence of insurance was not required, you would not purchase coverage.

Like many competent businesspeople, you may only purchase the required coverages, because you are already exposed to considerable business risks, and are feeling significant money pressures. People operating at this end of the buying spectrum see their situation as temporary, and expect to purchase more meaningful insurance later, when financial circumstances permit. Their position may not be enviable, but it can make perfect sense depending on one's position.

Perhaps you find yourself at the other end of the insurance buying spectrum. You are very serious about being fully protected against anything that can possibly happen. Like others, your worst fear may be the loss of what you have accumulated. You have fought hard to build your business, and you have no intention of losing any of it to bad luck. If this is the case, you will be looking for maximum protection against liability losses, and every other contingency that may surface. You are willing to pay the price, but you find complete insulation against risk is impossible. For all practical purposes, many hazards are simply uninsurable — such as war, nuclear damage, normal depreciation, termites, and dryrot.

Perhaps you are in between the two extreme motives discussed above. You need the evidence of insurance, which is what initially sent you to the marketplace. But while purchasing insurance, you are interested in arranging the most sensible coverage you can afford. You may have decided there are certain financial losses you could never afford to sustain, and wish to transfer those risks to a solid insurance company. One day you may hope to become a buyer who purchases full protection, but recognized that for now, some risks will have to remain uninsured because of a lack of cash flow.

Use Caution When Focusing on the Cheapest Price

Should you decide to purchase the minimum coverage at the cheapest price, keep in mind that buying for price is risky. If you have decided you only want the cheapest price no matter what the circumstances, inferior products are available. For example, by focusing on price only, you may purchase coverage from a nonadmitted insurance company. Should the company become insolvent, you will discover your state's guarantee fund will not protect you. Your claims will go unpaid, your insurance will be null and void, and you will find yourself purchasing a replacement policy from a second insurance company. Of course, you will see no return of the premium paid for the worthless insurance. If you financed the premiums through a premium finance company, you may find the finance company has the contractual right to collect the payments from you for the worthless insurance, because they paid the premium on your behalf. You may find what looked like a good deal turned out to be your worst option.

By doing a little extra preliminary buying work, you may find you can meet your objectives, and still decrease your exposure to risks.

Be aware when getting the cheapest premium from an insurance company — the company may already be experiencing financial difficulty. No matter how quickly you need insurance coverage in force, invest the time to make sure you know exactly what you are doing. By doing a little extra preliminary buying work, you may find you can meet your objectives and still decrease your exposure to risks. You may find you can get the same coverage, at the same price, from a stronger company or a more attentive agent.

The buyer looking for the cheapest deal should investigate the marketplace as thoroughly as the buyer looking for quality.

The buyer looking for the cheapest deal should investigate the marketplace as thoroughly as the buyer looking for quality. By presenting your insurance specifications to a wider number of insurance providers, you increase the chances you will purchase exactly what you want. After a careful search, you should find an agent willing and able to sell you a stripped down policy with a solid company, providing only the coverages you must have at the resulting price you desire. Be sure you are fully informed of the inevitable coverage compromises you make with such a purchase.

Tips for Paying for High Quality

Perhaps you have decided to pay whatever it costs for the highest quality. With the completed Business Insurance and Workers' Compensation Coverage Checklists and the Insurance Agency Information Profiles, you are well equipped to inspect for quality. Carefully verify referrals. You have made sure your submissions were accurately presented to the insurance companies by presenting your completed Underwriting Information Questionnaire.

Evaluate Your Quotes

As you close in on making your buying decision, make sure you have done your homework: your underwriting information should be complete and accurate. With the help of agents, you should have made an intelligent selection of coverages on the Business Insurance and Workers' Compensation Coverage Checklists from chapters 5 and 6. You should have proposals that provide comparable coverages at various prices. You are now in a position to make an informed decision.

To help make sure you don't overlook an important consideration, evaluate the proposals on a comparison worksheet. The quote comparison worksheets on the following pages help you look at all aspects of your purchasing decision, and hopefully help you make the wisest decision to satisfy your purposes. If you don't have enough information about one of the key issues for a quote you are considering, investigate that issue before spending your money.

If your business has employees, you will also want to read Chapter 6 and complete the Workers' Compensation Quote Comparison Worksheet, which is located on the following pages.

After you use the comparison worksheets, you should begin to favor a particular proposal more than the others. Unfortunately, you may favor a particular agency that has a proposal of equal quality at a higher price. Your next step is to target your favored agency and apply some negotiation tactics to lower its pricing. Chapter 8 will help you accomplish this task.

Notes

Quote Comparison Worksheets

Business Insurance Quote Comparison Worksheet

Workers' Compensation Quote Comparison Worksheet

Business Insurance Quote Comparison Worksheet Instructions

Important: The worksheet on the following page is a master copy. Make photocopies and enter information on your copies.

For each quoting agency, complete this form and compare your subjective ratings. To obtain the best coverage for your money, consider the four main variables and rate each by circling a number, one through ten — ten being the highest rating. Once you have rated each area, total the numbers and use this total as a guideline when making your purchasing decision.

1. Competency of agent — Consider referrals, experience with your type of business, attitude, credentials, and professional designations.
2. Strength of insurance company — Consider its financial rating in Best's, Moody's, and Standard and Poor. Consider the location of its servicing office. (Refer to Chapter 3.)
3. Adequacy of coverages — Ask yourself, "How suitable are the coverages presented?" and "Do the coverages meet my established specifications?"
4. Capacity of agency to serve your business' needs — consider location, staff size, insurance companies, attitudes of the staff, and referrals. (Refer to your completed Agency Profile.)

For agencies with similar or equal ratings, consider each firm's strengths and weaknesses by reviewing the Insurance Agency Profiles from Chapter 3. After reviewing the completed profiles about your quoting agencies, you should be prepared to make your buying decision.

Business Insurance Quote Comparison Worksheet

Date: ____________________

Name of agency: ____

Quoted price: $____________________

	Poor			Average				Excellent		
1. Competency of agent	1	2	3	4	5	6	7	8	9	10
2. Strength of insurance company	1	2	3	4	5	6	7	8	9	10
3. Adequacy of coverages	1	2	3	4	5	6	7	8	9	10
4. Capacity of agency to serve our business' needs	1	2	3	4	5	6	7	8	9	10

Total rating: (sum of circled numbers from 1–4 above) ____________________

Agency's greatest strengths: ____

Agency's greatest weaknesses: ____

Workers' Compensation Quote Comparison Worksheet Instructions

Important: The worksheet on the following page is a master copy. Make photocopies and enter information on your copies.

Compare agency proposals on the following form to make an informed buying decision. On the following page, enter the values from your completed Workers' Compensation Coverage Checklist from Chapter 6. When comparing your proposals, look at three main areas: dividends, cash flow, and service. Insurance agents and brokers should provide you with the information you need for the quote comparison worksheet.

1. Dividend considerations:
   a. The retention percentage represents the percentage of your premium the insurance company will keep even if you have no losses.
   b. The IBNR percentage is a result of multiplying a percentage by your premium to allow for possible claims that have occurred but have not yet been reported.
   c. Generally, the policy with the lowest total of retention percentage plus IBNR percentage, and the quickest dividend payment, is the superior value from a short-term viewpoint. The more assistance you need to lower the modification or to keep it low, the more significant is insurance company service in the buying decision. Earning a low modification factor can be very profitable, but there is a point of diminishing returns as modifications rarely get below 60 percent.
   d. The number of dividend payouts helps you understand whether the whole dividend is being released at once, or whether two or three partial payouts will be made. See the section on the timing of dividend check payouts in Chapter 6.
   e. Enter the expected payout dates in terms of number of months after your policy expiration. To do this, take your policy expiration date, then add the stated number of months to arrive at the dividend payout date. This step helps avoid confusion about the timing of dividend checks.
   f. Be sure to indicate the length of the dividend plan, to avoid comparing plans with different length terms. Read the section called comparing one-, two-, and three-year plans in Chapter 6.
2. Cash flow:
   a. Deposit amount is the amount you will have to pay to get the policy issued.
   b. After paying the deposit, you must report actual payroll and pay the premiums based on the reports. Be sure to find out how frequently the reports are due, because this will inform you how often you will make payments.
3. Service:
   a. Ask for an indication of case load per claims person. You might infer that the higher the number, the less time the agency will devote toward getting claims closed out as quickly and inexpensively as possible. While this is somewhat arbitrary, this question helps quantify the claims service you might expect.
   b. Asking how many loss control representatives are located at a local office can provide you with interesting insight. Your purpose in asking is to know how much actual loss control service and material you can expect to receive.
   c. Be sure to check the Best's rating so you have some idea about the financial status of the company. Refer to Chapter 3.
   d. Be sure the Insurance Agency Profiles are complete before you make your buying decision. Ideally, you will have profile for five quoting agencies.

Workers' Compensation Quote Comparison Worksheet

Name of insurance company: ______________________________

Address: ____

1. Dividend considerations

a. Retention percentage: ________________

b. IBNR percentage: ________________

c. Total: ________________

d. Number of dividend payouts: ________________

e. Dividend payout dates: ________________

____

____

f. (Check one) ☐ One-year plan ☐ Two-year plan ☐ Three-year plan

2. Cash flow

a. Deposit amount: ________________

b. Frequency of audit reports: ☐ Monthly ☐ Quarterly ☐ Annually

3. Service

a. Case load per claims person: ________________

b. Number of loss control representatives: ________________

c. Best's rating: ________________

d. Results of Insurance Agency Profile comparisons: ______________________________

Notes

After the Purchase

Section III

Chapter 10

How to Receive Quality Service

You Are Entitled to Quality Service

At this point, you have boldly approached the insurance marketplace. After careful thought and comparison, you have made your insurance purchase. How does it feel to be an informed buyer?

Now that you have made the best selection, with all the pertinent information about your business organized and effectively covered for losses, you must continue to follow up to ensure top quality service. You must learn to effectively deal with your insurance people after the purchase.

Services an Agency-Brokerage Can Provide

Most business insurance buyers don't understand the meaning of quality insurance service. If you were to ask a sampling of business insurance buyers, many would expect their policy within 60 days after its inception and to make changes during normal business hours, Monday through Friday. Unfortunately, this level of service is the only degree of service most buyers have come to expect. Fortunately, the informed buyer can receive much more.

Obviously, not all insured people will get the same level or number of service.

Obviously, not all insured people will get the same level or number of service for two reasons. First, business operations vary so widely in complexity that subsequent insurance service needs vary correspondingly. Second, both companies and agencies are governed by the premium size of the buyers' policies, since only a limited number of dollars are figured into the premium and commission to provide top quality service.

However, even the smallest accounts should expect certain services from their agency.

Naturally, the level and consistency of service is a major consideration in evaluating your relationship with insurance providers.

This chapter discusses the various services available from the insurance industry. The Service Schedule Checklist, located at the end of this chapter, will help you compare future service possibilities with what you currently receive. You can use the checklist as a guide to identify the services you consider most important, and make sure your insurance agency is doing its job in serving you. With your service priorities clearly identified, you will be prepared to present your expectations to insurance agencies, and determine which agencies meet your needs. Further, the checklist can help you establish a service standard to evaluate the level of service you receive in the coming years. Naturally, the level and consistency of service is a major consideration in evaluating your relationship with insurance providers.

Service Levels: Mandatory Versus Desirable

While you deserve to receive every service possible, you must realize your account size will have a bearing on the types of services you can expect. Many of the services are marked as *mandatory* because they are essential for all businesses purchasing insurance. Other services are marked *desirable* because they may not be provided by all agencies for all accounts, or may not be needed by all accounts. As a result, there is a list of some essential minimums, and the complete Service Schedule Checklist contains additional services which may be considered optional by some buyers. The larger your premiums, the more likely all applicable services will be labeled mandatory. As your premium increases, so does your ability to get more of the desirable services provided as though they were mandatory too.

Design Your Service Schedule Checklist

The Service Schedule Checklist is found at the end of this chapter and may be duplicated to serve your business' insurance purchasing purposes only. Present the blank checklist to prospective agents and ask them to indicate what you can expect from their agency. You can customize your Service Schedule Checklist as you add special services you desire into a clear statement of your service objectives. You may begin using the checklist anytime, whether you are obtaining quotes as part of your renewal process or in the middle of your policy year. Service counts — year round.

The Policy Year and Service

Service on most insurance policies is clustered around the all-important *inception date* — the date coverage begins for your new policy year and, coincidentally, ends for your old policy. Keep in mind, service prior to inception is the same as service just before expiration. The way you, your agent, and your insurance company view the service issue varies greatly. If you have recently changed insurance companies, your new company is looking at an opportunity to get your annual premium paid in full. The new company will seek ways to impress you with top quality service in hopes of generating cash flow in its business. The new company wants to perform well by getting the policy issued and enjoy twelve months of claims-free harmony. The losing company wants to wrap up any unsettled claims, if possible. On the other hand, the losing company wants to finish its final audit, and collect additional monies from you. Normally, you are interested in the inception date because it means your agency must prepare to pay the renewal premiums and wait for its new policies.

The remainder of the policy year can seem uneventful compared to the hustle of renewal time. However, some of the most critical cost containment, loss reduction, and prevention activities will occur during the remainder of the year. Take a look at your policy year relative to the different phases that should occur as the year progresses.

Policy Phase I – Proposal Acceptance to Policy Inception Date

The initial phase of the service cycle begins from the actual quote presentation through the policy inception date — the day coverage begins. All services in this first phase are considered mandatory for all businesses, regardless of the size of the premium. Make sure you get written evidence of insurance when you order coverage. For instance:

- All binders must be delivered by the policy inception date — If you don't have completed written binders, you are exposed to the many unnecessary risks that result from poor business practices. Insist on receiving your binders any time between the time you accept the proposal to the actual inception date. Receiving a binder after the inception date is considered inferior, sloppy service, and should be avoided whenever possible. Frequently, some amount of payment is expected when binders are delivered. Work this out in advance with your insurance professional.
- Certificates of insurance and evidence of insurance forms are mailed to specified recipients — Insist that certificates of insurance and evidence of insurance forms are sent at the same time the binders are prepared. These certificates show all interested people you are competently managing your insurance and meeting your commitments to carry coverage. Failure to send the certificates causes unnecessary follow-up calls and letters. Failure to send the certificates can also result in you being charged for insurance by lenders or others. Request confirmation copies to be sent to you as well.

Failure to send the certificates causes unnecessary follow-up calls and letters.

- Verify cash flow projection for the coming year — To bind coverage, the cash flow projection should be established before the final approval is given. When making your deposit payment, confirm that the premium will be as quoted, with no surprise fees. Verify that the payment plans are as originally agreed. This makes sure your purchasing decision is an informed one that details premium financing or installment charges.

- Invoices delivered, with deposit premium specified — Request an invoice before making a premium payment. The invoice will clearly document what you are paying for. The invoice also provides a policy number or binder number, as well as an invoice number, and the coverage period involved. Sound business practice dictates that you insist on receiving invoices when making premium payments. You should get reasonable advance notice for all payments due, and a realistic projection of future payments.

You have a right to expect telephone access to a competent, friendly, and cooperative person with whom you can resolve problems.

- Identify your customer service person to contact at the agency — You need to know who to contact for coverage change requests and routine administrative matters. This person should be someone who is in the office during business hours to answer your questions and respond to your requests. You have a right to expect telephone access to a competent, friendly, and cooperative person with whom you can resolve problems. You should also be able to reach the service person or a backup individual on the same day you call. Not being able to contact a service person is unacceptable because you would not be able to order needed coverage on short notice.
- Identify your claims contact at the agency or company, or both — Your agent should explain the procedure for reporting claims. This procedure needs to be clarified before the policy inception date. Many companies are using toll-free numbers that are available 24-hours a day, 365 days a year. This is particularly true of the exclusive and direct writers.
- Verify receipt of vehicle insurance identification cards — Many states mandate you keep specific evidence of your vehicle insurance in your vehicles. Vehicle insurance I.D. cards should be made available immediately, and be placed safely in your vehicles.
- File all Public Utility Commission filings and other legally required filings — Timely filings must be made to all government bodies, as required by the various state and federal laws. Copies of these filings should be sent to you. You can produce these copies as evidence of your compliance as needed.

Policy Phase II – The First 60 Days after Policy Inception

This phase normally concludes the agent's heavy involvement in the service of your policy for the remainder of year. By now, you should have started to develop a rapport with your customer service representative.

Mark your calendar and make sure you receive your insurance policy within a reasonable time period.

- Policy delivery — Mark your calendar and make sure you receive your insurance policy within a reasonable time period. You are always advised to read the policy completely, although most people never try. At the very least, examine the *declarations pages* — the cover pages to your policies that itemize the various coverages — to make sure they comply with your expectations. If necessary, ask your agent to explain the policy.

- Verify the policy coverages and pricing are as quoted — Your agent owes it to you to deliver what was promised; specific coverages at specific prices. Any discrepancies or changes should be clearly identified. Sometimes, circumstances beyond their control cause changes to appear. While they may not be able to correct the changes, they owe it to you to clearly identify exactly how the policy or rates deviate from what you purchased.
- Receive copies of all applications sent to insurance companies representing your account — Often, insurance buyers never see the applications that were sent in for them. The applications include your representations to the company, and you should be allowed to inspect the copies for accuracy. In addition, a copy in your shopping file can be useful in keeping your Underwriting Information Questionnaire current. See Sample Letter I in the Appendix.
- Schedule the date for loss control inspections, if applicable — This inspection will follow up the precoverage inspection, assuming you had one. The loss control inspection should verify that any insurance company recommendations have been implemented into your normal operations. If there was no inspection prior to policy inception, this inspection may take its place.
- Audit preparation and introduction to audit procedures — Audit preparation includes introduction to specific audit procedures, including specific documentation you are expected to produce to segregate classifications in payroll and receipts. Too often, the audit preparation issue is ignored. To avoid problems, clarify exactly how the premium will be computed at the end of the policy year. See the discussion on audits on the following pages.

Policy Phase III – Year-Round Policy Service

Some services are ongoing and should be continued throughout the year. Beyond normal customer service, you can expect written confirmation of all coverage changes, loss control assistance, and scheduled claims follow up.

- Written confirmation of all coverage change requests — Many coverage change orders are set over the phone. For your protection, get written confirmation of the changes as they are requested. Ideally, get price quotes for the changes you request. The best you can usually hope for is an estimated guess, due to the cumbersome rating process.

Many coverage change orders are set over the phone. For your protection, get written confirmation of the changes as they are requested.

- Loss control assistance with safety programs — When your account size merits loss control assistance, you are usually promised the assistance. Unfortunately, many policy years slip by where the loss control service never actually materializes. If you are entitled to loss control services, insist they be delivered, because they can be very valuable to you. Loss control assistance can include the following:

- Drivers training;
- Material handling training;
- Work station setup and design assistance;
- General training materials and safety meeting ideas;
- Hazardous materials handling;
- Hazard identification and assessment training;
- Preemployment checklist and physical assessment;
- Safety program review;
- Sound level and air quality tests; and
- Physical location inspections.

Refer to the end of this chapter for further discussion of loss control assistance.

- Monthly, quarterly, or semiannual claims follow up — Follow up should include taking all necessary steps to get you quickly indemnified for insured losses you incur, and professional attention to all liability situations. You are also entitled to loss runs. Refer to handling claims effectively in Chapter 12.
- Normal customer service and problem solving, as needed — You should expect good customer service and problem solving if problems arise.

Policy Phase IV – 120 Days Before Expiration

During the fourth phase of the policy cycle, preparations are made for the coming policy year. Mark your calendar with the following items to be completed by predetermined dates. The items in this fourth phase are not found on the Service Schedule Checklist, because they are inappropriate to give to agents.

- Selection of agents or brokers to quote the renewal — If you are going to shop your account this year, this is the time to get serious about inviting agents to quote your renewal. Refer to Chapter 3 for more information on shopping the marketplace.
- Update your Underwriting Information Questionnaire — Now is the time to prepare or update your previous year's information. See Chapter 4 for instructions.

As a part of receiving quality service, you are entitled to loss runs.

- Request copies of updated loss runs for the past three policy years — These loss runs will show current valuations of your losses for all policies expiring in the next 120 days. Use Sample Letter C in the Appendix to request your loss runs.

Policy Phase V – 90 Days Before Expiration

During the fifth phase, you will want to focus on one important area — renewal of coverage specifications.

Review your coverages with your current agent to update your coverage specifications. Be especially alert for changes needed due to modifications you have made in your operation since your last coverage analysis and evaluation. Be sure to carefully examine all property values, liability limits, and deductibles. Also, screen for coverages no longer necessary. Ask your current agent and other quoting agents for any additional coverages they feel are necessary, and examine those ideas too.

By now you should have received three to five years of updated loss runs for all your policies from your past agencies. It is now time to provide renewal information to quoting agents.

Policy Phase VI – 30 Days Before Expiration

Now it is time to spend your money. The thirty days before your expiration is crucial to making the right buying decision. Ideally, you will have several quotes from which to choose and you should wrap up any open claims reviews.

- Receive renewal quotes and competitive quotes for review — Encourage agents to submit the quotes early. Even though the winning quote may be late, start now to give yourself as much time as possible to compare proposals. Getting bids from companies this early is difficult — because agents know the sooner you get quotes, the longer you have to work on negotiating the price. Inform each quoting agent of your quote deadline. See Sample Letter T in the Appendix.
- Review premium financing terms and options — You will be expected to make a deposit for the new or renewal policy. At this point of the year, you want to be informed about this important budget item. Check now to see what options you have.
- Complete the Business Insurance and Workers' Compensation Coverage Checklists — The quotes should arrive with the completed coverage checklists for comparisons. If you have an attractive quote without the checklist completed, ask the agent to complete it, so you don't make an uninformed decision. You may wish to use Sample Letter A in the Appendix to explain your request.
- Final claims review of open claims — Aggressively pursue the final resolution of any open claims. Getting claims closed can save you money, because they tend to close lower than the estimated reserves. While claims are open, underwriters take the reserves at face value. To keep this process moving, see Sample Letter P for workers' compensation claims, and Sample Letter S for all other types of open claims. Both sample letters are in the Appendix.

Aggressively pursue the final resolution of any open claims.

Policy Phase VII – The Policy Expiration Date Arrives

Renew your coverage. Your previous policy has expired. Make sure you have new coverage binders, and begin the service schedule again for the new year.

- Prepare for the final audit of your policies — Since this is the expiration of your old policy and the beginning of your new policy, you will have two sets of insurance policies. Focus on the audit on your old policy. You will receive either a request in the mail for year-end figures or a visit from an insurance company representative to audit your books and records. If you have used the strategies in this book, you have already done most of the work by setting up your records to prepare for audits. If not, immediately contact your agent and discuss the segregation of payroll and contracts necessary to give the correct figures to your auditor.

Prepare for Your Final Audit

A common mistake made by insurance buyers is failure to understand how the commercial general liability premium is calculated. You need to know whether the calculation is based on payroll, receipts, square footage, units, or some other measure.

To better anticipate your business' costs, insist on clarification regarding potential audits, and on what your premium will be based upon.

Most general liability policies are audited once a year. Insurance buyers are frequently surprised shortly after the end of the policy year by an additional audit billing coming due. How can you run a business without anticipating and accruing costs? How can you choose the most effective insurance program without understanding the rating basis? You must insist on clarification regarding potential audits and how your premium will be calculated. This will also assist you in instructing bookkeepers and accountants on how they can assist you with the preparation of the data necessary for an insurance auditor. This can save you time and energy for use elsewhere in your business' operation.

If you are unclear as to how an audit may affect you with your current policies, take steps to clarify your position immediately.

If you are unclear as to how an audit may affect you with your current policies, take steps to clarify your position immediately. First, ask your agency if your policy is subject to audit. If it is subject to audit, ask your agent to explain exactly what the premium will be based on. Your agent should be able to show you the policy page that spells out the policy audit procedures. Inspect the values that were used as the basis for the estimated premium. You may prefer to send a letter like Sample Letter U, located in the Appendix, to obtain clarification from your current agency.

Includable Payroll for General Liability Policy Premium

If your policy charges a significant premium based on payroll, you must be very clear about what payroll will be included in your audit calculations. If there are several general liability classifications in your policy, you must be able to prove what specific payroll belongs in the lower-cost categories. Now is the time to find out exactly what the auditor will want.

Omit any payroll that is exempt from charges for general liability. Company practices vary, so establish an agreement with the company's audit department during the final quoting stages to avoid serious problems. Generally, companies agree not to charge liability premiums for the following types of payroll:

- Tips received by employees;
- Payments to group health plans, pensions, and possibly Section 125 Cafeteria plans;
- Special rewards for invention or discovery;
- Severance payments;
- Administrative employees;
- Salespeople, collectors, or messengers;
- Drivers — employees who work principally in or with vehicles;
- Draftspersons; and
- Overtime excess payroll.

When payroll is the basis of rating for a general liability policy, the owners, partners, and executive officers are usually assigned a fixed value of payroll to be used as their minimum and maximum includable amounts, rather than the real amount of compensation they receive. This is common throughout the industry. This assigned payroll may be eligible for exclusion, when the executive works in administrative operations or as a salesperson. If you feel this exclusion may apply to you, get clarification from the audit department of your insurance company by using Sample Letter V located in the Appendix.

General Liability Premiums Based on Subcontractor Costs

To be safe, always get certificates of insurance from subcontractors.

Some general liability policies charge a rate based on the amounts paid to subcontractors. If this amount is significant in your situation, be clear about what is included. The total costs to subcontractors can include all payments made to them, but can also include the costs of materials and equipment you provide for them to do their jobs. Costs also can include fees, bonuses, and commissions. Payments made to uninsured subcontractors will generally be treated as regular payroll, which can be expensive. Payments made to insured subcontractors are usually charged at a much lower rate. Ask the audit department for written clarification, if there is any confusion over these issues. To be safe, always get certificates of insurance from subcontractors, which proves they have insurance. If you question a subcontractor's validity, ask your agency staff to help verify it for you.

General Liability Premiums Based on Sales

Some general liability policy premiums are based on sales. If your policy is based on sales, clarify what sales will be included for your premium calculation. Ask your agency to write out exactly what is to be included. The following revenues may be exempt:

- Sales and excise taxes
- Returns and allowances
- Finance charge income
- Freight charges
- Collected royalty income

Other Premiums Subject to Audit

Some commercial automobile and all reporting forms on business personal property are subject to audit. If you obtained more vehicles during the policy period, that were automatically covered, you may owe additional premium. If you sold any vehicles, whereby reducing the insurance company's exposure to loss, you may have a refund coming. See discussion in Chapter 5 regarding business auto coverage symbols. Review the various numbers for coverage on automobile insurance to see which vehicles are covered, and determine if you may have an additional charge for newly acquired vehicles. If you have been reporting low figures or reporting late on the business personal property, you may jeopardize your coverage and have a large audit too.

Workers' compensation is always subject to audit.

Workers' compensation is always subject to audit and is based on the amount of remuneration you give to your employees on a yearly basis. See the discussion on workers' compensation in Chapter 6 for important information on this subject. Make sure all payroll and other remuneration is properly recorded in the proper classifications.

Loss Control Assistance with Safety Programs

Embracing the loss control process can enhance your image as a competent and progressive manager, and make your business more attractive to insurance company underwriters. Demonstrating a progressive attitude toward loss control can save you a fortune in some situations.

The smaller and less hazardous your operation, the lower the chance you will see loss control personnel.

The trend today is to only inspect the larger and more hazardous risks in an attempt to reduce insurance company costs. The smaller and less hazardous your operation, the lower the chance you will see loss control personnel. Your agent may be asked to inspect your business by completing supplemental applications or renewal questionnaires about any changes to your business.

If you had a prequote loss control inspection, you have already met your loss control representative. The second time you may see a loss control representative is during the policy period for a routine visit to recheck your operation. This is more likely when the first visit turned up several important loss control recommendations for improvement, and they are looking for responsiveness on your part.

The lack of a loss control visit is not always a fortuitous occurrence. Some insurance companies hire very talented loss control personnel — some are industrial hygienists or engineers by degree and certification. Other companies have loss control personnel and provide in-house training. No matter how the loss control personnel are trained, the quality and quantity vary substantially.

Most insurance companies can supply a wide variety of films, videos, slides, books, tapes, handouts, and articles on safety. Some of the better equipped companies will have all sorts of electronic gadgets to bring to your site to measure sound, heat, dust, contamination of various types, and to identify hazards in the workplace. Some insurance companies even have approved laboratories to do material or process analysis. They are qualified and equipped to assist you in developing plans to reduce your losses, personnel injuries, and subsequent down time. All of this can translate into money in your pocket.

Loss Reduction through Disaster Plans

Now, what if the worst does happen? Through a process called loss reduction, you may profit greatly from a written plan to deal with the worst case scenario. Suppose tomorrow at 3:00 A.M. you get a phone call that your business is now a pile of smoldering ashes. What do you do? Who do you call? What will the staff do when they come in?

The odds of a major loss occurring may be remote, so the need for the loss reduction plan may sound silly — until you need it. Should the worst occur, disaster preparation could make the difference between swiftly restoring your business or ending your enterprise forever. Ask the people of San Francisco, California if the years of practice drills for earthquakes paid off in October of 1989. Prior planning is always preferable to flying by the seat of your pants, particularly in a catastrophe where there may be a great deal of competition for emergency help.

Should the worst occur, disaster preparation could made the difference between swiftly restoring your business or ending your enterprise forever.

Here are a few simple things you can do to be ready:

- Analyze your needs for a replacement facility, perhaps talking with an area realtor every so often to be aware of possible alternatives.
- Determine your needs for floor space, utilities, access control, phones, and electricity to support your requirements.
- Decide how you will get the desks, computers, and other business equipment you will need.
- Make a vendor list for tools and machines to restart the business.

- Identify key employees and their alternative functions should a catastrophe occur.
- Calculate the financing you can anticipate being available for use.
- Check your state and local civil defense office for more help specific to your area.

Ask your insurance company loss control person and your agent to review your plan. Insurance companies prefer to insure a business with foresight. With a disaster plan in place, you will have a head start on surviving a catastrophe, no matter what occurs. Obviously, this has not been an all-inclusive discussion, but hopefully, the disaster planning idea will get you started. Incorporate the plan highlights into your personnel manual, so all your staff can be aware of the plan.

You now have a good idea of what services are available to you and what constitutes quality service. Continue to utilize your Service Schedule Checklist throughout your policy. In addition, now that you know what to expect both before and after your purchase, you can implement strategies to avoid costly pitfalls as discussed in Chapter 11.

Service Schedule Checklist

Service Schedule Checklist

Our agency agrees to provide the services indicated below.

Proposal Acceptance to Policy Inception Date

Yes	No	
☐	☐	All binders delivered by policy inception date.
☐	☐	Certificates of insurance or evidence of insurance mailed to the specified recipients of these documents.
☐	☐	Verify cash flow projection for the coming year.
☐	☐	Invoices delivered, with deposit premium specified.
☐	☐	Identify the agency's customer service or contact person.
☐	☐	Identify claims contact at agency and company, or both.
☐	☐	Verify receipt of vehicle insurance identification cards.
☐	☐	File all public utility commission filings and other legally required filings.

The First 60 Days after Policy Inception

Yes	No	
☐	☐	Policy delivery.
☐	☐	Verification by agency that the policy coverages and pricing equal what was quoted.
☐	☐	Copies of all applications sent to insurance companies representing our account.
☐	☐	Introduction of specific audit procedures to expect.

Year Round Policy Service

Yes	No	
☐	☐	Written confirmation of all coverage change requests.
☐	☐	Loss control assistance with safety programs.

(Check the following that apply)

____ Drivers training

____ Materials handling training

____ Work station setup and design assistance

____ General training materials and safety meeting ideas

____ Hazard identification and assessment training

____ Hazardous materials handling

____ Pre-employment checklist and physical assessment

____ Safety program review

____ Sound level and air quality tests

____ Physical location inspections

Service Schedule Checklist (continued)

Yes No

☐ ☐ Monthly, quarterly, or semiannual claims followup.

☐ ☐ Normal customer service and problem solving, as needed.

90 Days Before Expiration

Yes No

☐ ☐ Develop renewal coverage specifications.

☐ ☐ Three years of updated loss runs provided for all lines.

30 Days Before Expiration

Yes No

☐ ☐ Renewal quote provided.

☐ ☐ Renewal financing presented.

☐ ☐ Coverages presented on our coverage checklists.

☐ ☐ Final claims review of all open claims.

The Policy Expiration Date

Yes No

☐ ☐ Renewal coverage in effect.

☐ ☐ Final audit assistance, as needed.

Notes

Chapter 11

Avoid Costly Pitfalls

Be Aware of Insurance Pitfalls

Your sound business practices avoid the problems of human negligence and discourage fraud. If you end up in litigation, your chances of victory are greatly increased.

When agents or companies take advantage of you — intentionally or not — you will end up paying the bill. One of the goals of this book is to make you aware of some of the pitfalls, so you will not walk naively into such traps. Should you become a victim, you will quickly recognize the situation and take corrective actions. By knowing the pitfalls before they happen, you gain control of your insurance management and increase your alternatives. Make sure you have all necessary information in your files, and because of your preparation, you can change agents overnight. Your obvious strength in managing your insurance will tend to keep your agency working for your interests. Your sound business practices avoid the problems of human negligence and discourage fraud. If you end up in litigation, your chances of victory are greatly increased. You cannot completely protect yourself from every costly pitfall, but applying the methods shown in this chapter greatly improves your chances of protection.

The Incompetent Agent

Agents can easily bluff their way into handling complex accounts by acting confident, but too often, they are in over their heads. They may overlook something important — possibly neglect to suggest an important coverage — or incorrectly write a complex coverage form. In spite of their pretensions to competence in your case, their oversight can lead to financial disaster.

For help in avoiding this pitfall, refer to Four Ways to Find the Right Insurance Organization in Chapter 3. Complete the Insurance Agency

Profile at the end of Chapter 3 and carefully select the agencies from whom you buy. Allow your policies to be inspected by competitors to make sure the coverages meet those outlined in the coverage checklists from chapters 5 and 6.

Raising the Price

Seasoned agents skillfully question prospective clients to reveal what factors will result in a buying decision. The agent will want to know if the client has been paying too much money for too little coverage. Insurance company underwriters also ask the agent what other quotes are available, probing for price sensitivity. In fairness to company underwriters, they may be asking for the competitive information in an attempt to assess the risk and charge a fair premium for the exposures. The agent may feel justified in offering the client an attractive quote, while still withholding the best value possible for commission reasons. The level of commission an agent receives varies among insurance companies.

The more familiar your agency is with your account, the more comfortable it becomes with predicting your actions. Once the agency knows what it takes to win your business, it is not likely to improve upon your expectations.

A primary defense to raising the price is to never show all your alternatives. Keep agents believing access to lower prices may develop. Your completed Underwriting Information Questionnaire and Business Insurance Coverage Checklist subtly suggest alternative quotes may already be in process. Never get specific about the other agencies who may be quoting; keep your current agent wondering. Agencies will tend to do their best to present the lowest possible price to avoid being underpriced by a competitor. Obtaining competitive quotes defends you from paying inflated prices. In addition, sending the appropriate sample letters, located in the Appendix, alerts your insurance agency that you are growing in your expertise in managing your insurance.

Blocking the Insurance Market

A blocked insurance market may enable an agent to extract more premium out of you.

When an independent agency sends your application to an insurance company, it has staked a claim with that company on your account. The agency has blocked other independent agencies from accessing this insurance company, which will decline to quote any later submissions on your account. An independent agency that desires your business will request a quote from every available company the same day it gets your underwriting information. The agency's hurry is to prevent any competing agency from getting to these insurance companies first. Once your submission is logged in by the insurance company, this company will only release one quote to the agency that made the original submission.

An independent insurance agency with access to many insurance companies can quickly block a large percentage of the companies willing to quote your account — this presents an opportunity for disservice. The agency knows you cannot get another agency to quote the lowest priced company, because it has blocked that insurance market. The agency may elect to present a higher-priced proposal from its favorite company to give itself a larger commission, or for other self-serving reasons. With the insurance market blocked, the agency is fairly well assured you will be forced to accept its proposal and pay a higher than necessary premium.

Additionally, an agency may neglect to conclude negotiations with an insurance company to whom it has sent your application. The agency may fail to respond to an information request, or, in some other way, stall the quote, so it is not available in time for the proposal. The agency can honestly tell you it is giving you the best available quote, but neglect to tell you it failed to obtain a quote that it started. The agency's neglect may prevent you from accessing the perfect insurance company for you. In fairness to agencies, insurance companies sometimes fail to deliver a quote in the available time, despite an agency's best efforts.

You are more vulnerable to the blocked insurance market pitfall when only a few companies are willing to quote your account.

Your vulnerability to the pitfall of blocked insurance markets increases as your premiums become larger. There isn't much insurance market blocking over the smaller accounts, but as accounts become larger, the insurance markets are blocked more aggressively. You are more vulnerable to the blocked insurance market pitfall when only a few companies are willing to quote your account. Your business operations may look less attractive to insurance companies because of a potential for large losses, or because of your claims history. The limited number of interested companies makes it easier for one agent to successfully gain control over the small marketplace and exercise monopolistic powers against you.

Ask each quoting agency to supply a list of companies it would like to approach for quotes. This practice gives you more control, because you can restrict the number of insurance companies each agency will approach. You benefit in two ways. First, you assure yourself multiple quotes by having more than one agency quote your insurance, since no one agency can block all the insurance markets. Second, this serves to avoid the problem of eliminating the enthusiasm of underwriters — which can happen when multiple agents submit your account to them. This blunder wastes everybody's time and clearly notifies an underwriter the account is being seriously shopped, and the time spent quoting your account will probably result in a no sale. You may need to use an agent-broker of record assignment letter to give an agent exclusive rights to specific companies. Refer to discussion in Chapter 7.

Low-Balling Your Payroll or Sales Figures

An insurance agency can easily deliver a lower-priced policy by understating your payroll, square footage, receipts, or sales volume in their applications for quotes. By the time you are aware of this problem, more than a year may have passed and you are facing a large final audit premium billing.

To defend your business from this problem, complete your Underwriting Information Questionnaire. This will clearly document what you told the agency in the way of payroll and sales values. As soon as you get your policy, inspect the rating pages to confirm the rating is based on your figures. Having another agency inspect your policy is an effective way of making certain the rating basis is correct. For detailed information on this subject, see Chapter 5, and use Sample Letter U in the Appendix.

Misrepresentation

Agents can materially misrepresent your exposures to insurance companies — without your knowledge or consent — to obtain lower quotes. If your agents do this, you are exposed to the possibility of claims denial for misrepresentation, or expensive audit premium billings. Your agents are also exposing themselves to legal actions and department of insurance disciplinary actions. For example, your agent may tell the company you have had no losses, when, in fact, you had a major loss six months ago. Your agents may delete bad drivers from your drivers list. An agent may even say your 75-year-old building is only ten years old.

By falsely describing your facilities or operations, the agents may reduce your premium or get you accepted in a company that would otherwise decline to insure you. You may think they are helping you, but in misrepresenting your business to the insurance company, they are exposing you to potentially serious problems. Worse, you may appear to be a party to their fraud without knowing it.

A completed Underwriting Information Questionnaire documents that you correctly represented your business. Be sure to keep a copy of your completed questionnaire! Also, a review of the applications that resulted in your current policies is an excellent defense. Sample Letter I in the Appendix helps you obtain your applications if you do not have them in your file. Ask a competent insurance professional — such as a competitor agent or risk manager — to review your policy. You may be able to contract a risk manager to review your policies for a very reasonable fee, while a competing agent may provide similar services at no charge.

Lack of Detailed Rating Information

Detailed rating information discloses the cost of each line of coverage, including the basis and the rate applied to the basis. For example, the basis may be payroll, sales, or property values. The basis multiplied by the rate equals the premium you pay. Without detail rating in your quote, you are unable to select specific coverage based on cost-benefit evaluations. For example, upon review of the detailed rating information, you may decide to eliminate a coverage that is not cost-effective. The details are often available; however, many agents decide it is too much trouble to disclose the information. Disclosure of detailed rates may result in you asking questions and making changes to fine-tune your program, creating more work for the agent at a lower price and subsequent lower commission.

Many premiums are calculated by insurance companies on rating worksheets. If you have trouble getting detailed rates, ask for the rating worksheets. You may have to persist, but you will find the worksheets can be valuable. Their value comes from understanding all rating detail and from being able to show these to competing agents. Once competing agents understand how a rate was compiled, they may see an alternate rating method that works to your advantage.

Use the Business Insurance and Workers' Compensation Coverage Checklist to have your quoting agents provide specific rating information to help you avoid this pitfall.

Neglect Status

Neglect status occurs when your account is designated unprofitable or undesirable by the agency's or agent's standards. The agency or agent decides it is no longer willing to provide you with meaningful service. This happens when your account is considered too small, or the agency's markets are turning away from your type of business. When your agency sees no future in handling your account, it may continue renewing your policy as long as you pay your renewal premium. Every year, more and more clients are placed on neglect status, as the agencies and companies redefine their target markets.

Every year, more and more clients are placed on neglect status, as the agencies and companies redefine their target markets.

The best defense is to shop the marketplace using the Underwriting Information Questionnaire and Business Insurance and Workers' Compensation Coverage Checklists. The importance of shopping your insurance cannot be overstated — not just for price considerations, but also for the services you desire. You may find companies perfectly suited to your needs, which you never imagined existed.

The importance of shopping your insurance cannot be overstated — not just for price considerations, but also for the services you desire.

Cancellation Due to Small Claims

Getting canceled due to small claims frequency may cost you dearly when you purchase replacement coverage. It makes no sense to carry low deductibles and turn in a series of small claims — because it leads to premium increases or to a cancellation. Your claims may disqualify you from getting a renewal in a preferred premium program.

Higher deductibles will lower your current premium and keep your claims experience more acceptable. Insurance is not a maintenance agreement. Use it for the larger losses you cannot afford to sustain yourself.

Insurance is not a maintenance agreement. Use it for the larger losses you cannot afford to sustain yourself.

Failure to Place Coverage

The coverage you requested last week may not be in effect today because your agency may have failed to forward a correct request to the insurance company. Someone in the chain may have procrastinated, forgotten, or written the change in error. The request may have been mailed to the wrong company. Failure to place coverage is one of the major causes of errors and omissions claims against agents — because there are so many things that can go wrong in placing coverage.

Confirmations are valuable protection. If your agency fails to place the coverage, its errors and omissions policy may reimburse you for any loss.

Follow the suggestions in the discussion, Twelve Rules to Avoid Problems, in Chapter 7. You always want to get prompt written confirmations on all changes or additions to your coverages. Confirmations are valuable protection. If your agency fails to place the coverage, its errors and omissions policy may reimburse you for any loss.

Renew-As-Is

Your agents may tell you they shopped the market for your renewal policy, when, in fact, little work was done for you. Agents find it is much easier to simply renew a policy than to put the applications together with current information, shop any other available markets, and prepare a new proposal for you to consider. If you are not competently managing your insurance situation, you won't shop the market for yourself, and you will just pay the renewal premium. The agency is happy to put your file away for a year, and pocket the commission.

Your best defense against this pitfall is to update your Underwriting Information Questionnaire and Business Insurance and Workers' Compensation Coverage Checklists. With these forms completed, you can easily volunteer your renewal information 90 days before your expiration date. This communicates to the agency you expect the job to actually get done. Naturally, you will collect other quotes from competing agencies; maybe not this year, but your agency doesn't have to know that.

The Incumbent Agent

Your current agency can get to the companies first, enabling it to systematically block insurance markets, year after year. Another company may be willing to write your account 10 percent lower, but you will never know what opportunities you were denied.

Maintain your completed Underwriting Information Questionnaire and your coverage checklists to protect you from this problem. This updated information will enable you to easily obtain competitive quotes. You can also ask your incumbent agent to show you the quotes he or she has obtained from other companies — assuming you are with an independent agency. Seeing the actual quotes will help assure you they are being obtained.

No Loss Runs

An agency or company may not give you loss runs or other vital information about your policies, which cripples your ability to shop prices elsewhere. Loss runs are vital for showing your profitability as a client to any interested insurance company. Request your loss runs by sending sample letters C or D in the Appendix. Follow up with the agency until you are satisfied.

The Installment Plan

Some very attractive installment programs are offered by insurance companies with only nominal installment charges, and low or no interest. Often, installment plans are not presented as options to you, because if you choose this type of plan, then the agent's commission is paid in installments, as opposed to an upfront commission.

Read about negotiating strategies in Chapter 8. Ask if there is a company installment plan offered, and you may end up profiting from it.

The Procrastinating Agent

A serious disservice occurs when your agents procrastinate when working on your renewal. Agents use time against you to limit alternatives, thus forcing your decisions. They may wait until your expiration date is upon you to surprise you with a large rate increase. The timing may leave you little choice but to accept the increase. As your renewal date approaches, your options tend to become more limited, until finally, you give in to the time constraint pressures and accept whatever they present.

As your renewal date approaches, your options tend to become more limited, until finally you give in to the time constraint pressures and accept whatever they present.

Adhere to your service schedule as discussed in Chapter 10. Mark your calendar to make sure the steps take place on time. If all your good efforts fail to get you prompt quotes, ask for an extension of your current policies. The extension should be arranged by your current agent for up to 30 days, depending on your company and your account history. Take the time to make a solid decision.

In many states, you have a specified amount of time to take a free look at a policy and then return it with no premium due. You usually do not need to specify any reason for your return. Contact your state insurance department to see what policies have this privilege in your state. Be aware that returning a policy in this manner leaves you with no insurance, so you will first need to arrange replacement coverage. The free look privilege relieves you from having to keep a policy, should a better deal become available shortly after your effective date.

In many states, you have a specified amount of time to take a free look at a policy and then return it with no premium due.

The Premium Is Higher than the Quote

Your policy may arrive with a higher premium than you were quoted. This can occur for various reasons, some beyond the agent's control. The problem increases as time goes by, because the earned premium will be greater than what you budgeted. For example, suppose you paid your deposit premium and accepted a coverage binder. Nearly two months later, your policy arrives with a higher price. Your agent attempts to explain it as a misunderstanding. Your agent may tell you he or she has reevaluated all your alternatives, and must recommend you accept the higher-priced policy.

Because you have shopped the market and obtained other quotes, you are in a position to seek assistance from other agencies.

By adhering to the service schedule discussed in Chapter 10, you insist quotes be done well in advance with correct information you provided from your completed Underwriting Information Questionnaire. Because you have shopped the market and obtained other quotes, you are in a position to seek assistance from other agencies.

The Minimum or the Fully Earned Premium

Beware of purchasing a policy for which the full annual premium is *fully earned.* This means no refunds are likely in the event of cancellation of the policy before the expiration date. Purchasing such a policy may be your only option in some cases, but be sure you understand the terms of premium payment and refunds. If you cancel three months into the policy, you may be surprised to get no refund whatsoever.

Typically, you encounter this pitfall when it is necessary for you to deal with an excess or surplus lines insurance company. When buying insurance, request that the agencies complete the coverage checklists. Any minimum premium or fully earned premium should be clearly displayed, when you are presented with the quote. A fully earned or minimum premium should be clearly marked on the declarations page of your policy.

The Insolvent Company

Insurance companies do go bankrupt. When this occurs, you are confronted with three problems.

- First, you must arrange replacement coverage, often with very short notice.
- Second, you will not receive any refund of your unearned premium to use to purchase the replacement coverage.
- Third, if you have a claim, settlement may be a slow process, perhaps through your state's guarantee fund — if you have been insured by an admitted carrier. A nonadmitted carrier won't be covered by the guarantee fund. See the discussion in Chapter 3 on Admitted Versus Nonadmitted Insurance Companies.

When possible, insure with companies that are financially sound, rated by one of the insurance company rating services, and admitted in your state. Refer to Chapter 3. If you can't find a rating or a record of the insurance company, call your state insurance department. Check on any complaints that may have been filed, and ask for any available data on the company.

Commingling of Funds

If you pay your premium directly to your agency, it may deposit your money in its premium trust account, then it pays the insurance company when billed. Funds in the trust account can possibly be misdirected, and the agency may become unable to pay your premiums to your insurance company. If your payment never gets to the insurance company, your policy will be cancelled — even though you paid the premium to the agency. Violation of the integrity of the premium trust account is a serious crime in many states, and a violation of the insurance industry's code of ethics. To avoid exposure to this type of pitfall, make your payments directly to insurance companies, whenever possible.

Bogus Policies

In some rare cases, an agency may take your premium, but never purchase a policy or place the coverage. You may receive binders or policies, but there is no coverage in force and these binders and policies are worthless. The agent is betting you won't have a major claim.

If you use the Insurance Agency Profile, your chances of screening out agents who would issue bogus policies are much better. Wise business insurance buyers will follow up on their service schedule and will be alerted to missing policies. When ordering coverage, insist on written confirmation from the agent to prove that coverage has been placed. This confirmation should be in the form of a letter or preferably a formal insurance binder. Sixty days later, you should follow up to make sure your policy has arrived. If there is any doubt about the authenticity of a policy or binder or in coverage being placed, call the insurance company directly. If a call becomes necessary, ask for the underwriting department of the insurance company. Take caution when selecting insurance people with whom you will deal and you can avoid the bogus policies pitfall.

Remember, you are better protected to select insurance companies rated favorably by the insurance company rating services, as discussed in Chapter 3.

Misrepresented Coverage

Claim checks should be drawn on insurance company bank accounts, not an agency's account.

Your agency may underinsure you, charge you for full coverage, and then pay your small claims out of its own account. Paying the small claims delays getting caught. The agency is betting you won't have any claims. Warning signals may include not getting your policy, or getting a policy that does not provide all the coverage shown in the quote. A major warning signal is getting a claim settlement check drawn on the agency checking account. Claim checks should be drawn on insurance company bank accounts, not an agency's account.

The distinction between the last three pitfalls is in the severity of the insurance company's known error. For further clarification:

- In the commingling of funds pitfall, the insurance agency issues a policy and hopes to pay the insurance company in time.

- In the bogus policies pitfall, the insurance agency does not issue a policy at all.
- In the misrepresented coverage pitfall, the insurance agency just issues part of the coverages it promised in the proposal.

To help defend your business against the misrepresented coverage pitfall, complete the Insurance Agency Profile and carefully select the agencies from whom you buy. Compare your policies to your quotes, and allow these prices and coverages to be inspected by competitors, to make sure the coverages meet those outlined in the Business Insurance and Workers' Compensation Coverage Checklists, which are located at the end of chapters five and six.

Chapter 12

Handle Claims Effectively

If Your Business Suffers a Loss

In the event you suffer a loss, this chapter will guide and assist you through the typical claims process. You will become familiar with the insurance company adjuster's point of view and recognize the potential for your use of a public adjuster along with alternative dispute resolution techniques. By acquainting you with your responsibilities, and understanding the adjuster's point of view, you will hopefully gain useful insight for making the process as painless as possible.

Know What Claims People Can Do for You

If a loss is significant, an insurance company will be represented by an adjuster. An *adjuster* is either an employee of the insurance company or an independent contractor representing the insurance company. In either case, the adjuster's job is to settle the claim in a fair and equitable manner.

A *public adjuster* is an independent contractor who you can elect to represent you. Public adjusters are frequently former insurance company adjusters who have decided to earn their living helping insurance buyers get all the benefits to which they are entitled from their respective insurance companies. They charge for their services either on an hourly basis, or for a fee, which is usually a percentage of the claim.

Alternative Dispute Resolution Techniques

Alternative dispute resolution techniques, also referred to as ADRs, are becoming very popular in the insurance industry and include appraisal, mediation, and arbitration.

- *Appraisal* is used in almost all property policies to resolve disputes over the value of an item that was damaged. The technique is more fully described in the property claims section later in this chapter.
- *Mediation* is used as a voluntary way for people who dispute claims to resolve their disagreements without the outcome being binding on either party. In mediation session, a mediator is present to act as a facilitator for the disputants to negotiate a settlement between themselves with no outside judgment being imposed. While the outcome is not binding on any party to the process, just the face-to-face confrontation is often a sufficient catalyst to get the parties involved to settle a claim without the need of legal action.
- *Arbitration* is written into both personal and commercial auto policies as a method of settling disputes in the uninsured motorist coverage section. Arbitration is also used in professional liability and commercial general liability claims as a preferred method to settle claims. The process is very similar to appraisal, except it deals in liability, not property claims, and the outcome is binding on all parties.

These three techniques allow for faster, more cost-effective claims settlements, without the formality and hostility often involved in litigation.

Rules to Follow when Any Type of Loss Occurs

The following rules are useful for achieving a satisfactory claim settlement and for avoiding aggravation in handling your claim. Each claim is unique and must be managed depending on its own circumstances. However, the first set of simple, easy-to-follow rules apply to all loss situations. The rest of the rules are arranged by type of loss and should be equally useful.

Record Your Experience of the Incident in Writing

After you are involved in an incident that will involve an insurance claim, write down all pertinent details — such as times, locations, observations, contacts, witnesses, and conversations — as soon as possible. Written details are very valuable to you in accurately reporting your claim, because you will be very clear about the events that transpired. Your written record will add credibility to the statement you give the adjuster. If a conflict develops about what actually happened, your written record will strengthen your position. If your time to write is limited, keep a small tape recorder with you and use it to record the data. The information can be transcribed at a later date. Keep the paper or recorder handy for several days after the loss as you may recall pertinent information about the loss more clearly after the initial shock wears off.

Identify All Possible Witnesses

Getting witnesses at the scene of a loss can make a big difference in the results of a claim. Be sure to write down their names, phone numbers, addresses, and their accounts of what happened. Witnesses can verify the facts and put the claim in its proper perspective. If you were directly involved, you will need to remain calm and collected to identify witnesses in the excitement of an incident — but the results can be very profitable to you. If a camera is available, photograph the incident. Better yet, use a video camera.

Notify the Appropriate Authorities

The police must be notified for all losses when a law is broken, such as burglary, theft, robbery, and uninsured motorist losses. The fire department should inspect all fires — even if you put it out yourself — because hidden smoldering embers can later reignite a building. Police reports are needed for traffic accidents — especially if you were not at fault — because the reports document the facts regarding the accident. Take note of the officer who takes your report, including name, badge number, and telephone number. Full written reports are often not available for more than ten days after an accident, so it can help to know which officer is working on your case if any leads develop. If you get a police report number, inform your adjuster.

Report the Loss to the Insurance Company Promptly

In most cases, you must call your agent or claims office during business hours, unless you were provided with a 24-hour number. You want to report the loss as soon as possible. Hopefully, from following the loss control suggestions, the correct telephone number for reporting claims is readily available. Have your policy number ready when you call, especially if you are calling a claims office rather than your agency. When you call, be prepared to give the claims contract person all the information you collected, and be sure to note the name of the person to whom you reported the claim, and the date and time it was reported. Ask for a claim number and write it down as soon as it is available.

Find Out the Name of Your Adjuster and the Best Time to Call

The adjuster is the person responsible for completing the documentation of your claim file, negotiating the settlement, and assuring you are paid. Once you have identified your adjuster and his or her telephone number, call to agree on the itinerary of the settlement of your claim.

Be Truthful and Cooperative when Reporting Your Claim

In most policies, your duty to cooperate in the settlement of any claim is clearly spelled out. As discussed in Chapter 7, you are always better off if you are friendly, cooperative, and honest. If adjusters feel you are trying to get compensation for more than you lost, they may put up their most defensive posture. Never try to collect more than what you are entitled to receive. You want no part of an adjuster's most defensive posture. Remember, your adjuster is responsible for completing the documentation of your claim file, negotiating the settlement, and assuring you are paid.

Read Your Policy for Actions to Take after a Loss

As soon as possible, after a loss has occurred, read your policy. Don't panic, you need not read it all — just the section that spells out your duties after a loss. This will give you valuable insight about what the insurance company will expect you to do to settle the claim.

For adjusters to release a claim check, they must first fulfill vital responsibilities and correctly document a file. They must confirm coverage is in force, and that no policy exclusion has stopped it from applying to your loss. Adjusters must verify the limits and conditions of your coverage, including the maximum limit, valuation methods, and any deductibles. Adjusters must usually collect your recorded statement as evidence the loss actually occurred. Often, they will need to conduct a physical inspection, take photographs, and obtain witnesses' statements and police reports. To certify the information and formalize your claim, your signature will be needed by the adjuster on a proof of loss form. Finally, the amount to be paid must be established, using accepted methods of valuation.

Call Your Adjuster for Advice if Your Claim Is Delayed

Dealing directly with the claims adjuster takes the agent out of the loop and can save days of phone tag, getting your claim settled faster.

Most adjusters have busy case loads, and many days may pass while adjusters wait for something you can easily provide. Many claims problems are solved by the proactive communication of the insurance holder. Dealing directly with the claims adjuster takes the agent out of the loop and can save days of phone tag, thus getting your claim settled faster.

Be Satisfied before You Accept a Check

Never sign a full release of all claims, then expect to collect additional payments later.

If you are accepting a check from your insurance company, make sure the claim remains open if you are not fully satisfied. Never sign a full release of all claims, then expect to collect additional payments later. However, many businesspeople fear accepting any partial payment claim checks until all the issues are settled. This is an unreasonable fear. In many circumstances, accepting payment from your own insurer does not affect your rights under your policy, as you can later collect additional sums to correctly adjust the loss. At some point, it may be necessary to contact your attorney, but it is beyond the scope of this book to define the point at which an attorney's services are needed. Before contacting an attorney, be certain that your problem is not simply based on poor communication between you and your adjuster.

Focus on the Facts and Key Issues to Solve Problems

If an adjuster is being unreasonable, contact that adjuster's supervisor. Also, the supervisor may be very helpful if your adjuster cannot be reached due to illness or vacation. In resolving your impasse, remember being hostile to claims people almost never profits your cause. Refer to Chapter 7 for discussion on how to motivate insurance people.

Listen Carefully and Ask for Written Confirmation if Your Claim Is Denied

The purpose of this action is twofold: you make sure the adjuster has a thorough knowledge of your case, and you have a clear document showing the position the insurance company has taken. With this data in hand, you can quickly and clearly communicate the problem to an attorney and efficiently explore any possibilities for generating better results.

An insurance company has a duty to act in good faith in the settlement of your claim. Fortunately, most insurance companies act in good faith because they are in business to service you when you have losses, and bad faith dealings have cost some insurance companies dearly in the past. However, the mention of bad faith is not always the way to encourage cooperation. Keep this in mind as a last resort because if you remind an uncooperative adjuster you expect them to act in good faith, it may change that adjuster's attitude. Adjusters and insurance companies want to avoid lawsuits where they must explain and justify actions before a jury. This is because juries are often unsympathetic to insurance companies. If all else fails, be prepared to turn to an attorney.

Rules to Follow for Property Claims

Property claims involve losses to your buildings, furniture, fixtures, inventory, and other business personal property. Property claims do not include losses caused by damage to automobiles, although business personal property in an automobile is often part of a property claim. Use the following rules as guidelines when handling your property claims.

Take Reasonable Steps to Minimize a Loss

You must make the judgment call as to what is reasonable based on the circumstances you face. But recognize you usually have a legal duty to take reasonable steps to avoid unnecessary losses. Therefore, if your building is on fire, you must call the fire department. You might also need to hire people to move your business personal property from your building to a safe location if the building next to yours is on fire.

Protect Your Property from Further Harm

This can mean boarding up windows if they are broken during a burglary, or covering an open hole in your roof if high winds have caused significant damage.

See if the Adjuster Wants to View the Damage

Don't make permanent repairs unless the adjuster says it is all right to proceed. Always get your adjuster's permission before you begin permanent repairs.

Prove the Loss

Property insurance usually requires that you produce a list of the property that was damaged, and sometimes an additional list of the items that were not damaged. The list should include a description of the item, its age, purchase date, an estimate of the cost when new, and the cost to replace the damaged item. Copies of receipts, canceled checks, or credit card statements are helpful. Photographs help prove the property existed, its quality, and its condition. If all else fails, offer signed affidavits from disinterested parties who confirm the existence of the property, its quality, and condition. By providing this information, you help the adjuster document your file and move toward settlement of your claim.

Know How to Handle Disagreements on Property Values

Replacement cost valuation disputes are often resolved by asking the adjusters to identify a supplier to replace your property. If you cannot find a supplier for the prices suggested by your adjuster, then offer your own supplier's prices, and let the adjuster produce an alternative.

Be sure you read the exact definition of replacement cost in your policy, so you understand the conditions and limitations. Conditions usually provide that you must actually replace the property, or receive only the actual cash value until you replace it. The presence of replacement cost coverage does not extend the coverage beyond the stated coverage limit in the policy. To do this, you will need an endorsement added to your policy called guaranteed replacement cost. Unfortunately, it is normally only available for buildings insured in personal lines policies.

Realize ACV Disputes Are More Complex than Replacement Cost Issues

Actual cash value (ACV) is usually defined as replacement cost minus depreciation, and depreciation is a subjective issue. Adjusters use depreciation tables — maintained by insurance companies — that serve as guidelines for general categories of property. But the actual condition of your specific items are important factors in their values. The valuation issue often boils down to two important questions:

- Where can you purchase a similar piece of property of like condition and age, and what would it cost?
- What could you have sold your property for immediately before the loss?

Substantiate Values to Solve the Valuation Issue

The idea is to propose your own valuation and substantiate your valuation method with evidence.

You need to show the price the marketplace puts on your property. Classified advertisements and appraisals are helpful evidence. The idea is to propose your own valuation and substantiate your valuation method with evidence. The adjuster's job is to fully document and justify each dollar spent, so if you assist with the documentation, you make the adjuster's job easier. You can help by filling your adjuster's file with evidence substantiating payments made to you. Sometimes, you and the adjuster will not agree on a value; but that is not an insurmountable problem.

Submit to Appraisal to Solve a Property Valuation Dispute

The ultimate remedy for a property valuation dispute is to submit to an appraisal.

The appraisal process is one of the alternative disputes resolution techniques built into property policies. The process involves you and the insurance company each hiring your own appraiser. Each party pays its own appraiser in full. Then, the two appraisers agree on a third appraiser to provide a third opinion, and this cost is split equally between you and the insurance company. A decision by any two is usually binding on all parties. This remedy is built into most property insurance contracts to simplify the resolution of disputes. The most difficult part of appraisal is finding an acceptable third appraiser. This difficulty may force you and the insurance company to compromise and resolve your differences and settle the claim.

Bypass Appraisal and Go to an Attorney, if Necessary

First, you must comply with all the conditions of the policy, so read the conditions carefully. The conditions involve filing a prompt proof of loss with the company. Notify the police if a law has been broken, such as a theft loss. Comply with other obligations you have as part of the insurance contract. Compliance with these duties is not difficult, you just need to comply in a timely fashion.

Rules to Follow for Auto Claims

When a loss occurs that involves an automobile, the loss requires a specialized automobile claims process. Collisions, theft, and vandalism are obvious examples of automobile losses; but even injuries that occur while getting in and out of a vehicle are included in an automobile claim. The following rules can help you when dealing with any automobile claim.

Take Pictures of the Accident Scene, if Possible

Photographs should include the location of the vehicles and the damage to the vehicles. Many companies equip their vehicles with disposable cameras in the glove compartment of the vehicle for use in the event of any accident. Some insurance companies also include a driver's report to be completed at the time of the accident by the driver. These reports are easy to create. Simply ask your agent or broker for the claim form your insurance company will want you to complete. You will identify what is necessary for the driver to record at the scene and that will be a good start toward completing the claim form.

File a Police Report, if Necessary

If any laws were broken or if the accident caused enough bodily injury or property damage to require filing a police report per your state laws, then file a police report immediately. If you are hit by an uninsured motorist, notify the police and describe the accident and the vehicle that hit you. A hit and run vehicle is considered an uninsured motor vehicle in most states.

Protect Your Property from Further Harm

This can mean storing your vehicle in a locked storage facility. Insurance policies prohibit your abandoning the vehicle and claiming a total loss. You must protect it from any further damage.

Do Not Repair Your Damaged Vehicle before Official Approval

In most cases, an insurance company wants the adjuster to see the damage before repairs are made. Some small losses, such as a broken windshield, may be handled directly by your agent or broker who will immediately issue a check to you.

Sometimes, differences of opinion will exist between you and the adjuster on the value of a vehicle. If this happens, you probably can ask for the appraisal process to settle the dispute. See the discussion on appraisal earlier in this chapter for details. Appraisal can work the same way in auto physical damage as in the property policy.

Rules to Follow for Liability Claims

All liability rules apply to an automobile policy, if you have been involved in an accident where you may be liable for bodily injury or property damage and subsequently sued. Here are some rules to know should you become involved in such a situation.

Forward All Summons and Complaints to Your Agent or Company

Immediately stamp a received date on any summons or complaints and keep copies for your records. Retain copies of all papers you receive regarding your claims.

Realize Your Company Should Defend You

This means the company will select an attorney and pay all your defense costs. This duty ends when the company actually pays someone the full amount of coverage available under the policy for this occurrence.

Be Aware Settlements Can Be Made without Your Permission

Don't be surprised if a claim is settled, and you are not even aware of it. The insurance company may make a small payment, even when your liability is questionable, to settle the claim and avoid the high cost of litigation — commonly known as the *nuisance claim payment*, which is permissible by an insurance contract. This can adversely affect your loss ratio, but not as severely as litigating a claim and losing the case. The company is only trying to protect itself from losses it can avoid.

Do Not Make an Admission of Guilt to a Third Party

No matter how morally obligated you may feel, make no payments to a third party without your insurance company's written permission. In the event a deposition is taken, remember all you say can and will go into the official court record. Confer with your attorney before the deposition is taken.

Rules to Follow for Workers' Compensation Claims

While every state has workers' compensation insurance, the rules vary by state. At this point in the book, you should have completed the bidding or renewal process and you know some of your state's laws regarding the sale of workers' compensation insurance. In addition, you should know what company is providing your coverage.

Become Familiar with Your State's Laws

In particular, you should know the laws on when and how to handle a work-related injury. Normally, quickness is of utmost importance in handling these claims, so make every effort to report claims to your company as soon as possible. Make sure you comply with your state's law. In addition, make sure your managers are aware of your state's laws. Everyone has to be involved in safety and the claim reporting process. Be sure to keep a log of claims and follow up on the progress of all injured workers.

Take an Active Interest in the Injured Worker's Return-to-Work Date

Find a way to assist the employee to return to light duty work as soon as possible. If rehabilitation is required for the employee, be sure to keep in touch and get a return-to-work date from the employee.

Review Open Claims at the Claims Review Sessions

You and your agent or broker have these sessions as part of the ongoing service you negotiated before the purchase of your policy. Make your time at these sessions valuable by continuing to review the status of open claims and assist in getting the claims closed or reduced.

Perhaps more than with any other kind of claim, workers' compensation claims are within your control. Your involvement is valuable to you in controlling your future insurance costs.

Beating the Claims Game

Hopefully, you business will be spared any loss that requires you to put the claims process into action. In the event that you do suffer a loss, however, you will be prepared to follow the general rules to handle the various types of claims. You are encouraged to use this chapter as a reference point to start a claim, because the chapter's text gives you inside industry tips that you may not have otherwise known.

Even if your business does suffer a loss, rest assured. By knowing the claims process beforehand, you can move your claims along smoothly and quickly.

Before you put this book down, read the conclusion on the remaining pages to give you an idea on how to start your search for the ideal coverages at the most affordable price!

Conclusion

Congratulations! If you have made it this far, you are on your way to becoming an informed business insurance buyer. Now that you have learned what it takes to approach the insurance marketplace and how to deal with the various insurance people, it is time to put your insurance buying skills into action. On the following pages, you are given five key objectives to help you get started.

Five Objectives to Get You Started

The five key objectives below will help you begin improving your insurance situation. The objectives are arranged in the order of their probable impact for better results. Each objective is followed by specific time-saving actions, designed to achieve the objective with the least amount of time and effort.

First Objective – Gather the Facts about Your Business

As you know, the Underwriting Information Questionnaire is the key to managing the important facts about your business. You have the option to complete the form provided in Chapter 4 or you can automate this information by using *The Insurance Assistant,* this book's companion software. To begin this important step, you can follow the time-saving actions listed below.

- Understand why you must reevaluate your insurance from Chapter 1.
- Obtain your latest insurance applications by using Sample Letter I in the Appendix.

- Obtain your loss runs by using Sample Letters C or D in the Appendix.
- Obtain your current policies from your agent's files by using Sample Letter K in the Appendix.
- Obtain your policy history by using Sample Letter O in the Appendix.
- Complete you Underwriting Information Questionnaire from Chapter 4. If you have purchased *The Insurance Assistant* you can begin compiling information on your computer.

Second Objective – Define the Coverages You Need

With all your business' essential data collected, it is time to confidently approach insurance people to quote your account. Follow the time-saving actions listed below to achieve optimum coverage options. Remember, thousands of agencies and brokerages are available to work for you.

- Know your business insurance coverage options by examining chapters five and six.
- Send Sample Letter B to your current agent to have your current coverages described on the Business Insurance and Workers' Compensation Coverage Checklists.
- Ask your current agent or competing agent to specify coverage recommendations on your Business Insurance Coverage Checklist, by providing the agent with your competed Underwriting Information Questionnaire from Chapter 4.

Third Objective – Improve Your Business' Image to Insurance Companies

You can enhance your business' appearance and receive lower premiums. You have the ability to maintain your business in a way that shows agents, brokers, and underwriters that you are not a risk to insure. Thus, you will be quoted for your needed coverages at reasonable prices. Because your business' image plays a key part in the insurance purchase, carefully follow these time-saving actions.

- Establish a loss control program for your business by following a service schedule as outlined in Chapter 10.
- Eliminate or minimize your red flags to appear less of a risk to insure, as discussed in Chapter 3.
- Know how to make your account more profitable to your agent or broker as discussed in Chapter 7.
- Understand the rules to avoid problems and strategies to approach new agencies as outlined in Chapter 7.

Fourth Objective – Obtain Alternative Insurance Quotes

One of your main goals is to shop the insurance marketplace. After reading this book, you should be fully equipped with the necessary information to gather at least three, preferably five, quotes from differing agencies or brokerages. To expedite this process, carefully observe the following time-saving actions.

- Know the key preparations for approaching the marketplace, as outlined in Chapter 3.
- Recognize your workers' compensation issues and learn how to control these costs, as discussed in Chapter 6.
- Expect your prequote loss control and know how to prepare for your inspection, as referred to in Chapter 4.
- Collect Insurance Agency Profiles on your current agent and prospective agents. You can use the master copy profile in Chapter 3 and reproduce as many as you need.
- Effectively negotiate your prices. Now that you are equipped with key negotiation tactics, you are ready to skillfully communicate with agents regarding price.
- Use the Quote Comparison forms to help you decide on the best proposal for your business.

Fifth Objective – Clarify Your Service Standards

As you apply the strategies in this book, you will be one of the few truly informed business insurance buyers. You know what it takes to negotiate, motivate, reevaluate, and most importantly, make the right purchasing decision. At this point, you know what quality service means and the importance of post-purchase progress. To fulfill your insurance service needs after the purchase, follow the time saving actions listed below.

- Use the key strategies to motivate insurance people to help you, as you learned from Chapter 7.
- Insist on quality service from your agent. Service guidelines are outlined in Chapter 10.
- Demand that you receive loss control assistance with safety programs, as outlined in Chapter 10.
- Discuss the Service Schedule Checklist with quoting agents and let them know you expect the services that are outlined on your schedule. Refer to Chapter 10.
- Be prepared for audits. You can effectively prepare for and expect any necessary audits. See Chapter 10 for more details.
- Know how to manage your claims properly, as outlined in Chapter 12.

Win the Battle!

Now it is time to take up your armor and defend your business from harm. You are now prepared to fight the insurance battle and win the right coverage at the right price.

How to Contact the Authors

If you have insurance questions or comments about this book, you can write or call the authors directly.

Write to:	**Don Bury** P.O. Box 6043 San Rafael, CA 94903	**Larry Heischman** P.O. Box 11656 Pleasanton, CA 94588-1656
To call:	Toll free (800) 493-1311 Direct (415) 491-1311 Fax (415) 472-3845	 (510) 426-9014 (510) 426-9014

Helpful Resources

Section IV

Appendix of Sample Letters

Glossary

Index

Appendix of Sample Letters

The following sample letters can become key parts to your business insurance management program. As owner of this book, you are entitled to use the suggested sample letter format for your business insurance purchasing purposes.

The sample letters suggest communications that are often useful in dealing with insurance situations. The letters can be customized for your specific situation, or they can suggest issues to address by phone. These letters will help you:

- Save time by not having to draft your own letters; and
- Show your agency that you are serious about quality service and committed to paying lower prices.

To simplify the process even more, you can opt to purchase *The Insurance Assistant*, the companion software to this book. The software will eliminate any further word processing and allows you to plug in the information specific to your business.

Sample Letter A – Coverage Checklist Completion Request to Quoting Agencies

Ask quoting agents to complete the Business Insurance Coverage Checklist when you arrange for a quote as discussed in Chapter 5. Sometimes, you will receive a quote on the agency's form. Use this letter to motivate agents to describe the quoted coverages on your standardized form — so you can easily compare quotes.

Insisting on completion of the coverage checklist greatly simplifies proposal comparisons and leads agents to make sure everything you request is included in the quoted price.

Your Business Letterhead

Date

Quoting Agency
P.O. Box 111
Anytown, USA 00000

Dear Agent:

We appreciate your effort involved in obtaining competitive quotes for our insurance program.

To help us understand the coverages you are quoting, please complete our enclosed coverage checklist. This will help us evaluate your proposal and make an informed purchase.

Thank you for your efforts.

Sincerely,

Informed Buyer

Enclosure: Business Insurance Coverage Checklist

Sample Letter B – Coverage Checklist Completion Request to Current Agent

Have your current agent specify your current coverages on your standardized format — the Business Insurance Coverage Checklist, as discussed in Chapter 5. Use this letter to introduce the coverage checklist to your current agent and request its completion.

Your Business Letterhead

Date

Current Agency
P.O. Box 111
Anytown, USA 00000

Re: Policy # ____________________

Dear Agent:

Please help us increase our understanding of our current insurance program. To help us, please indicate the coverages we now purchase on our enclosed coverage checklist. Your effort will help us appreciate the value of our coverages and may suggest other coverages we should consider purchasing.

We are sure you will agree that review of our program is a worthwhile effort. We appreciate your assistance and thank you for your continuing efforts to serve our insurance needs.

Sincerely,

Informed Buyer

Enclosure: Business Insurance Coverage Checklist

Coverage design improves with agent attention and effort. Having your agent complete the Business Insurance Coverage Checklist gets that person's expertise focused on your coverage design.

Sample Letter C – Loss Runs Request from Current Agent

Collecting your loss runs at least once a year is vital. Send this letter to the agent(s) who provided your policies over the past five years. If you don't have current loss runs, request them now. Don't wait for the expiration date. By obtaining complete loss runs, getting updates before each policy expiration is much easier. Refer to the Index for locations of loss runs discussions, as well as the Underwriting Information Questionnaire.

Obtaining loss runs is simple when you request them in writing and follow up by phone. They should arrive within ten days.

Your Business Letterhead

Date

Current (and past) Agency
P.O. Box 111
Anytown, USA 00000

Dear Agent:

Please provide us with loss runs for all policies we have purchased through your firm for the past five years. We need the following information for each policy:

- Date of loss;
- Cause of the loss;
- Amount paid on the claim;
- Status of claim (is it open or closed?); and
- Current reserve.

We appreciate your assistance in obtaining this information from our insurer(s).

Sincerely,

Informed Buyer

Sample Letter D – Loss Runs Request for Issuing Insurance Company

If you don't get the desired response from an agent, request loss runs directly from the insurance company. Send a letter to each company issuing you a policy in the past five years. Indicate the policy periods and policy numbers and provide your phone number. Call the insurance company and ask for a commercial underwriter, who will advise you to whom and where to send this letter. If you don't find the insurance company's phone number on your policy, try directory assistance, an insurance agent, or the *Best's Key Rating Guide Property Casualty,* located at your local library.

Your Business Letterhead

Date

Attn: Branch Manager
Current (and past) Insurance Company
P.O. Box 555
Anytown, USA 00000

Dear Manager:

Please provide us with loss runs for all policies we have purchased through your agency for the past three years. We need the following information for each policy:

- Date of loss;
- Cause of the loss;
- Amount paid on claim;
- Status of claim (is it open or closed?); and
- Current reserve.

Policy Dates		Policy Number
From ________	To ________	________________
From ________	To ________	________________

Sincerely,

Informed Buyer

Once you have the right contact at the insurance company, you can more quickly and easily get loss runs directly — rather than going through an agent.

Sample Letter E – Pending Workers' Compensation Dividends Status Inquiry

Many buyers do not know what the dividend potential is from their current workers' compensation policy, or from policies they have carried in recent years. All too often, the communication in this area is lacking. This letter is designed to obtain a status report of your situation. As a businessperson, you naturally need to be aware of potential income, so you will want to know of any incoming dividend checks. See Chapter 6.

Treat dividends just like any other receivable. Engage in active collection to make sure you receive any monies you are due on a timely basis.

Your Business Letterhead

Date

Current Workers' Compensation Agency
1111 Paper Shuffle Court
Los Angeles, CA 99999

Re: Workers' Compensation Policy # _______________
Policy period: From _________ To __________

Dear Agent:

In reviewing our workers' compensation program, we find the need to clarify our dividend status. Please help us understand what workers' compensation dividends we may be eligible to receive for our current policy and for the policies we have carried over the past three years. We are interested in your estimate of when checks will be released and any indication of the amounts of these checks.

We appreciate your help.

Sincerely,

Informed Buyer

Sample Letter F – Current Experience Modification Worksheet Request

When your workers' compensation is subject to an experience modification factor, keep a copy of the annual worksheets in your workers' compensation file. If you pay a significant workers' compensation premium, keep copies of the worksheets of your experience modification calculations. With this record, you can make sure your open claims are as low as possible before the next calculation date and your underwriters can have this information to prepare your dividend quotes. See the discussion in Chapter 6.

The experience modification worksheet is an essential piece of your workers' compensation cost containment program, because it affects your rates for the entire year.

Your Business Letterhead

Date

Current Workers' Compensation Agency
1111 Paper Shuffle Court
Los Angeles, CA 99999

Re: Workers' Compensation Policy #________________

Dear Agent:

Please obtain a copy of our current workers' compensation experience modification worksheet for us. This letter shall act as your authority to obtain the worksheet from any insurance company, or the (Place appropriate workers' compensation agency name here. Names vary from state to state).

It is our business practice to keep apprised of our experience modifications by maintaining a copy of the current worksheet. Thank you for your assistance in keeping us informed.

Sincerely,

Informed Buyer

Sample Letter G – Alternative Coverage Quote Request

Often, business insurance buyers are better served to raise deductibles on property and vehicle physical damage coverages, and then apply the premium savings to increasing liability limits. You can only make these choices when provided with premium quotes for alternative coverage combinations. Often, agents and companies resist providing these quotes because of the rating work involved. This letter may be appropriate. See Chapter 8 for a detailed discussion.

Ask your agent to make thoughtful suggestions regarding using your insurance dollar wisely.

Your Business Letterhead

Date

Current Agency
P.O. Box 111
Anytown, USA 00000

Re: Alternative Coverage Quotes

Dear Agent:

Please help us make the best possible coverage selections by providing rate quotes for some variations in coverages. We suspect carrying a higher deductible on our property and vehicle physical damage coverages may help conserve premium dollars that could be better used to increase liability limits.

As you know, these decisions cannot be made wisely until the cost-benefit alternatives are understood. We want to review alternative price quotes for increased liability limits and deductibles. We welcome your suggestions for modifying our coverage selections based on the rates you obtain.

Thank you for your continued assistance in managing our insurance program.

Sincerely,

Informed Buyer

Sample Letter H – Insurance Agency Profile Completion Request

An effective way to get background on a quoting agent is to send this letter with the Insurance Agency Profile. Use this letter to introduce the form and motivate the agent to provide the information. Of course, the blank form can be handed to the agent or completed by you at an interview. See Chapter 3 for further discussion.

If an agent will not complete the profile, you can assume the individual is not very interested in your business.

Your Business Letterhead

Date

Current Agency
P.O. Box 111
Anytown, USA 00000

Re: Agency Profile

Dear Agent:

Please help us learn more about you and your agency by providing the information requested on the enclosed Insurance Agency Profile. We hope you will welcome this opportunity to better inform us regarding your strengths and credentials.

Thanks for your time and interest in our business.

Sincerely,

Informed Buyer

Enclosure: Insurance Agency Profile

Sample Letter I – Copies of the Applications that Produced Current Policies Request

The applications your agent submits to insurance companies to quote your account are often intentionally not released to you, because having the applications makes it too easy for you to shop your account and scrutinize your agent's work. The copies may reveal errors or misrepresentations that were made on your behalf, and they can save you time in completing your Underwriting Information Questionnaire. Obtaining the applications informs your agent you expect full disclosure. For more information, refer to the Underwriting Information Questionnaire in Chapter 4 and the conclusion of this book.

Read the applications when they arrive, and see how well they present your business. How can they be improved?

Your Business Letterhead

Date

Current Agency
P.O. Box 111
Anytown, USA 00000

Re: Copies of applications

Dear Agent (or Customer Service Person):

In reviewing our records, it appears we are lacking copies of the applications you submitted to produce our current policies through your agency. Please help us complete our files by providing us with copies of the complete submissions.

We feel that maintaining copies of the applications is a sound business practice to help avoid errors or misunderstandings. Thank you for your continuing assistance in managing our insurance account.

Sincerely,

Informed Buyer

Sample Letter J – Letter of Recommendation for Current Agency

A letter of recommendation should help motivate your agent to make your account a priority, and put you on the preferred client list. After your agent has shown the letter to prospective clients, your continued satisfaction will be vital to his or her new sales. Send this letter only when he or she has earned it, and expect your service needs to be met with top priority in the months ahead. Use of this letter is discussed in Chapter 7.

Your Business Letterhead

Date

Current Agency
P.O. Box 111
Anytown, USA 00000

To whom it may concern:

This is to confirm my business has been insured with ABC Insurance Agency since 19__. I feel the service I have received has been excellent, and I never hesitate to recommend the agency to my friends who are in need of business insurance.

In my opinion, ABC Insurance Agency is very professional and renders excellent services and competitive pricing. I would welcome any phone calls regarding this agency's quality of service.

Sincerely,

Informed Buyer

This letter costs you next to nothing and may motivate your agent to treat you well.

Sample Letter K – Copies of Current Policies Request

If you discover you lack copies of your current policies, you must immediately request them. You may have misplaced the policies, or you may have never received them. Whatever the reason, it is absolutely essential you have your policies readily accessible for your review. Refer to the Underwriting Information Questionnaire for more details.

If you don't have copies of policies you purchased over 90 days ago, fax this letter to your agent today!

Your Business Letterhead

Date

Current Agency
P.O. Box 111
Anytown, USA 00000

Re: Policy copies for ______________ coverage

Dear Agent:

In reviewing our records, we cannot locate a copy of the above mentioned policies we hold through your agency.

Because it is vital we have such records, please assist us by faxing a copy of each declarations page to us no later than ______________. Please mail complete replacement policies to us no later than ______________.

We appreciate your effort in assisting us in maintaining complete records of our insurance program.

Sincerely,

Informed Buyer

Sample Letter L – Billing Clarification Request

To resolve accounting problems, request the statement for the shortest period of time necessary — because you want to avoid making unnecessary work for your bookkeeper. When the statement arrives, you should be able to clearly follow the transactions and see why your agency is billing you for the current balance. Make sure all your payments have been credited and inspect each charge to make sure it is correct. Any errors or discrepancies will be obvious. A call to your bookkeeper will now quickly correct any apparent error.

Your Business Letterhead

Date

Current Agency
P.O. Box 111
Anytown, USA 00000

Re: Billing Clarification

Is the billing coming from the agency or from the insurance company? Make sure you are communicating with the right office.

Dear Agent (or Customer Service Person):

We are experiencing difficulty in following the transactions leading to our current balance with your accounting department.

To help us clarify this matter, please return a statement itemizing all our transactions for the period from January 1, 19__ to January 1, 19__.

We hope the statement will display all the charges and credits to our account, so we can reconcile our records.

This correspondence is more powerful than a phone call, because it documents your concern. Written requests are paid more attention than phone calls.

Thank you for your continuing assistance with our insurance matters.

Sincerely,

Informed Buyer

Sample Letter M – Confirmation of Insured Vehicles and Equipment Request

When you want confirmation that all your vehicles and equipment are correctly insured, use this letter. Often, many change orders create a flurry of endorsements, and it pays to get a summary of your current status. See chapters 4 and 5.

Many equipment and vehicle schedules have serious errors, creating coverage gaps.

Your Business Letterhead

Date

Current Agency
P.O. Box 111
Anytown, USA 00000

Re: Vehicle and Equipment List Clarification

Dear Agent (or Customer Service Person):

Please provide us a current schedule of our insured vehicles and equipment and indicate the coverages provided for each item. We need to confirm all our vehicles and equipment are correctly scheduled and that the valuations are correct.

We appreciate your help in managing our insurance account.

Sincerely,

Informed Buyer

Sample Letter N – Problem Issues Clarification Request

Any dispute regarding valuation, cancellations, accounting, or claims, is quickly solved when you clearly understand the problem. Asking the perpetrators of the problem to document their position in writing gives them an opportunity to carefully think through the matter. They may come up with a better solution. For further discussion see Chapter 7.

Your Business Letterhead

Date

Current Agency
P.O. Box 111
Anytown, USA 00000

Re: Issue Clarification

Dear Agent (or Customer Service Person):

To improve my understanding regarding the issue of __________, would you please send us a letter clarifying your position? Your written explanation will help us understand the situation and the issues affecting it. We expect your communication will help us identify the best course of action to resolve the issue.

Thank you for your assistance in helping us resolve this situation.

Sincerely,

Informed Buyer

If you feel you are getting the runaround, this letter can be worth thousands of dollars to you.

Sample Letter O – Policy History Information Request

Completing the policy history section of the Underwriting Information Questionnaire can be a major challenge for some businesses whose records are not easily accessible. If the information is not readily available from loss runs, why not enlist your agent's help in obtaining the information? You can have your current and past agents provide the information by customizing this letter to your situation. See the Underwriting Information Questionnaire in Chapter 4.

Call ahead to see if you can get this information over the phone. Make sure this letter goes to an individual who will help.

Your Business Letterhead

Date

Current Agency
P.O. Box 111
Anytown, USA 00000

Re: Insurance History

Dear Agent (or Customer Service Person):

We are assembling our business' policy history for the past five years. Would you please help us complete our records by indicating which policies you provided during that period? We welcome any documentation you can provide — such as the name of the insurance company, policy number, premium, and expiration date for policies you provided.

Sincerely,

Informed Buyer

Sample Letter P – Workers' Compensation Open Claim Status Reports Request

Send this letter if your business is subject to an experience modification factor for workers' compensation coverage. The letter should be sent three to four months before your next calculation date, to minimize your next year's workers' compensation costs. See the workers' compensation discussion beginning in Chapter 6.

Your Business Letterhead

Date

Current Agency
P.O. Box 111
Anytown, USA 00000

Re: Workers' Compensation Open Claim Status Reports

Dear Agent:

Our records indicate our new experience modification should be calculated in the month of __________ 19__. We are endeavoring to make sure the claims reported on the Insurance Company's Unit Statistical Reports are minimal, so our resulting modification factor will be as low as possible.

Please help us obtain open claim status reports for the three years that will affect our upcoming modification calculation. We want to conduct a review of all open claims with you to close any necessary claims or reduce reserves.

We appreciate your help in working towards improving our modification factor.

Sincerely,

Informed Buyer

Mark your calendar to send this letter four months before your next experience modification calculation date. Don't let the calculation date slip past you. You could be overcharged for claims that should have been closed.

Sample Letter Q – Rented Vehicles Coverage Clarification Request

Never tolerate uncertainty whether rental vehicles are insured. If you depend on your agent to cover you, use this letter to get written confirmation that the right coverage is in place before renting a car. See the discussion in Chapter 5.

Today, too much bad advice is given regarding rental car coverage. Get the facts in writing from your agent.

Your Business Letterhead

Date

Current Agency
P.O. Box 111
Anytown, USA 00000

Re: Rented Automobile Coverage

Dear Agent:

I expect to rent a vehicle in the near future, and I need your help in deciding whether or not to purchase insurance from the car rental company. The car will be rented from _____ to _____. It will be used for ____, during this period.

Please clarify if my current coverage extends to rented vehicles and if so, identify the coverage's limitations. For instance, will my liability, comprehensive, and collision coverages apply to a vehicle I rent?

Thank you for taking the time to look into this matter. I will await your reply.

Sincerely,

Informed Buyer

Sample Letter R – Late Payment Notification to Agent

When you make a late payment, communicate this to your agent. Typically, your agent will get a copy of the late notices and wonder if a call to you is appropriate. This letter will be appreciated and gives the agent some responsibility to call you in the event of a lapse in coverage.

Your Business Letterhead

Date

Current Agency
P.O. Box 111
Anytown, USA 00000

Re: Insurance Premium Payment
Policy # ________________

Dear Agent:

This is to let you know our payment in the amount of $_________ is being sent for the above mentioned policy on __________. We share your concern that our policies stay in force, and are making every effort to see the premiums are paid on a timely basis. Please contact the insurance company to make sure coverage will remain continuously in force, and telephone us if we must act to prevent a lapse.

We appreciate your assistance in seeing us through this period, when our premium is being paid so close to the deadline.

Sincerely,

Informed Buyer

Some companies will deposit your late check and refuse to reinstate your policy. Later, they issue you a check for any refund due. A phone call from your agent to the insurance company can win the reinstatement and save you from having to purchase your insurance all over again.

Sample Letter S – General Coverage Open Claim Status Reports Request

Your business may have open claims that adversely affect renewal rates. An open claim is assigned a monetary reserve — an estimate of the expected loss. Reserves are often higher than the final cost of the closed claim. If you have open claims, send this letter to win the attention you need to minimize reserves. Make sure you get the requested status reports, then discuss the claim with the adjuster to help close it. If the claim won't close, ask the adjuster to reduce the reserve. Make sure any quoting agents learn of any improvements you achieve on your open claims. See chapters 4 and 10.

Many open claims can be closed after a discussion with your claims adjuster.

Your Business Letterhead

Date

Current Agency
P.O. Box 111
Anytown, USA 00000

Re: Open Claim Status Reports

Dear Agent:

To minimize our outstanding losses in time for our coming policy renewal, we want to close any open claims and set reserves as low as possible.

Please help us obtain open claim status reports for the three years that will affect our coming renewal. We appreciate your help in working towards reducing our premiums.

Sincerely,

Informed Buyer

Sample Letter T – Send Quotes 30 Days before Expiration Date Request

Send this letter to all quoting agents four to five weeks before your expiration date. Set your quote deadline for at least two weeks before your expiration date. Refer to Chapter 10 for discussion.

Your Business Letterhead

Date

Current Agency
P.O. Box 111
Anytown, USA 00000

Re: Pending Quote

Dear Agent:

Thank you for your efforts in obtaining quotes for our soon-to-expire insurance program. Please remind the underwriters we will need the quotes by ____________________, for decision-making purposes.

Should any additional information be needed to complete the quote, please let us know.

Sincerely,

Informed Buyer

To avoid being cornered into last minute comparisons and decisions at the expiration date, assert a sensible quote deadline.

Sample Letter U – Commercial General Liability Coverage Rating Information Request

Send this letter if you are unclear about your general liability insurance rates. This will protect you from painful surprises at the year-end policy audit, or help make sure you get any refunds due to you. Refer to chapters 5, 9, and 10 for discussions.

When you get these rates, your cost accounting can be much more accurate, and you can better anticipate any final audit billing or refund.

Your Business Letterhead

Date

Current Agency
P.O. Box 111
Anytown, USA 00000

Re: Commercial General Liability Rating Information

Dear Agent:

Please help us understand how our commercial general liability is rated, so we can better anticipate the policy year-end audit adjustment. We need to know the actual rates and the basis to which they are applied.

Thank you for taking the time to describe the rating information, so we can avoid surprises at the policy year-end audit.

Sincerely,

Informed Buyer

Sample Letter V – Clarification of Payroll Exclusion Request

Send this letter if your general liability rates are based on payroll. See discussion in Chapter 10.

Your Business Letterhead

Date

Current Agency
P.O. Box 111
Anytown, USA 00000

Re: Exclusion of General Liability Payroll from Basis for Owners

Dear Agent:

I understand our commercial general liability rates are based on payroll and a fixed amount of payroll is assigned to owners, officers, or partners. I believe the payroll assigned can be excluded from the rating basis under certain conditions.

Please help me determine what payroll will be excluded for our owners, officers, or partners. I believe owners, partners, or officers may be excluded when they are involved only in administrative or sales duties.

I understand you may have to contact the audit department of our insurance company to get these facts.

Thank you for helping to clarify this matter and avoid misunderstandings at the year-end audit.

Sincerely,

Informed Buyer

Too many businesses have paid for owner's payroll when they shouldn't have. This letter helps you avoid overpaying possibly thousands of dollars.

Sample Letter W – Coverage Change Request

Send this letter to document your request for coverage changes. Make sure you discuss the letter with your agent, to ensure your request is received and is being honored. See Chapter 5 for further discussion.

Verbally ordering coverage changes is dangerous, because your change may not happen. Always get written verification of coverage changes, or use this letter to create your own proof.

Your Business Letterhead

Date

Current Agency
P.O. Box 111
Anytown, USA 00000

Re: Coverage Change Request

Dear Agent:

Effective ________________, please make the following change(s) to our policy:

____

____

Please send us confirmation of this change and call us for any information you may need.

Sincerely,

Informed Buyer

Sample Letter X – Service Schedule Checklist Request

Use this letter to introduce the Service Schedule Checklist to your current agent, or quoting agents. Refer to Chapter 10 for a full discussion.

Your Business Letterhead

Date

Current Agency
P.O. Box 111
Anytown, USA 00000

Dear Agent:

In our efforts to continue improving the quality of our insurance purchasing program, we are adopting the enclosed Service Schedule Checklist. We hope this will help optimize the services we receive from our insurance vendors, and avoid missed opportunities to reduce costs.

Please review the checklist, and indicate the services we can reasonably expect from your agency. We look forward to receiving your completed checklist. Let's discuss any areas that may need improvement, and mark our calendars to make sure no opportunity escapes our attention.

Sincerely,

Informed Buyer

Enclosure: Service Schedule Checklist

Never hesitate to request excellent service. The very survival of your company is at stake, and you are the one who pays top dollar for the service.

Notes

Glossary

account A term used by many insurance people to refer to insurance clients.

accounts receivable coverage This coverage compensates you for losses due to the destruction of your records, resulting in your inability to collect receivables. The destruction of the records must be caused by a covered peril like a fire, a tornado, or an earthquake.

actual cash value A method of property valuation, which is defined as replacement cost (at the time of loss) minus depreciation.

advertising liability Liability from copyright infringement and misappropriation of advertising ideas.

agency bill A premium collection method where an insurance company bills an agency for your insurance premium, and an agency bills you for the premium. Ultimately you owe an agency the premium.

agent For the purpose of this book, an entity licensed to transact insurance business for insurance companies with whom it has contracts. An agent is legally viewed as representing the insurance company in all its dealings with both the insurance buyer and the insurance company.

agent-broker of record assignment letter A letter that assigns your selected broker or agent exclusive rights to act as your agent or broker with a named insurance company. The newly chosen agent or broker is empowered by this letter to obtain information about your policies, and make coverage changes for you. This is a convenient method of changing agents or brokers.

agreed amount An alternative to having coinsurance in a property insurance policy. When the agreed amount method is used, the value of an insured item is agreed upon between an insurance company and an insured, usually at policy inception. All covered losses are paid in full, subject to the settlement clause, whether actual cash value or replacement cost, and the coverage limit of the policy.

all risk coverage A misleading term used to describe property insurance special form, which provides coverage for risks of physical loss not specifically excluded.

all states endorsement A workers' compensation endorsement adding coverage for employees temporarily working out of your home state, but not in a monopolistic fund state.

appraisal A method of claims dispute resolution for property valuation issues. Typically, you and an insurance company each select an appraiser and pay the appraisers' expenses. The two appraisers select a referee appraiser. The agreement of any two appraisers as to valuation is binding. The expense of the referee is divided equally between the disputing parties.

arbitration A method of: 1) resolving disputes, particularly with valuation issues in claims, where a third party is empowered to decide a fair settlement, in lieu of turning to the courts; 2) settling an uninsured motorist claim dispute, similar to appraisal, specified in an automobile insurance policy.

audit The process of obtaining factual information regarding your business' payrolls, receipts, and sales, for premium determination purposes. Audits are called voluntary when the information is requested by mail. Auditors also visit business premises to review financial information — including financial statements, tax returns, payroll records, and sales figures.

audit billing A billing accompanied by an audit statement, itemizing payroll or revenues on which the billing is based. Frequently, this is a final audit, summarizing your full year's figures.

binder A document prepared by an insurance agent or company to evidence temporary insurance coverage that is in effect until the policy can be delivered. The binders are usually only valid for a maximum of 60 to 90 days, depending on your state's laws.

bodily injury A term used to describe physical injury to humans, including death.

bodily injury liability insurance An insurance coverage protecting against losses from lawsuits and judgments against you for bodily injuries you have caused to a third party. Normally, you must be found legally liable for causing the injuries.

broker An entity licensed to transact insurance business, legally viewed as representing an insured client, rather than an insurance company.

business insurance The term used in this book to refer to all coverages purchased by a business to transfer its risks to insurance companies. This includes commercial auto, property, liability, inland marine, workers' compensation, boiler and machinery, crime, farm, and umbrella. This book does not cover life, disability, group medical, or employee benefits issues. The risks associated with your business are usually excluded by your personal policies, such as homeowners, personal auto, and personal umbrellas.

business interruption coverage Coverage designed to compensate you for lost profits and continuing expenses that result from interruption of your business operations due to a covered peril such as fire, lightning, or explosion that causes damage to an insured's buildings or property.

business personal property Your inventory, furniture, fixtures, stock, and tenant improvements and betterments. Coverage may include property of others if it is temporarily in the insured's possession.

cancellation The termination of insurance coverage as a result of either an insured's request, or an action of the insurance company prior to a normal expiration date. When canceled by an insurance company, the company must send you a formal notice specifying the date and time that the coverage terminates and the reason for the action.

claims made liability policy A commercial liability policy that triggers coverage of claims based on the date the claim is made (reported) to you or an insurance company. Commercial general liability policies are usually written on an occurrence basis, rather than a claims made basis. In an occurrence policy, the trigger for coverage is the date when the loss occurred.

coinsurance clause Used in property insurance policies to encourage you to insure to an amount equal to or greater than a set percentage, usually 80 or 90 percent of the property's actual cash value or replacement cost at the time of loss. If you comply, losses are paid in full; if not, you become a coinsurer and the loss payment is reduced by application of a penalty. The penalty is discussed in Chapter 5.

collision coverage Insurance applying to physical damage to vehicles caused by collisions or upset — which is a rollover of the vehicle.

combined single limit This term is used to describe the liability coverage limit that combines both bodily injury and property damage into one aggregate amount. Another common method of coverage is split limits when bodily injury and property damage each have their own limit of coverage. Examples of the appearance of combined single limit are $100,000 versus split limits of $50,000/100,000/50,000.

commercial general liability A policy protecting you against monetary damages from suits, as a result of bodily injury, property damage, or both, to third parties, for which you are legally liable as a result of your business operations. The policy includes coverage for defense, as well as for claims settlement.

commercial lines insurance Another phrase for business insurance. See: business insurance.

commission Money paid to an insurance agency by an insurance company, usually a percentage of your premium, to compensate for the efforts expended in selling you insurance and serving your insurance needs.

company appointments A contractual agreement between an agency and insurance company that empowers the agency to bind coverage and transact insurance for the insurance company.

completed operation Work that you or your employees have completed and you have permanently left the work site.

composite rate The price per $100 or $1,000 of insurance coverage (either property or liability) used for calculating the insurance premium. This occurs when the rate for various kinds of insurance have been combined into the one rate figure. The rate figure is multiplied by the exposure base — such as sales, payroll, or property values — to determine the premium.

comprehensive coverage Insurance that applies to physical damage to vehicles, caused by perils other than collision or upset. Some exclusions do apply to this coverage, which is very broad in its scope. Usually includes losses involving fire, theft, vandalism, glass breakage, earthquake, flood, and collisions with animals.

contingent business interruption Coverage designed to compensate you for lost profits and continuing expenses that result from interruption of your business operations, caused by an insured peril — such as fire, explosion, tornado — to one of your customer's or supplier's buildings or business personal property.

continuing expenses The expenses you must continue to pay — such as leases, payroll to key personnel, and taxes — even when the business is shut down.

coverage checklists The standardized coverage presentation designed to simplify coverage comparisons. In this book, you are provided with the Business Insurance Coverage Checklist and the Workers' Compensation Coverage Checklist.

covered/insured peril The perils of loss you are protected against by an insurance policy. Examples of perils are fire, lightning, theft, vandalism, and the threat of a lawsuit.

customized vehicles Vehicle modifications, unlike original factory installations, are usually excluded unless specifically added for coverage. For example, a truck body with special racks welded on to hold machinery is considered a customized item.

death benefit The amount of money a surviving spouse or child receives from workers' compensation insurance after the death of a spouse or parent from a work-related cause.

deductible A specified amount you pay of any loss, over which an insurance company pays the rest of the loss, up to the limit of a policy.

defense cost The costs to defend you in a lawsuit for either bodily injury or property damage; usually, an unlimited amount of coverage is available. These costs include attorney fees, court costs, taxes, and fees assessed against you by the court.

deposit premium The amount of premium paid at policy inception, held through the policy year and credited at a final audit.

direct bill A premium collection method where the insurance company bills you directly for your insurance premiums. You ultimately owe the insurance company the money.

direct writer Any company soliciting insurance without using an agent or broker, usually, by direct mail or telemarketing techniques.

discrimination/wrongful termination Unfair treatment of the general public and improper dismissal of employees. These acts are frequently excluded by commercial general liability policies.

drive-other-car coverage An endorsement to commercial auto insurance that provides coverage for named employees who do not own a personal vehicle and use company-provided vehicles for their personal use.

earned premium Part of the premium that an insurance company is entitled to keep after coverages have already been provided.

employer's nonowned auto liability Commercial auto bodily injury and property damage liability insurance coverage provided to employers for injuries to third parties, caused by employees driving their personal vehicles in the course of company business.

employer's stop gap coverage Usually, an endorsement to the commercial general liability policy covering lawsuits from employees or their families, as a result of work-related injuries. This coverage is only needed in the six monopolistic fund states of Nevada, North Dakota, Ohio, Washington, West Virginia, and Wyoming, where workers' compensation policies do not cover employer's liability.

endorsement An amendment to an insurance policy to make some kind of change to a policy.

errors and omissions coverage Professional liability coverage purchased by insurance agents and brokers to defend and indemnify for losses caused by an agent's or broker's negligence in the rendering of their services. See: professional liability insurance.

estimated cost new As requested on vehicle schedules, the vehicle's cost when new is used for premium determination purposes for comprehensive and collision coverages. This is not a coverage limit.

experience modification A number representing the safety of an employer, calculated by the insurance rating bureau. This number is usually between 0.5 and 2.5. The number 1.0 is considered to be the normal range; numbers below 1.0 represent lower losses than normal, while numbers above 1.0 represent higher than normal losses. The experience modification is a factor applied to the basic manual rates to calculate an individual employer's premium. For further discussion, see Chapter 6.

expiration date A commonly used term referring to your policy anniversary date. The last day of coverage provided by your policy. Property casualty policies do not have grace periods. For information on choosing your expiration date, refer to Chapter 4.

exposures The term referring to potential areas of financial loss. For example, property loss exposures presented by the ownership of a building. If the building is damaged or destroyed, the business will lose the value of the buildings' assets.

extended discovery The time after the expiration of a claims made liability policy, when claims may still be presented and honored.

extra expense A coverage that reimburses you for the expenses you would not have incurred had a loss not occurred. These expenses include temporarily using other locations, equipment, and services during the period of restoring business operations after a loss caused by a covered peril, such as a fire.

fire legal liability Coverage for fire and smoke damage to premises you lease, caused by your negligence. See: waiver of subrogation.

first dollar defense A provision in a liability policy that provides defense costs without an insured having to pay any part of the costs; no deductible applies.

flat cancellation A policy cancellation method that cancels a policy from its inception date (the very beginning). It is as though the policy never existed, thus you owe no earned premium.

flat charge This term indicates the policy premium is not subject to audit, but is fixed at the inception of the policy.

forms The insurance policy and endorsements that can be attached to the policy. Frequently, these forms need approval by the state department of insurance before an insurance company can use them.

functional replacement cost A method of property valuation that permits replacement of damaged items with new items that utilize more modern technology, but perform the same functions as the damaged items — such as, replacement of an old printing press with a new modern printing press, instead of the older, hard-to-find model.

general aggregate The maximum amount a commercial general liability policy will pay for claims in any twelve month period, normally the time from policy inception to policy expiration. The only exceptions to this are products and completed operations claims that have a separate aggregate.

gross vehicle weight The legally licensed, laden weight of a vehicle, used in commercial auto rating, often found on a vehicle registration form.

hard insurance market A condition caused by insurance companies lacking sufficient capital to accept new business. Sometimes this causes a sharp rise in pricing and coverage availability diminishes. Compare: soft market.

hired auto liability Automobile liability coverage extending to vehicles your business leases, rents, or borrows from others, but not from your employees.

host liquor liability Liquor liability coverage for those businesses who do not manufacture, distribute, sell, or serve alcohol. This covers losses from occasional serving of liquor and subsequent bodily injury and property damage losses caused by intoxication of the persons served.

"if any" An expression in insurance applications or policies describing an exposure base, such as payroll, when coverage is desired and the exposure is minimal. Typically found in liability insurance.

incumbent broker A term describing the agent-broker currently controlling the insurance for an insured, sometimes termed the writing agent-broker.

indemnify A fundamental principle of insurance, meaning: 1) to make an insured whole after a loss; 2) to make an insured as he or she was immediately before the loss occurred.

insurance agency profile The form provided in this book that you can use to obtain crucial information about insurance agencies for comparison purposes.

insurance carrier A term commonly used to refer to insurance companies.

insurance specifications 1) The information you provide on the Underwriting Information Questionnaire and the coverage checklists. 2) The guidelines developed to tell an insurance agent, broker, or company what a business owner needs or wants insured and the amounts and types of coverage the business needs.

insured perils See: covered perils.

Jones Act A federal law that mandates benefits for bodily injuries to regular crew members of vessels operating in navigable waters.

liability insurance An insurance policy that protects you against monetary losses due to liability from your negligent acts or failures to act.

limit The dollar amount of insurance coverage provided by a policy.

line A single type of insurance, such as auto, property, or inland marine.

liquor liability Liability coverage for a business that manufactures, distributes, sells, or serves alcohol, for losses stemming from intoxication of its customers. Compare: host liquor liability.

loss control inspector The insurance company representative sent to your premises to evaluate the potential for bodily injuries or property losses from your operations and premises, including management's attitude toward safety and loss prevention.

loss of refrigeration A coverage for losses caused by damage to refrigeration units from a covered peril that results in damage to refrigerated items — such as food in a cooler cabinet that spoils when the refrigeration unit is hit by lightning.

loss prevention Actions taken by an insured to prevent either bodily injury or property losses from occurring, such as cutting dry weeds around a building to reduce the potential for fires.

loss runs Reports generated by insurance companies displaying losses incurred — including dates, categories of losses, causes of losses, and the amounts paid or reserved. Sometimes premiums paid are also reported. The reports may be generated annually, quarterly, or monthly depending on the size of the premium.

malpractice insurance See: professional liability insurance.

marketplace All the insurance companies willing and able to insure a business.

market value The current selling price of a property item in your local area that is frequently used as a reference point to establish actual cash value. You will not find this term used or defined in most insurance policies. Sometimes inland marine, auto, and property forms use the term.

material misrepresentation False information presented to insurance providers to induce them to offer coverage, which the providers may otherwise have refused to insure, at a reduced price. Material misrepresentation can result in your coverage being voided, rescinded, or canceled. Always carefully present the facts about your operation.

medical payments (auto) Coverage provided to pay medical bills for injuries to occupants of an insured vehicle, regardless of the driver's liability for the injuries.

medical payments (premises) Coverage provided to pay medical bills for injuries to individuals other than owners, their employees, and their tenants, regardless of the owner's fault.

minimum earned premium The minimum premium an insurance company keeps regardless of audit results at policy expiration. If the policy cancels prior to an expiration date, an insurance company keeps at least the minimum earned premium. In some cases you may benefit from a prorated refund due to a cancellation, or you may get a refund after short-rate cancellation charges.

mono-line insurance policy An insurance policy covering only one line of insurance, such as auto.

monopolistic fund state One of the six states (Nevada, North Dakota, Ohio, Washington, West Virginia, Wyoming) where only the state government is allowed to sell workers' compensation insurance.

multi-line insurance policy An insurance policy covering two or more lines of insurance, such as auto and property.

named perils A method of providing property insurance coverage where the perils insured against are named in the policy. Losses caused by perils not named or specified are not covered. See: specified perils coverage.

no-fault automobile insurance A coverage mandated by the passage of a no-fault insurance law in some states. Usually this only covers bodily injury claims to people in your automobile. It does not cover the automobile. It replaces medical payments coverage and adds loss of income coverage, with death and survivor benefits. These benefits are available regardless of fault — who caused the accident.

nonowned auto liability Auto liability insurance coverage provided to employers if employees or others drive their own vehicles in the course of company business.

off-premises power failure Coverage for property losses resulting from power outages caused off-premises by insured perils. For example, lightning that strikes a transformer not on your premises could cause your heat to fail, thus causing frozen and burst water pipes.

overinsured This occurs when a business purchases property coverages with limits greater than the value of the item insured.

owner's and contractor's protective Protection provided to owners or general contractors for property damage or bodily injury caused by contractors or subcontractors performing work for an owner or general contractor.

peak season A property coverage endorsement that provides an increase in the total coverage limit for a set time period, usually 90 days or less. If you feel a need for peak season coverage, discuss your fluctuating values in depth with your insurance professional.

perils Things that cause a reduction of quality, quantity, or value of assets. Fire, lightning, theft, and vandalism are examples of perils frequently insured against by property insurance. The covered peril in liability insurance is the threat of a lawsuit.

personal injury A legal term for actions, normally including libel, slander, false arrest, wrongful eviction, defamation of character, wrongful entry, invasion of privacy, and malicious prosecution. Frequently, attorneys refer to personal injury instead of bodily injury. Sometimes, umbrella insurance policies will use this terminology instead of bodily injury because the term, personal injury, is broader in scope.

personal injury and advertising liability A legal term for actions, normally including libel, slander, false arrest, wrongful eviction, defamation of character, wrongful entry, invasion of privacy, and malicious prosecution. Frequently, attorneys will refer to personal injury and advertising liability instead of bodily injury. Sometimes umbrella insurance policies will use this terminology instead of bodily injury because the term, personal injury, is broader in scope.

personal property Business personal property refers to a business' inventory, furniture, fixtures, stock, and tenant improvements and betterments. Coverage can include property of others.

pollution Damage to the environment, normally to land, water, or air. The damages and cost of cleanup are normally excluded from coverage by all insurance policies.

premium The dollar cost of insurance, or the money you pay for insurance.

products Those items that an insured manufactures, sells, or distributes.

products and completed operations Liability coverage that pays for bodily injury or property damage, resulting from products you sell or completed operations you have performed. For example, if a wooden picnic table you manufacture and sell collapses and injures those seated on it, then your products liability coverage will respond. For completed operations, assume you built a deck addition onto a home. After its completion, the deck collapses and causes injury to people standing on it. Completed operations coverage will respond to any subsequent lawsuits for bodily injury or property damage.

professional liability insurance Liability insurance providing coverage for damages resulting from improperly rendering or failing to render professional services. Malpractice insurance is the term for coverage for bodily injury caused by the medical profession. Errors and omissions coverage is used for attorneys, accountants, insurance agents, and other professions and positions that have professional exposure, but no bodily injury exposure.

property damage liability insurance Liability insurance coverage for damage to the property of others, for which you are legally liable, which is not in your care, custody, and control. Property damage includes loss of use of damaged property. For example, assume you splatter paint on a car next to the building you are painting. The damage to the car will be a property damage liability claim.

proposals The formal presentations of insurance price quotes and coverages provided.

pro rata cancellation Cancellation of insurance coverage, whereby the insurance company retains a portion of the premium based on a number of days the coverage was in force.

punitive damages Amounts awarded to plaintiffs that are payable by a defendant as punishment for the defendant's actions, which are so heinous, the court wants to make the individual an example to society. These amounts are awarded in excess of general damages and specific damages. See Chapter 5 for further discussion.

quotes Estimates of insurance policy premiums, often generated in agencies or brokerages, that, normally, can only be confirmed upon receipt of a policy.

registered letter Service provided by the United States Postal Service that documents and proves correspondence was received by an addressee.

renewal A term used to describe the policy intended to replace your expiring policy. The renewal date refers to the date your current policy expires.

rental reimbursement Coverage intended to pay for the cost of rented vehicles for automobiles temporarily removed from service due to covered losses. Typically, a daily maximum limit is specified for the rental reimbursement for a specified number of days.

replacement cost A method of property valuation, which is defined as replacement cost (at the time of loss) with no depreciation considered. This is one of the most desirable valuation methods for property policies.

reporting form Property insurance coverage that requires periodic (quarterly, monthly, or semiannually) reporting of insurable values to an insurance company. Often used when a business' personal property values frequently fluctuate.

rescind The act of voiding insurance coverage; as though a policy never existed and coverage was not provided.

retro date In claims made liability forms, any occurrences that give rise to loss and occur prior to this date are excluded from coverage, regardless of when the occurrences are presented.

risk management A process of determining the level of acceptable loss an entity is willing to tolerate. The process begins by an identification of potential loss exposures and various alternatives on how to prevent or minimize the losses. Next, the best alternative is selected and implemented, and its outcome is monitored. If the desired outcome is not achieved, the process is repeated until the acceptable level of losses is achieved.

risk manager One who performs risk management. Frequently, in the insurance industry, this person only deals with insurable exposures of loss (fire, explosion, and lawsuits). A risk manager does not deal with all the possible loss exposures faced by a business, such as economic depressions and recessions.

self-insured retention (SIR) The dollar amount of losses an insured must handle completely without the assistance of an insurance company. Once a loss exceeds this amount, an insurance company will become involved. Compare and contrast to a deductible in Chapter 5.

short rate cancellation Cancellation of insurance coverage when the premium an insurance company retains is based proportionate to the number of days coverage was in force. An additional amount, typically 10%, is retained by a company as penalty for the premature cancellation of a policy.

soft market A condition where insurance premiums are lowered and the availability of insurance high. Insurance companies are anxious for business and good deals are abundant. Compare: hard market.

specified causes of loss A form of physical damage coverage for vehicles that usually provides coverage for fire, lightning, theft, vandalism, flood, earthquake, windstorm, hail, explosion, and some perils of transportation. The alternative coverage is called comprehensive coverage, which does not list the perils it covers, but covers everything it does not exclude.

specified perils A method of providing property insurance coverage where the insured perils are named in a policy. Any loss that occurs from a peril not named or specified is not paid. See: named perils.

tenant improvements and betterments A value you should include in your total business personal property for the labor and materials used in improving your landlord's building — including remodeling, carpeting, shelving, and painting. Your lease may specify improvements for which you are responsible to provide property coverage.

territory This is the geographic territory where insurance coverage from a policy applies. If a loss occurs outside the territory or if a suit is brought against an insured outside the territory, the insurance policy will not cover the loss. Normally this is defined in the policy as the United States, its territory or possessions, Puerto Rico, and Canada.

towing An optional auto coverage that provides limited coverage for covered autos that become disabled and require towing or on-the-road repairs. The coverage pays for towing or repair, minus any parts subject to the limit of coverage.

underinsured motorist Someone driving an automobile without sufficient insurance coverage in force to pay for damages that individual causes to a third party by bodily injury or damage to the third party's property.

underwriters Employees of insurance companies who select risks to insure so their company can make a profit. They determine whether to quote your insurance and at what price. They make their decisions based on information they receive from agents, brokers, inspectors, and claims people.

Underwriting Information Questionnaire The standardized form to help you accumulate and present necessary information about your premises and operations for the purpose of obtaining insurance quotes. An automated version of this form is available in this book's companion software — *The Insurance Assistant.* For more information on this software, contact The Oasis Press.

uninsured motorist Someone driving an automobile without proper insurance coverage in force as required by state law. Refer to Chapter 5 for an in-depth discussion.

USL&H coverage An endorsement extending workers' compensation coverage to include the benefits mandated by the United States Longshoreman's and Harborworker's Compensation Act. Many risk managers will suggest you add this coverage on an "if any" basis, when there is any possibility your employees work near or on a dock, wharf, or ship.

valuable papers coverage A coverage for manuscripts, blueprints, plans, contracts, specifications, and any documents that will cost money to replace in the event of destruction due to a fire or other covered peril. The amount of coverage should be the cost to reproduce or replace the documents and the information contained in the documents.

voluntary compensation coverage An endorsement to workers' compensation coverage that provides coverage for workers that are normally exempt from coverage. Providing coverage for them on a voluntary basis may avoid litigation under employer's liability coverage.

waiver of subrogation A commonly used clause in leases between landlords and tenants that releases the right to collect from each other for damage to one another's property. The waiver usually relieves a tenant from the need to purchase higher limits of fire legal liability coverage.

worldwide coverage An expansion of the geographic territory where an insurance policy coverage applies to encompass the entire world. Inland marine, ocean marine, homeowners, and dwelling policies routinely provide coverage on a worldwide basis for either all or part of their coverages. For liability policies, products liability can be provided either on a limited worldwide coverage or on true worldwide coverage.

Index

A

B

C

SmartStart
Your
(State)
Business

Successful Business Library

A Complete Franchise Solution.

From The Oasis Press®

Understand the nuances of running a franchise or turning your existing business into a successful franchise model. Each of these books offer unparalleled expertise in helping you make the most of operating a franchise in today's marketplace...

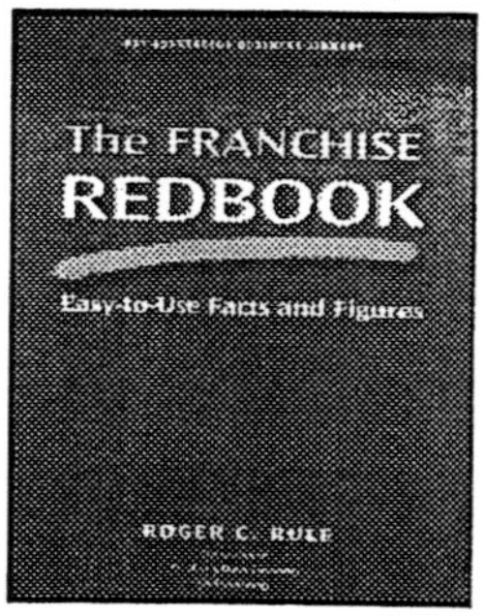

The Franchise Redbook

Easy-to-Use Facts and Figures

ROGER C. RULE

An accurate and user-friendly reference that will help determine your best franchise opportunity. While there are several other reference books available, *The Franchise Redbook* is up-to-date, comprehensive, and by far the easiest to use to determine your franchise options. The organized listings make it easy to weigh the pros and cons of the franchises within your area of interest. Ideal for selecting a franchise, doing market and comparative analysis, preparing a marketing or business plan, preparing contact lists, or doing any other research on franchises.

PAPERBACK $34.95

ISBN 1-55571-484-6
750 PAGES

No Money Down Financing for Franchising

ROGER C. RULE

An essential resource for securing finances and building the foundation to a winning franchise. Broken down into three logical progressions, this book explores every resource available for franchise financing, including many methods that require no money down and explains the vital points that will prepare you in obtaining these goals.

PAPERBACK $19.95

ISBN 1-55571-462-5
240 PAGES

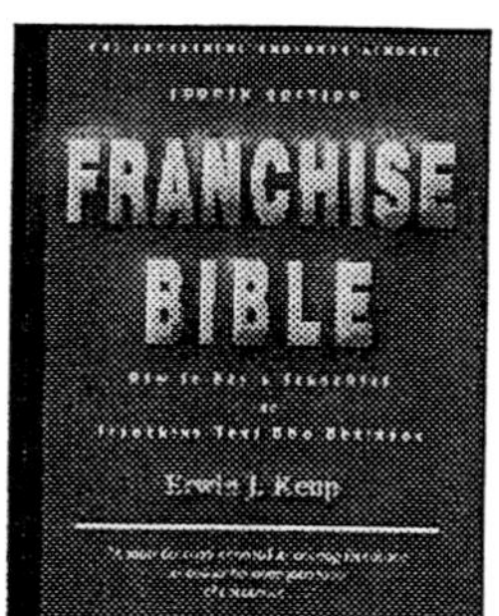

Franchise Bible, 4th edition

How to Buy A Franchise or Franchise Your Own Business

ERWIN J. KEUP

If you are thinking about acquiring a franchise or franchising your own business, this indispensable and recognized guide will tell you how to do it, and save you time and money in the process. You'll learn the advantages and disadvantages of the franchise system and familiarize yourself with the terms and concepts that are essential in operating a franchise today. A recognized, must-read if you are interested in the world of franchising.

PAPERBACK $27.95

ISBN 1-55571-526-5
274 PAGES

TO ORDER CALL 1-800-228-2275 OR VISIT YOUR FAVORITE BOOKSTORE

From The Leading Publisher of Small Business Information

Books that save you time and money.

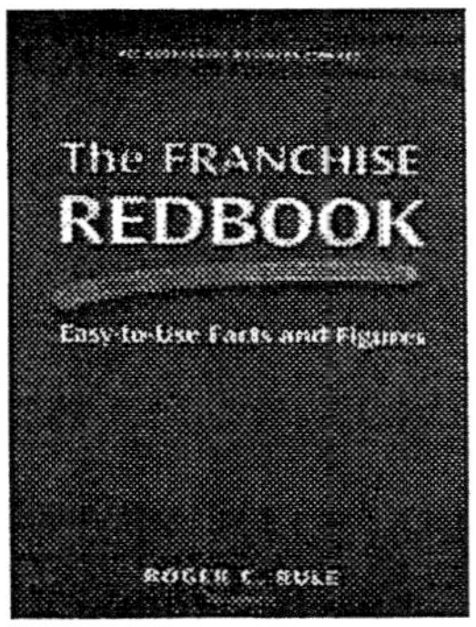

The Franchise Redbook
Paperback: $34.95
Pages: 750
ISBN: 1-55571-484-6

An accurate and user-friendly reference that will help determine your best franchise opportunity. While there are several other reference books available, *The Franchise Redbook* is up-to-date, comprehensive, and by far the easiest to use to determine your franchise options.

What's It Worth?
Paperback: $22.95
Pages: 234
ISBN: 1-55571-504-4

Determine what your business or investment is really worth. Whether you're buying or selling a business or franchise, this unique guide will quickly show you how to get the best deal. This book is ideal for anyone wanting to purchase a new business, to establish a fair selling price for a going business, or simply to have a better understanding of a professional appraiser's process.

No Money Down Financing for Franchising
Paperback: $19.95
Pages: 240
ISBN: 1-55571-462-5

Explores every source of financing available for franchising, including many ways that require no money down. Reviews the preliminaries of financing, rating your credit, developing financial statements and understanding the necessary investment requirements.

The Rule Book of Business Plans for Startups
Paperback: $18.95
Pages: 338
ISBN: 1-55571-519-2

Business plans have become a virtual prerequisite to gaining financing as well as for effectively managing most businesses. *The Rule Book of Business Plans for Startups* presents each step in business plan development in a logical, straightforward manner, with numerous examples and forms that are adaptable to most new ventures.

ALL MAJOR CREDIT CARDS ACCEPTED

CALL TO PLACE AN ORDER
— or —
TO RECEIVE A FREE CATALOG
1-800-228-2275

International Orders **(541) 245-6502** ***Fax Orders*** **(541) 245-6505**
Web site **http://www.psi-research.com** ***Email*** **sales@psi-research.com**

PSI Research P.O. Box 3727 Central Point, Oregon 97502 U.S.A.

From The Leading Publisher of Small Business Information

Books that save you time and money.

Prospecting for Gold
Paperback: 14.95

Pages: 150
ISBN: 1-55571-483-8

A hands-on book that gives you specific, practical ideas for building and implementing a sales plan, from personal assessment and goal setting to 101 ideas for prospecting new sales sources.

Business Owner's Guide to Accounting & Bookkeeping
Paperback: $19.95

Pages: 184
ISBN: 1-55571-381-5

Makes understanding the economics of your business simple. Explains the basic accounting principles that relate to any business. Step-by-step instructions for generating accounting statements and interpreting them, spotting errors, and recognizing warning signs, Discusses how creditors view financial statements.

Connecting Online
Paperback: 21.95

Pages: 450
ISBN: 1-55571-403-X

"The authors' combined expertise in technology and public relations have led to a complete reference for anyone who is interested in promoting a positive image on the Internet."

— David Siegel, Author, Creating Killer Web

Before You Go Into Business Read This
Paperback: 17.95

Pages: 208
ISBN: 1-55571-481-1

Ensures you that the simple things are kept simple, and that the complex things are made simple. It is designed to give the average entrepreneur basic definitions of terms and conditions in industry, and the general concepts of running a business.

ALL MAJOR CREDIT CARDS ACCEPTED

CALL TO PLACE AN ORDER — or — TO RECEIVE A FREE CATALOG 1-800-228-2275

International Orders **(541) 479-9464** ***Fax Orders*** **(541) 476-1479**
Web site **http://www.psi-research.com** ***Email*** **info@psi-research.com**

PSI Research P.O. Box 3727 Central Point, Oregon 97502 U.S.A.

HOW TO ORDER

Mail: Send this completed order form and a check, money order or credit card information to: PSI Research/The Oasis Press®, P.O. Box 3727, Central Point, Oregon 97502-0032

Fax: Available 24 hours a day, 7 days a week at 1-541-245-6505

Email: info@psi-research.com (Please include a phone number, should we need to contact you.)

Web: Purchase any of our products online at our Website at http://www.psi-research.com/oasis/

Inquiries and International Orders: Please call 1-541-245-6502

Indicate the quantity and price of the titles you would like:

TITLE	BINDER ISBN	PAPER ISBN	BINDER	PAPERBACK	QTY.	TOTAL
Advertising Without An Agency		1-55571-429-3		□ 19.95		
Before You Go Into Business Read This		1-55571-481-1		□ 17.95		
Bottom Line Basics	1-55571-329-7 (B)	1-55571-330-0 (P)	□ 39.95	□ 19.95		
BusinessBasics		1-55571-430-7		□ 16.95		
The Business Environmental Handbook	1-55571-304-1 (B)	1-55571-163-4 (P)	□ 39.95	□ 19.95		
Business Owner's Guide to Accounting and Bookkeeping		1-55571-381-5		□ 19.95		
businessplan.com		1-55571-455-2		□ 19.95		
Buyer's Guide to Business Insurance	1-55571-310-6 (B)	1-55571-162-6 (P)	□ 39.95	□ 19.95		
California Corporation Formation Package		1-55571-464-1 (P)		□ 29.95		
Collection Techniques for a Small Business	1-55571-312-2 (B)	1-55571-171-5 (P)	□ 39.95	□ 19.95		
College Entrepreneur Handbook		1-55571-503-6		□ 16.95		
A Company Policy & Personnel Workbook	1-55571-364-5 (B)	1-55571-486-2 (P)	□ 49.95	□ 29.95		
Company Relocation Handbook	1-55571-091-3 (B)	1-55571-092-1 (P)	□ 39.95	□ 19.95		
CompControl	1-55571-356-4 (B)	1-55571-355-6 (P)	□ 39.95	□ 19.95		
Complete Book of Business Forms		1-55571-107-3		□ 19.95		
Connecting Online		1-55571-403-X		□ 21.95		
Customer Engineering	1-55571-360-2 (B)	1-55571-359-9 (P)	□ 39.95	□ 19.95		
Delivering Legendary Customer Service		1-55571-520-6 (P)		□ 14.95		
Develop and Market Your Creative Ideas		1-55571-383-1		□ 15.95		
Developing International Markets		1-55571-433-1		□ 19.95		
Doing Business in Russia		1-55571-375-0		□ 19.95		
Draw the Line		1-55571-370-X		□ 17.95		
The Essential Corporation Handbook		1-55571-342-4		□ 21.95		
Essential Limited Liability Company Handbook	1-55571-362-9 (B)	1-55571-361-0 (P)	□ 39.95	□ 21.95		
Export Now	1-55571-192-8 (B)	1-55571-167-7 (P)	□ 39.95	□ 24.95		
Financial Decisionmaking		1-55571-435-8		□ 19.95		
Financial Management Techniques	1-55571-116-2 (B)	1-55571-124-3 (P)	□ 39.95	□ 19.95		
Financing Your Small Business		1-55571-160-X		□ 19.95		
Franchise Bible	1-55571-366-1 (B)	1-55571-526-5 (P)	□ 39.95	□ 27.95		
The Franchise Redbook		1-55571-484-6		□ 34.95		
Friendship Marketing		1-55571-399-8		□ 18.95		
Funding High-Tech Ventures		1-55571-405-6		□ 21.95		
Home Business Made Easy		1-55571-428-5		□ 19.95		
Improving Staff Productivity		1-55571-456-0		□ 16.95		
Information Breakthrough		1-55571-413-7		□ 22.95		
Insider's Guide to Small Business Loans		1-55571-488-9		□ 19.95		
Keeping Score: An Inside Look at Sports Marketing		1-55571-377-7		□ 18.95		
Kick Ass Success		1-55571-518-4		□ 18.95		
Know Your Market	1-55571-341-6 (B)	1-55571-333-5 (P)	□ 39.95	□ 19.95		
Leader's Guide: 15 Essential Skills		1-55571-434-X		□ 19.95		
Legal Expense Defense	1-55571-349-1 (B)	1-55571-348-3 (P)	□ 39.95	□ 19.95		
A Legal Road Map for Consultants		1-55571-460-9		□ 18.95		
Location, Location, Location		1-55571-376-9		□ 19.95		
Mail Order Legal Guide	1-55571-193-6 (B)	1-55571-190-1 (P)	□ 45.00	□ 29.95		
Managing People: A Practical Guide		1-55571-380-7		□ 21.95		
Marketing for the New Millennium		1-55571-432-3		□ 19.95		
Marketing Mastery	1-55571-358-0 (B)	1-55571-357-2 (P)	□ 39.95	□ 19.95		
Money Connection	1-55571-352-1 (B)	1-55571-351-3 (P)	□ 39.95	□ 24.95		
Moonlighting: Earning a Second Income at Home		1-55571-406-4		□ 15.95		
Navigating the Marketplace: Growth Strategies for Small Business		1-55571-458-7		□ 21.95		
No Money Down Financing for Franchising		1-55571-462-5		□ 19.95		
Not Another Meeting!		1-55571-480-3		□ 17.95		
People-Centered Profit Strategies		1-55571-517-6		□ 18.95		

Sub-total for this side:

TITLE		ISBN	BINDER	PAPERBACK	QTY.	TOTAL
People Investment	1-55571-187-1 (B)	1-55571-161-8 (P)	□ 39.95	□ 19.95		
Power Marketing for Small Business		1-55571-524-9 (P)		□ 19.95		
Proposal Development	1-55571-067-0 (B)	1-55571-431-5 (P)	□ 39.95	□ 21.95		
Prospecting for Gold		1-55571-483-8		□ 14.95		
Public Relations Marketing		1-55571-459-5		□ 19.95		
Raising Capital	1-55571-306-8 (B)	1-55571-305-X (P)	□ 39.95	□ 19.95		
Renaissance 2000		1-55571-412-9		□ 22.95		
Retail in Detail		1-55571-371-8		□ 15.95		
The Rule Book of Business Plans for Startups		1-55571-519-2		□ 18.95		
Secrets of High Ticket Selling		1-55571-436-6		□ 19.95		
Secrets to Buying and Selling a Business		1-55571-489-7		□ 24.95		
Secure Your Future		1-55571-335-1		□ 19.95		
Selling Services		1-55571-461-7		□ 14.95		
SmartStart Your (State) Business		varies per state		□ 19.95		
Indicate which state you prefer:						
Small Business Insider's Guide to Bankers		1-55571-400-5		□ 18.95		
Start Your Business		1-55571-485-4		□ 10.95		
Strategic Insights		1-55571-505-2		□ 19.95		
Strategic Management for Small and Growing Firms		1-55571-465-X		□ 24.95		
Successful Network Marketing		1-55571-350-5		□ 15.95		
Surviving Success		1-55571-446-3		□ 19.95		
TargetSmart!		1-55571-384-X		□ 19.95		
Top Tax Saving Ideas for Today's Small Business		1-55571-463-3		□ 16.95		
Truth About Teams		1-55571-482-X		□ 18.95		
Twenty-One Sales in a Sale		1-55571-448-X		□ 19.95		
WebWise	1-55571-501-X (B)	1-55571-479-X (P)	□ 29.95	□ 19.95		
What's It Worth?		1-55571-504-4		□ 22.95		
Which Business?		1-55571-390-4		□ 18.95		
Write Your Own Business Contracts	1-55571-196-0 (B)	1-55571-487-0 (P)	□ 39.95	□ 24.95		

Success Series	ISBN		PAPERBACK	QTY.	TOTAL
50 Ways to Get Promoted	1-55571-506-0		□ 10.95		
You Can't Go Wrong By Doing It Right	1-55571-490-0		□ 14.95		

Oasis Software	FORMAT	BINDER		QTY.	TOTAL
Company Policy Text Files CD-ROM	CD-ROM □		□ 49.95		
Company Policy Text Files Book & CD-ROM Package	CD-ROM □	□ 89.95 (B)	□ 69.95 (P)		
Winning Business Plans in Color CD-ROM	CD-ROM □		□ 59.95		

Subtotal from other side	
Subtotal from this side	
Shipping	
TOTAL	

Ordered by: *Please give street address*

NAME TITLE

COMPANY

STREET ADDRESS

CITY STATE ZIP

DAYTIME PHONE EMAIL

Ship to: *If different than above*

NAME TITLE

COMPANY

STREET ADDRESS

CITY STATE ZIP

DAYTIME PHONE

Shipping:

YOUR ORDER IS:	ADD:
0-25	5.00
25.01-50	6.00
50.01-100	7.00
100.01-175	9.00
175.01-250	13.00
250.01-500	18.00
500.01+	4% of total

PLEASE CALL FOR RUSH SERVICE OPTIONS.
INTERNATIONAL ORDERS, PLEASE CALL FOR A QUOTE ON CURRENT SHIPPING RATES.

Payment Method:

☐ CHECK ☐ MONEY ORDER
☐ AMERICAN EXPRESS ☐ DISCOVER
☐ MASTERCARD ☐ VISA

CREDIT CARD NUMBER

EXPIRATION (MM/YY) NAME ON CARD (PLEASE PRINT)

SIGNATURE OF CARDHOLDER (REQUIRED)

Fax this order form to: (541) 245-6505 or mail it to: P.O. Box 3727, Central Point, Oregon 97502
For more information about our products or to order online, visit http://www.psi-research.com

OASIS PRESS BOOKS & SOFTWARE

04172000